Third Edition

Teaching Children Gymnastics

Peter H. Werner, PED

University of South Carolina at Columbia

Lori H. Williams, PhD

The Citadel

Tina J. Hall, PhD

Middle Tennessee State University

Human Kinetics

Library of Congress Cataloging-in-Publication Data

Werner, Peter H.
  Teaching children gymnastics / Peter H. Werner, Lori H. Williams, Tina J. Hall.
-- 3rd ed.
        p. cm.
  Includes bibliographical references.
  ISBN-13: 978-1-4504-1092-2 (soft cover)
  ISBN-10: 1-4504-1092-8 (soft cover)
  1. Gymnastics for children--Coaching.   I. Williams, Lori H. II. Hall, Tina J.
III. Title.
  GV464.5.W47 2012
  796.44083--dc23
                                                                    2011028520
ISBN-10: 1-4504-1092-8
ISBN-13: 978-1-4504-1092-2

The web addresses cited in this text were current as of June 22, 2011, unless otherwise noted.

Acquisitions Editor: Scott Wikgren; **Managing Editor:** Amy Stahl; **Assistant Editor:** Rachel Brito; **Copyeditor:** Jan Feeney; **Permissions Manager:** Dalene Reeder; **Graphic Designer:** Joe Buck; **Graphic Artist:** Yvonne Griffith; **Cover Designer:** Keith Blomberg; **Photographer (cover):** Neil Bernstein; **Art Manager:** Kelly Hendren; **Associate Art Manager:** Alan L. Wilborn; **Illustrations:** © Human Kinetics; **Printer:** McNaughton & Gunn, Inc.

Printed in the United States of America

10 9 8 7 6 5 4 3 2 1

The paper in this book is certified under a sustainable forestry program.

Human Kinetics
Website: www.HumanKinetics.com

United States: Human Kinetics
P.O. Box 5076
Champaign, IL 61825-5076
800-747-4457
e-mail: humank@hkusa.com

Canada: Human Kinetics
475 Devonshire Road Unit 100
Windsor, ON N8Y 2L5
800-465-7301 (in Canada only)
e-mail: info@hkcanada.com

Europe: Human Kinetics
107 Bradford Road
Stanningley
Leeds LS28 6AT, United Kingdom
+44 (0) 113 255 5665
e-mail: hk@hkeurope.com

Australia: Human Kinetics
57A Price Avenue
Lower Mitcham, South Australia 5062
08 8372 0999
e-mail: info@hkaustralia.com

New Zealand: Human Kinetics
P.O. Box 80
Torrens Park, South Australia 5062
0800 222 062
e-mail: info@hknewzealand.com

E5463

CONTENTS

PREFACE

In my parochial elementary school, physical education was not offered. Fortunately, I was an active child. I remember swinging and sliding on playground equipment and playing sandlot baseball, football, and basketball. When I attended middle school and high school, I was excused from physical education because I was an athlete. As a result, I reached late adolescence with only a few informal gymnastics experiences. In college, as a physical education major in the early to mid-1960s, I enrolled in two gymnastics courses. One was in tumbling, and the other was in apparatus gymnastics. Because I was attending a former German Turnverein program at the University of Wisconsin at LaCrosse, both courses were presented very formally and progressively, using an Olympic system. My experiences with Dr. Gershon as my teacher were excellent and thorough. I learned good fundamental skills and good body mechanics, but I felt cheated! I didn't start gymnastics early enough or get to do it long enough to become competent in doing back handsprings, somersaults, and the like—the flashy stuff. I never really felt satisfied because I never got to put a whole routine together. We learned and were tested on single skills.

When I started teaching, I was convinced that gymnastics was good for children and that it should be an integral part of the physical education curriculum. I began to search for ways to enhance my background. I attended workshops led by Joan Tillotson, Bette Jean Logsdon, Kate Barrett, Jane Young, and Pat Tanner. I read all the British books on movement education I could get my hands on. I experienced a lot of growth in my knowledge of all the content areas of physical education—games, dance, and gymnastics. The work of Rudolf Laban and the movement framework, including the concepts of body, space, effort, and relationships, became my main source of influence. Graduate work and a doctorate followed.

As I began teaching at the university level in the early 1970s, college curriculums started to change. With the expansion of knowledge in disciplines such as exercise physiology, kinesiology, and motor learning, content courses in skills were cut. During the 1990s and now, in the 21st century, it is not unusual for physical education majors to receive but one course in gymnastics. Often such courses earn just one credit and meet twice a week for the semester. How much gymnastics expertise can a teacher develop in one course? As a teacher, how can I give my students what they need in order to feel confident about teaching gymnastics to children?

For me, some answers emerged during two sabbatical leaves in England in 1987 and 1994. There I studied with Bob Smith of the Loughborough University of Technology. I also attended workshops on gymnastics led by John Wright from Nonington College, Martin Underwood from Exeter University, Joyce Allen from the Chelsea School of Human Movement, and Victor Sabin from the Northamptonshire education department. Although gymnastics suffers the same plight in England as in the United States—poor teaching and lack of emphasis in the curriculum—these leaders have taken a positive stance, bringing gymnastics to its rightful place in the national curriculum.

This third edition of *Teaching Children Gymnastics* brings on board two new coauthors: Lori Williams and Tina Hall. Each has an extensive teaching background at the elementary and middle school levels. In addition to teaching gymnastics to children, they have conducted gymnastics workshops for teachers at state, regional, and national levels. Each also has a background in the revised national standards for physical education and assessment in physical education. Both Lori and Tina are also coauthors of the book *Schoolwide Physical Activity,* with Judy Rink (Human Kinetics 2010).

In a sense we have been accumulating the content of this book for over 40 years. These ideas represent our growth as teachers. They combine our knowledge of gymnastics and of teaching. These ideas combine the best facets of developmental skills, health-related fitness, and conceptual learning from the field of human movement. They represent what we think is possible to achieve in the real world with gymnastics education. In the third edition of this book, these ideas show how we have grown over the past 15 years.

In this book we present gymnastics in a way that has meaning for teachers. It is through you that children can enjoy the many developmental benefits of a gymnastics system focused on body management. This book is for both novice and experienced physical education teachers who want to enhance their background in gymnastics. The contents are packaged in two parts.

PART I

Part I begins with an introductory chapter that includes a definition of gymnastics; gives a brief history of the sport; and discusses how gymnastics contributes to the psychomotor, cognitive, and affective domains. New to this chapter is an update of the National Standards for Physical Education. Chapter 2 discusses adapting gymnastics to your teaching situation. Virtually no two teaching situations are identical in physical education. Suggestions on how you can structure your program to fit the idiosyncrasies of your school are provided. This chapter includes ideas for teaching lessons with limited space, equipment, and time. New to this chapter are sections on behavior management, inclusion (accommodating individual differences), and advocacy. As this chapter explains, quality programs can be developed in less-than-ideal situations, but it's not easy. Chapter 3 is restructured to include a new scope and sequence table for gymnastics for grades K to 5. Information on developing sequences in gymnastics has been moved to a separate chapter in part II.

The final chapter in part I concerns assessment. In addition to providing examples of how to assess students in the psychomotor, cognitive, and affective domains, this revised chapter relates assessment to the national standards, offers suggestions using performance-based outcomes, and addresses assessing both analytic and holistic means of accountability in gymnastics.

PART II

The unique aspect of this book is the series of detailed learning experiences in part II for each of the skill themes of traveling, statics, and rotation. Each chapter further divides work into categories. Categories of traveling in chapter 5 include steplike actions using the feet; steplike actions using the hands, feet, and knees; weight transfer; and flight. Characteristics, principles, and types of balance are the categories of statics in chapter 6. Chapter 7 focuses on the principles of rotation, movement around three axes, and rotation of the body. The process variables of human movement—body, space, effort, and relationships—support all work (see table 3.8 on page 57).

Learning experiences do not develop in only one dimension. Although one skill theme is chosen as the primary focus in each learning experience, other skill themes are used to support the development of that concept through sequence work. The themes develop parallel to and dependent on one another. What this means is that a lesson will never be only about forward rolls, cartwheels, balances, or jumping and landing. Rather, after a warm-up period, the main focus of the lesson is developed. Students learn and refine the new material. Then, a sequence is developed that integrates the main focus with other previously learned skills. For example, if the children work on rolling skills, by the end of the lesson they might integrate a jump, hop, land, and roll of choice, finishing in a balance at a low level.

The concept behind the lesson is focusing on specific skill development and then combining that skill with other skills in logical pieces of work. For example, students learning to perform rolls may link two different rolls together with a balance. Students focusing on traveling actions may jump, jump, jump with a turn or shape; land; and resolve the movement with a balance.

Whereas the second edition of this book included 10 learning experiences for each of the skill themes, this edition expands the number of learning experiences to 11. Each learning experience follows the components described in part I of this book. Also new to this edition are some modifications for additional gymnastics learning experiences.

We added an eighth chapter to this third edition of this book. It focuses on sequence work in gymnastics. It provides a guide to help teachers develop sequence work with children. We provide samples of sequence work to help teachers get started in developing their own ideas.

Most books on gymnastics present an Olympic menu of stunts, tumbling, and apparatus skills. A few texts follow an educational or informal approach using Laban's themes of body management. We give strength to this book by integrating Olympic and educational gymnastics in a way that challenges students and links gymnastics skills into meaningful sequences in each learning experience.

Peter Werner

ACKNOWLEDGMENTS

Any undertaking of this size cannot be done by one person. We are grateful to all of the teachers and coaches with whom we have studied for their contributions to our developing knowledge of gymnastics. We thank Terry Sweeting, Sharon Brown, Liz Jones, Gina Barton, Adelaide Carpenter, and present or former graduate students who reviewed, taught, and made suggestions about lesson plans in the developmental phase of this book. In addition, we thank Kym Kirby, physical education teacher at A.C. Moore Elementary School, Richland District 1, Columbia, South Carolina (1998-2002), for allowing us to teach her children and experiment with our ideas for developing content in gymnastics. Mary Werner prepared the tables and figures, and without her super job this book would have been void of aesthetic essentials. Our involvement with Scott Wikgren and others at Human Kinetics has been superb. What a group of encouraging professionals!

PART I

Developmentally Appropriate Gymnastics

In 1992 the National Association for Sport and Physical Education (NASPE) published a document titled *Developmentally Appropriate Physical Education Practices for Children*. The document, developed by the executive committee of the Council on Physical Education for Children (COPEC), represents the collective wisdom of many physical educators about what good elementary physical education is. This document was revised in 2000 under the title *Appropriate Instructional Guidelines for Elementary Physical Education* and most recently in 2010 under the title *Appropriate Instructional Practice Guidelines for Elementary School Physical Education*. The principles NASPE espoused in each of these documents guided the development of this book.

Part I begins with an overview of developmentally appropriate gymnastics, why it should be part of a quality elementary physical education program, and how this approach differs from what has been traditionally taught in physical education. Chapter 1 includes a brief history of gymnastics in its many forms. Chapter 1 also includes a definition of the physically educated person using the National Standards for Physical Education, including psychomotor, cognitive, and affective performance standards and a discussion of the significance of this definition for children's gymnastics instruction.

Virtually no two teaching situations are identical in physical education. Chapter 2 identifies similarities and differences in school settings. It provides several suggestions on structuring your program to fit the idiosyncrasies of your school. This chapter includes ideas for teaching lessons with limited space, equipment, and time. It also includes a discussion about planning, the development of a positive learning environment, the inclusion of all children in physical education, safety guidelines, and advocacy. As explained in this chapter, quality programs can be developed in less-than-ideal situations, but it's not easy.

A complete description of the content, including definitions of terms specific to the content area, is provided in chapter 3. The specific focus of this chapter is to outline a developmentally appropriate gymnastics curriculum designed to provide children with a logical progression of tasks leading to skill in, and enjoyment of, gymnastics. Stages of gymnastics from beginning skill development to more advanced sequence development are discussed, in addition to how you can use extending, refining, and applying tasks in designing learning experiences for children. In addition, information on teaching styles, student demonstrations, accountability, and good body mechanics precedes a discussion of each of the skill themes for gymnastics and the process variables that are used in developing learning experiences. To set the stage for part II of this book, components of a learning experience are outlined. You will quickly see that they contain much more than games and activities that simply keep children occupied for 30 minutes or so.

The final chapter in part I concerns assessment. Chapter 4 has been revised with regard to the national standards and performance-based outcomes. It differentiates between alternative assessment and traditional testing and describes authentic and performance-based assessment. It provides practical ways to assess how well children are learning the concepts and skills related to the content being taught. In the 21st century, educators are increasingly being required to document, in realistic ways, the progress their students are making. This requirement presents unique challenges to an elementary school physical educator who may teach 400 or more children each week. Chapter 4 provides some realistic suggestions for analytically and holistically assessing what children are learning.

CHAPTER 1

Why Is It Important to Teach Children Gymnastics?

After reading and understanding this chapter, you will be able to

- explain how gymnastics can contribute to human motor development in both sport-related skills and everyday life experiences;
- define gymnastics in your own words;
- describe the rich history and the many branches of gymnastics;
- discuss the outcomes of a quality physical education program with reference to gymnastics and specific performance outcomes at selected grade levels;
- explain how gymnastics contributes to child development in the psychomotor, cognitive, and affective domains; and
- discuss how gymnastics should be taught with reference to research on teaching and the study of pedagogical and content knowledge.

From infancy we are eager to master the possibilities of human movement. We crawl. We gain upright locomotion. We seek out ways to develop and vary our movement repertoire, venturing on to learn traveling, balancing, and rotation. Each of these skills is related to gymnastics in a broad sense.

As youngsters, you and your siblings and friends most likely pushed back the sofa, chairs, and coffee table in the living room to prepare a space for play. Maybe your father, another adult, or the strongest sibling would lie on his or her back and lift you, into the air or support you horizontally with his or her feet at your waist. Part of your acrobatics may have included rolls. Furniture may have served as equipment.

You may remember many similar activities outdoors:

- An adult holding you firmly by the arms to spin you round and round
- Riding high up on someone's shoulders or riding piggyback
- Rolling down a grassy hill
- Doing cartwheels on the lawn
- Climbing trees
- Jumping over logs in the woods
- Climbing on the jungle gym
- Crossing the monkey bars and challenging your peers to see how many rungs they could skip
- Twisting the chains of a swing around as tight as you could get them and then spinning around while lying or sitting on the seat

- Swinging from grapevines or ropes hung from a tree
- Crossing a creek or brook by jumping from one rock to another or leaping all the way across
- Sliding down an icy hill in winter while spinning on a plastic saucer or garbage can lid
- Walking on the rails of the railroad tracks, trying to keep balanced
- Hanging upside down from a tree limb or playground ladder
- Turning flips or doing handstands in the swimming pool

Although children's play equipment has changed over the years, the intent of play has not. Maybe as a child you jumped a Lemon Twist; walked on stilts and Romper Stompers; jumped on pogo sticks, pogo balls, and Hippity Hops; rode on roller skates; or twirled a hula hoop. Perhaps your play was similar to that of today's children who enjoy the challenge of skateboards, snowboards, in-line skates, and scooters. More recent play and challenges for children and adults include electronic balance activities such as those found in Wii Fit Balance. All these activities that emphasize traveling and balancing are great fun regardless of the generation of play.

Children of all ages seem fascinated by rides that stimulate their vestibular awareness (sense of balance) and their body's position in space. Youngsters enjoy riding elevators and escalators. Carnival and amusement park rides, such as the merry-go-round, Tilt-a-Whirl, Scrambler, Magic Mountain, roller coaster, and Ferris wheel stimulate their awareness of linear and rotary motion. Children will walk on any narrow surface such as a curb, a wall, or a fallen tree. They can't seem to get enough.

In years when the Olympic Games are held, there is a huge increase in the number of parents who enroll their children in gymnastics centers. In the past, girls would dream of becoming Mary Lou Retton, Cathy Rigby, Nadia Comaneci, Olga Korbut, Shannon Miller, Dominique Dawes, Kerri Strug, Dominique Moceanu, Svetlana Khorkina, Liu Xuan, Kim Zmeskal, or Betty Okino. Boys would dream of becoming Bart Conner, Kurt Thomas, Mitsuo Tsukahara, Vitaly Scherbo, Alexei Nemov, Li Xiaopeng, Mitch Gaylord, or Trent Dimas. Children today may aspire to be the next Shawn Johnson, Nastia Liukin, Carly Patterson, Paul Hamm, or Jonathan Horton (see figure 1.1). Other children pursue gymnastics hoping one day to become cheerleaders, acrobats, or circus clowns.

Figure 1.1　Many children dream of competing in the Olympics.

Despite the excitement and challenge of moving our bodies in different ways, only a handful of youngsters pursue gymnastics beyond childhood. These are the elite few who aspire to the Olympics or college team competition, although many youngsters use gymnastics skills as an avenue toward cheerleading. Cheerleading today has become a competitive team activity requiring advanced gymnastics skills to make the team.

Gymnastics plays a role in sports and everyday life by helping people learn to manage their bodies efficiently and safely. A bicycle rider, seeing a dog suddenly cross his path, tumbles to the ground, rolls, and staves off serious injury. A painter miscalculates a rung on a short ladder, stumbles, but recovers before total disaster. A softball player runs, makes a diving catch, rolls, and comes up throwing to catch the runner at first. A football player gets blocked, rolls back to his feet, pursues, and makes the tackle. A volleyball player digs a ball to keep it from hitting the floor, rolls, and returns to her feet. An equestrian rider is thrown from a horse and curls and rolls to prevent injury. All of these actions are variations of gymnastics movements, used by people who are not Olympic gymnasts.

DEFINING DEVELOPMENTALLY APPROPRIATE GYMNASTICS

Gymnastics may be globally defined as any physical exercise on the floor or apparatus that promotes endurance, strength, flexibility, agility, coordination, and body control. At its best, it is body management through the use of functional movement. As such, it is different from games (which promote the mastery of objects and the accomplishment of a purpose such as overcoming an opponent) and from dance (which promotes the expression or communication of feelings, attitudes, ideas, and concepts).

Gymnastics is like many other childhood activities, however, in that it includes learning to develop locomotor and balance skills as well as body and spatial awareness. Beyond enhancing body awareness, gymnastics is an activity involving movement in a controlled manner. It is also an enjoyable aesthetic activity that uses a variety of stimuli (apparatus, group work, and music) to promote development of the body and mind in addressing specific tasks.

A developmentally appropriate physical education program includes tasks that accommodate both the ability and confidence level of the students. A variety of experiences both off and on equipment that include traveling, taking flight, balancing, rolling, and transferring weight will accommodate the individual differences of the learners.

A physical education program featuring gymnastics benefits children in many areas. It improves body management and control and aids in the development of locomotor, nonlocomotor, and manipulative skills. Gymnastics promotes coordination, flexibility, agility, muscular strength and endurance, and bone strength. These abilities in turn relate to health and fitness and promote more physically active lifestyles. In fact, the *2008 Physical Activity Guidelines for Americans* (U.S. Department of Health and Human Services 2008) has determined that children and youth need a minimum of 60 minutes or more of physical activity, including at least three days a week involved in activities that promote muscle and bone strengthening (see figure 1.2). In addition, gymnastics can improve cognitive and affective outcomes in the areas of problem solving, body mechanics, and aesthetics. Each of these components will be developed later in more depth, but first, some observations on the history of gymnastics demonstrate how it can benefit a physical education curriculum.

BRIEF HISTORY OF GYMNASTICS

As early as 2600 b.c. the Chinese practiced a series of medical exercises called *kung fu*. They thought diseases resulted from inactivity of the body, so they developed medical gymnastics, or kung fu, to combine movements with breathing exercises to help the organs function, prolong life, and ensure the soul's immortality.

Summary of Physical Activity Guidelines for Children and Youth

Children should do 60 minutes (1 hour) or more of physical activity daily.

- **Aerobic:** Most of the 60 or more minutes a day should be either moderate- or vigorous-intensity aerobic physical activity and should include vigorous-intensity physical activity at least three days a week.
- **Muscle strengthening:** As part of their 60 or more minutes of daily physical activity, children and adolescents should include muscle-strengthening physical activity on at least three days of the week.
- **Bone strengthening:** As part of their 60 or more minutes of daily physical activity, children and adolescents should include bone-strengthening physical activity on at least three days of the week.

It is important to encourage young people to participate in physical activities that are appropriate for their age, that are enjoyable, and that offer variety.

Figure 1.2   Children and youth should spend a minimum of 60 minutes daily on physical activity including aerobics, muscle strengthening, and bone strengthening exercises.
Reprinted from U.S. Department of Health and Human Services 2008.

The Greek culture also developed the relationship between body and mind. Philosophers such as Socrates, Plato, and Aristotle promoted physical training, seeking beauty, strength, and efficiency in movement. Concepts of medical gymnastics, massage, and health-related fitness trace back to ancient Greece.

In the Roman empire, society promoted physical activity to facilitate military training of its male citizens. As a result, Roman youths developed strength, stamina, and courage through physical conditioning. Among the array of sport activities, which included ball games, running, jumping, and throwing, acrobatics appeared as a form of gymnastics.

In early 19th-century Europe, schools began to become available to all classes of society. Physical education played an integral role in the curriculum. In Germany, Johann Friedrich Guts-Muth, and later Friedrich Ludwig Jahn, used physical education to further political aspirations toward nationhood and freedom from the repression of Napoleonic France. Jahn's system of gymnastics was widely adopted at outdoor and indoor gymnastics centers, marking the beginning of modern Olympic gymnastics. Schoolboys performed gymnastics exercises regularly in the hope that sovereignty would follow the development of strong, sturdy, and fearless German youths. Guts-Muth and Jahn saw a direct link between gymnastics and fitness, or a military gymnastics.

Nationalism also motivated Sweden's P.H. Ling to develop a physical education system. Ling hoped that a vigorous youth would help recapture Sweden's dignity after its loss of territory in wars with Russia in the late 1700s and early 1800s. Ling also thought that his gymnastics system, based on an extensive study of anatomy and physiology, would enhance aesthetic, educational, and health values. The Swedish gymnastics system was based on apparatus work, including the use of swinging ladders and rings, ropes, vaulting horses, and stall bars. Careful attention was given to the development of exercises in a progression from simple to complex.

Before the mid-19th century there was no formal system of physical education in the United States. Puritanical religious beliefs and harsh living conditions allowed little time for recreation and pleasure. A notable exception was the development of the Jahn Turnverein gymnastics program in Massachusetts in the mid-1830s. At that time Catherine Bucher adapted German gymnastics in the United States, developing a system of simpler, lighter calisthenic exercises done to music. Bucher's work resulted in the birth of rhythmic gymnastics.

Between the 1870s and World War I, military training had an obvious influence on the physical preparedness of young men. At the same time there was more concern for preventive medicine. As a result, leaders such as Dio Lewis, Edward Hitchcock, and Dudley Sargent promoted both German and Swedish gymnastics programs in the United States.

Another figure in the development of educational gymnastics was Rudolf Laban, who fled from Germany to England just before World War II, establishing himself as a leader in modern dance there. He developed movement themes based on body and spatial awareness, effort, and relationships (BSER). His thematic approach to movement encouraged people to solve and interpret movement problems in new and creative ways. Laban's influence carried over into gymnastics and games; movement education programs became popular in England.

At the same time, Liselott Diem in Germany developed programs based on exploration of structured environments using gymnastics apparatus. Her programs subsequently gained widespread popularity in the United States and other parts of the world in the 1960s.

Movement education is a significant departure from previous programs in physical education. Unlike the more structured system of progressive content development, in which all students are expected to perform to the same standard, educational gymnastics encourages individuals to resolve movement problems in unique ways that correspond to their ability levels. For example, rather than have all students attempt a headstand, teachers may ask children to find a way to balance in an inverted position on three body parts.

GYMNASTICS TODAY

Gymnastics has branched in many directions over the years. It is the umbrella (see figure 1.3) that includes many forms of movement, much as dance assumes many forms (e.g., jazz, tap, modern, folk, square, ballet, aerobic). Clearly, it is for you as the teacher to decide which elements of gymnastics are most appropriate in given situations. At times children need to learn specific skills such as a forward roll or cartwheel. This may best be accomplished through a direct teaching style using an Olympic (formal) approach to teaching gymnastics. At other times gymnastics could be used in a remedial (medical) model designed to build strength and flexibility of selected muscles and joints. Educational gymnastics using concepts as learning themes may be most appropriate when you require the children

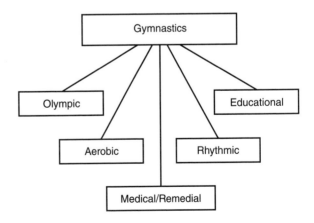

Figure 1.3 The many branches of gymnastics.

to solve movement problems in multiple ways, giving each child a way to resolve the problem based on individual ability and interests. The approach used in this book can best be defined as a combination of formal and educational gymnastics.

NATIONAL STANDARDS FOR PHYSICAL EDUCATION

The standards-based reform movement began in response to the 1983 document *A Nation at Risk*. By 1996, in response to the Goals 2000: Educate America Act of 1994, experts in the various disciplines began to develop national content standards. The National Association for Sport and Physical Education (NASPE) developed seven physical education content standards. A decade later, in 2004, the standards were condensed into the current six (see figure 1.4).

A Physically Educated Person

- **Standard 1:** Demonstrates competency in motor skills and movement patterns needed to perform a variety of physical activities.
- **Standard 2:** Demonstrates understanding of movement concepts, principles, strategies, and tactics as they apply to the learning and performance of physical activities.
- **Standard 3:** Participates regularly in physical activity.
- **Standard 4:** Achieves and maintains a health-enhancing level of physical fitness.
- **Standard 5:** Exhibits responsible personal and social behavior that respects self and others in physical activity settings.
- **Standard 6:** Values physical activity for health, enjoyment, challenge, self-expression, and/or social interaction.

Figure 1.4   The National Content Standards for Physical Education.

From National Association for Sport and Physical Education (NASPE), 2004, *Moving into the future: National standards for physical education,* 2nd ed. (Reston, VA: NASPE), 11.

The physical education content standards define what students should know and be able to do as a result of a quality physical education program. Further, they provide a framework for instructional alignment (that is, they allow you to align instructional practices and assessment with program-level and grade-level performance outcomes). Using performance outcomes as goals can help you plan lessons and assess students' progress in becoming physically educated. A few sample performance outcomes are included in *Moving Into the Future: National Standards for Physical Education* (2004) and are listed by standard and grade range (grades kindergarten to 2 and 3 to 5 for elementary school). Grade range is used to represent learning across three-year spans. Following are sample performance outcomes you may choose to include in an elementary physical education program. While most of these examples are specific to gymnastics, a few cross all areas of the curriculum. The performance outcomes are listed by learning domain (psychomotor, cognitive, and affective) national standard, and grade range. While figure 1.5 represents many possible performance outcomes, the scope of this text does not allow for all possible options.

Psychomotor Domain (Content Standards 1, 3, and 4)

Standard 1: Demonstrates competency in motor skills and movement patterns needed to perform a variety of physical activities.

Grades K to 2

- Travel in a variety of locomotor patterns (e.g., skips, hops, gallops, slides) using mature form.
- Demonstrate clear contrasts between slow and fast movement when traveling.
- Travel forward and sideways, using a variety of locomotor skills, changing directions quickly in response to a signal or obstacle.
- Match a sequence of traveling actions on the floor with a partner.
- Maintain momentary stillness bearing weight on various body parts as a base of support.
- Balance, demonstrating momentary stillness, in symmetrical and asymmetrical shapes on a variety of body parts and at different levels.
- Balance using a variety of inverted balances on different bases of support, shapes, and levels.
- Balance using a variety of symmetrical and asymmetrical shapes with a partner (mirror and match) both on and off low equipment.
- Balance using various bases of support on low equipment.
- Starting form in a squatting position, rock smoothly and repeatedly on the back, maintaining a round body shape, alternating touching hands behind head and returning feet to mat.
- Roll in various directions (sideways, forward), maintaining a round body shape without hesitating or stopping.
- Roll sideways with control, maintaining a narrow body shape and tight muscles.
- Jump, land, and roll in at least one direction.
- Jump and land using a variety of take-offs and landings in relation to various equipment.
- Jump over objects using yielding landings.
- Jump off equipment and make various body shapes in the air.
- Jump and land using various patterns: one foot to the same (hop), one foot to the opposite (leap), two to two, one to two, and two to one.
- Design and perform simple sequences involving traveling, balancing, and rolling and incorporate change of level and shapes.
- Momentarily transfer weight from feet to hands, making the legs land in various places around the body.

Grades 3 to 5

- Jump and land for height and distance using mature form.
- Run and leap for height and distance using a mature pattern.
- Jump on, over, or from one object to another using buoyant landings.
- Travel and then use a spring take-off, landing safely on an apparatus.
- With a partner, jump off of equipment and in flight make a variety of matching body shapes (e.g., wide, narrow, round, twisted, symmetrical, and asymmetrical).
- Jump onto equipment using a variety of take-offs and landings.

(continued)

Figure 1.5 Sample performance outcomes relevant for gymnastics.

Based on NASPE 2004; Hopple 2005.

- Jump off equipment and rotate while in flight (quarter, half, three-quarter, or full turns).
- Balance in inverted positions with the center of gravity over the head (e.g., frog stand, tripod, headstand).
- Balance on equipment using a variety of bases of support, body shapes, and levels.
- Balance with a partner using principles of counterbalance and countertension.
- Design and perform a small-group balance by controlling or supporting each other's weight.
- Balance in a variety of upright and inverted positions, move smoothly into a roll, and end in a balanced shape.
- Move smoothly from one balance to another in a variety of ways.
- Balance on a variety of moving objects (e.g., stilts, balance boards).
- Balance with weight partially on equipment and partially on the floor.
- Perform a variety of rolls (e.g., forward shoulder roll, forward roll, backward shoulder roll, and/or backward roll) demonstrating a mature pattern starting and landing on feet.
- Use various body shapes to begin and end rolls.
- Travel, jump over low equipment, land, and roll.
- Stretch to catch an object or strike a ball, then roll in one direction with enough momentum to return to feet.
- Roll on low equipment (e.g., bench, wedge mat).
- Design and perform gymnastics sequences that combine traveling, rolling, balancing, and transferring weight into smooth flowing sequences with intentional changes in direction, speed, and flow.
- Design and perform a partner routine on and off equipment (include rolling, weight transfers, and balances and vary the movements using the concepts of levels, shapes, directions, and speed).
- Transfer weight from feet to hands at fast and slow speeds using large extensions (e.g., mule kick, handstand, cartwheel).
- Use a variety of body actions to move from feet to hands and return to feet using large extensions (e.g., cartwheel, round-off, twisting to various landing positions on one or two feet).
- Step into weight transfers from feet to hands over low equipment.
- Transfer weight by placing hands on equipment and springing off of two feet to traverse the equipment.

Standard 3: Participates regularly in physical activity.

Grades K to 2

Participate in a wide variety of activities that involve locomotion, nonlocomotion, and manipulation of objects outside of physical education class.

Engage in moderate to vigorous physical activity on an intermittent basis.

Select a skill to improve on and practice it on your own to get better.

Participate actively at recess.

Grades 3 to 5

Participate in purposeful physical activity at recess and after school.

Identify a sport or activity to practice and improve.

Seek opportunities in before- and afterschool programs or in the community for structured physical activity.

Figure 1.5   *(continued)*

Standard 4: Achieves and maintains a health-enhancing level of physical fitness.

Grades K to 2
- Sustain moderate to vigorous physical activity.
- Demonstrate sufficient muscular strength to support body weight while climbing, hanging, and momentarily taking weight on hands.
- Move each joint through a full range of motion.
- Engage in a series of locomotor activities without tiring easily.
- Travel hand over hand along a horizontal ladder (e.g., monkey bars).
- Move transversely along a rock wall with little or no assistance from a teacher.

Grades 3 to 5
- Engage in appropriate activity that results in the development of each component of physical fitness.
- Support, lift, and control body weight in a variety of activities.

Cognitive Domain (Content Standards 2 and 4)

Standard 2: Demonstrates understanding of movement concepts, principles, strategies, and tactics as they apply to the learning and performance of physical activities.

Grades K to 2
- Identify body planes (i.e., front, back, side).
- Identify various body parts (e.g., knee, foot, arm, palm).
- Recognize appropriate safety practices.
- State that best effort is shown by trying new or more difficult tasks.
- Repeat cue words for motor skills and then demonstrate and explain what is meant by each.
- Correct movement errors in response to corrective feedback.
- Explain that quality practice improves performance.
- Identify and use a variety of relationships with objects (e.g., over and under, behind, alongside, through).
- Identify and begin to use proper technique (leg flexion) to soften the landing in jumping (e.g., squash the landing).
- Identify the critical elements of selected locomotor and nonlocomotor actions (e.g., hop, jump, roll, balance).
- Explain the difference between symmetrical and asymmetrical.
- Identify critical elements of basic movement patterns.

Grades 3 to 5
- Explain how quality practice improves performance.
- Identify physical and psychological benefits that result from long-term participation in physical activity.
- Accurately recognize the critical elements of a skill performed by a fellow student and provide feedback to that student.

(continued)

Figure 1.5 *(continued)*

- Detect, analyze, and correct errors in personal movement patterns.
- Identify proper warm-up and cool-down techniques and the reasons for using them.
- Identify basic practice and conditioning principles that enhance performance.
- Explain that one's center of gravity should be over the base of support for inverted balances.
- Describe the principles of counterbalance and countertension.
- Explain that a combination of maintaining a round body shape and momentum can help a person to roll and return to feet.
- Identify critical elements of specialized movement patterns.

Standard 4: Achieves and maintains a health-enhancing level of physical fitness.

Grades K to 2

- State the immediate effects of physical activity on the heart.
- Express the relationship between participating in enjoyable activities and fitness.

Grades 3 to 5

- Recognize that physiological responses to exercise are associated with fitness level.
- Explain the personal consequences of poor flexibility on ability to perform various activities.
- Identify strengths and weaknesses based on the results of fitness testing.

Affective Domain (Content Standards 5 and 6)

Standard 5: Exhibits responsible personal and social behavior that respects self and others in physical activity settings.

Grades K to 2

- Follow the rules for participating in class.
- Work in a group setting without interfering with others.
- Respond to teacher's signals.
- Handle equipment safely.
- Share equipment and space.
- Choose partners without regard to personal differences (e.g., race, gender, disability, skill level).

Grades 3 to 5

- Make responsible choices toward becoming an independent learner.
- Choose a partner whom he or she can work with productively.
- Assist a partner by sharing observations about skill performance during practice.
- Seek out, participate with, and show respect for persons of similar and different skill levels.
- Work productively with a partner to improve performance of a partner sequence (e.g., take into account differences in abilities, share in the decision making, practice synchronizing).
- Arrange gymnastics equipment safely in a manner appropriate to the task.
- Take seriously his or her role in assisting other classmates in improving performance.
- Indicate respect for people from different cultural backgrounds.
- Use time wisely when given the opportunity to practice and improve performance.

Figure 1.5   *(continued)*

- Remain on task in a group activity without close monitoring from a teacher.
- Demonstrate concern for safety in self-designed activities.
- Encourage others and refrain from put-down statements.
- During class performances show respect and appreciation for others.
- Accept responsibility for selecting movement and equipment choices that are suitable and safe for your ability.

Standard 6: Values physical activity for health, enjoyment, challenge, self-expression, and/or social interaction.

Grades K to 2

- Recognize that physical activity is good for personal well-being.
- Exhibit both verbal and nonverbal indicators of enjoyment while participating alone and with others.
- Identify feelings that result from participation in physical activities.
- Accept the feelings resulting from challenges, successes, and failures in physical activity.
- Willingly try new movements and skills.
- Continue to practice when not successful.

Grades 3 to 5

- Design unique gymnastics sequences.
- Celebrate personal successes and achievements as well as those of others.
- Recognize the role of gymnastics in getting to know and understand self and others.
- Describe the benefits of physical activity.
- Exhibit an eagerness to be physically active.

Figure 1.5   *(continued)*

Psychomotor Domain

Psychomotor development refers to the physical development of the body. In the psychomotor domain, performance outcomes address motor skill and physical fitness development. In effect, they correspond to content standards 1, 3, and 4 of the National Content Standards document presented in figures 1.4 and 1.5.

Skill Development

The wide range of movement activities that children experience in gymnastics can be categorized as locomotor (traveling), statics, and rotation. (These concepts are developed in more detail in chapter 3.) The point here is that early experiences should develop basic skills; in time, the tasks become more complex and more difficult. Some basic skills, for example, are traveling on the feet, balancing, and rolling. Learning concepts of body awareness and spatial awareness help children develop a variety of movement responses to use with given challenges or tasks. Children can also work on refining these basic movement responses.

As children develop physically, cognitively, and socially, additional concepts focusing on effort actions and relationships are gradually added. In general, levels of skill proficiency should form the guidelines (Graham, Holt/Hale, & Parker 2010). In the primary grades (K to 2), most children are operating at precontrol and control levels. Learning experiences should include work on skills to become efficient, effective, and adaptable movers under simple conditions. In practical terms, children will first run, jump, roll, and balance, focusing on these skills individually and then progress to combining the skills into simple sequences. Experiences should include movements both on and off of equipment. In the upper elementary grades (3 to 5), assuming quality gymnastics experiences have occurred in the early years, most children will be functioning at the control or utilization level. Their increasing competence and confidence allow them to work on more difficult skills. Students are ready to combine complex skills in sequences and routines in relationships with partners, small groups, and equipment and apparatus.

Physiological or Physical Fitness Development

As mentioned earlier, gymnastics is a critical part of the physical education curriculum that aids in both health-related and skill-related fitness concepts. Over time, units in gymnastics should emphasize health-related cardiorespiratory development, muscular strength and endurance, and flexibility. During periods of warm-up, children can derive cardiorespiratory benefits by running, hopping, skipping, and jumping. They can also use traveling actions to approach, jump onto, move along, and jump off benches, boxes, beams, and other pieces of equipment to achieve continuous movement. Continuous repetition of simple sequences, such as running on the floor and rolling or wheeling across mats, can also achieve a cardiorespiratory effect. The critical factor is to keep people moving in a gymnastics-like, aesthetic manner. This is not jogging, a race, or aerobic dance. It is being a gymnast who is moving continuously: running, jumping, vaulting, and rolling with good mechanics.

Cardiorespiratory fitness does not take place in a vacuum, however. It cannot be achieved in a one- or two-day-a-week program or in a five-minute warm-up. When gymnastics is combined with other aspects of the physical education curriculum (dance and games), physical activity breaks during the school day, walking and running programs, and an overall school physical activity and physical education program, it will contribute to cardiorespiratory development.

Focusing on the strength of various muscle groups and bones can be a part of the conditioning phase of each lesson. Taking weight on the hands builds muscles and bones in the arms and shoulder girdle. Making bridges with the body, supporting the body's weight in front- and rear-support positions, and holding balance positions also develop arm strength. Rolling, rocking, balancing, traveling on the feet, and vaulting develop the muscles and bones supporting the abdomen, buttocks, and legs. Most gymnastics skills require strong, tight bodies for control. Lifting, supporting, and propelling the body into the air each requires a tremendous amount of strength. Done repetitively over time, these activities develop muscular endurance and bone strength as well.

During many gymnastics movements as well as the cool-down phase of a lesson, body flexibility can be developed and maintained. Gymnasts need to have a good range of motion in all of the joints. Straddle and pike positions, back bends, happy and angry cat positions, and various other actions promote flexibility of the shoulder, back, hip, and ankle joints.

Skill-related fitness involves balance, coordination, agility, power, speed, and reaction time. Skill-related fitness, sometimes referred to as motor fitness, may contribute to a person's ability to acquire fundamental and specialized motor skills, participate regularly and in a greater range of physical activity options, and prevent injuries. Consequently, people with motor fitness have a variety of lifetime activity options to help them achieve and maintain a health-enhancing level of physical fitness. Early body-management experiences and continued challenges in gymnastics are ideal contributors to motor fitness.

Cognitive Domain

The cognitive domain refers to the development of a knowledge base in children. In the cognitive domain, performance outcomes address basic knowledge and higher-order thinking skills through application of concepts and principles. For development in the cognitive domain, review standard 2 and related performance outcomes in the NASPE standards outlined in figures 1.4 and 1.5.

Basic Knowledge

Gymnastics should provide children with a variety of experiences to develop cognitive abilities. At the simplest level, children can acquire a knowledge of their body parts and how to move them in and through space. Their movements should reflect a knowledge of shape, level, direction, pathway, extension, time, force, flow, and relationships (BSER framework). Over time, children should learn a variety of biomechanical principles such as rotation, center of gravity, base of support, balance, counterbalance, momentum, and force application.

Higher-Order Thinking Skills

As children develop basic movement skills, present them with opportunities for higher-order thinking skills. Open-ended, process-oriented tasks provide opportunities to solve problems by developing the students' comprehension and abilities to apply, analyze, synthesize, and evaluate movement. For example, have the children think of a balance with a wide base and a low center of gravity. Next, let them do a balance with a wide base and a high center of gravity. Then ask them, "Which one is more stable? Why?" You can also ask the children to create a movement sequence using each of the body's three axes for rotation. Ask the children what the three axes are and which skills they use for rotation around each axis. The program in gymnastics should be an education in both motor skills and understanding of movement.

Affective Domain

The affective domain refers to the development of attitude and value systems in children. In the affective domain, performance outcomes address behaviors and values; for development in the affective domain, review standards 5 and 6 and related performance outcomes in the NASPE standards outlined in figures 1.4 and 1.5.

Responsible Personal and Social Behavior

In gymnastics settings, students have opportunities to learn and use acceptable behaviors for physical activity. The focus is directed toward understanding safe practices and applying classroom rules and procedures specific to gymnastics. Students learn how to take care of equipment, safely move equipment, and use it appropriately. They learn to work independently and productively for short periods. Students also begin to understand the concept of cooperation through opportunities to share space and equipment with others.

Understanding and Respect for Differences Among People

Opportunities in gymnastics help to build a foundation for successful interpersonal communication. Children learn to play and cooperate with others regardless of personal differences such as sex, ethnicity, and ability level. They recognize the attributes that people with differences can bring to group activities. They learn to treat others with respect and to resolve conflicts in socially acceptable ways.

Opportunities for Enjoyment, Challenge, Self-Expression, and Social Interaction

Gymnastics provides a setting for children to try new movement activities and skills. By engaging in gymnastics activities, students can learn to enjoy participation alone and with others. They can learn to associate positive feelings with participation. As students gain competence, they master simple skills and become ready for the challenge of progressively more difficult work. When given opportunities to develop movement sequences based on developmental skill levels, students can demonstrate their work as a means of self-expression. Working with a partner and in small-group settings also provides students with opportunities to interact with friends.

Aesthetic Development

Gymnastics does not have the same aesthetic concerns as dance. Dancers are concerned with the body as an instrument of expression. Gymnasts are more concerned with the function of movement. The beauty of gymnastics movement derives from a concern for the shape and line of action. Gymnasts strive to link actions, or to create a flow of action from one movement to another. There is a kinesthetic satisfaction in performing an action just right. In terms of outcomes, gymnasts know and apply movement concepts and principles to achieve a satisfying, proficient, aesthetic performance of a single skill or a sequence. As observers and appraisers, gymnasts also can appreciate watching the movement of others.

Creative Development

True creativity in gymnastics is relatively rare because there are only so many ways the body can move. New moves (such as the Endo or Tsukahara) sometimes are invented and christened. With children, however, creativity means putting together a series of movements, a process that may be novel to the individual. Rather than always telling youngsters what skills to perform and in what order, it is wise sometimes to give children choices: Perform a roll and finish in a balance. Choose a traveling action to approach and mount the bench, balance on the bench using a symmetrical (or asymmetrical) shape, and exit the bench with a rolling (or sliding or wheeling) action.

Psychological Development

Children learn what they can and cannot do with their bodies. In a gymnastics system that promotes body management, children will discover appropriate challenges within their ability level. Challenges require some risk taking, courage, and perseverance. If you present tasks, lessons, and units in a logical sequence, children will challenge themselves to do their best work, overcome some fears, learn their limits, and develop confidence in their abilities while respecting the strengths and limitations of others.

HOW GYMNASTICS SHOULD BE TAUGHT

To teach a system of basic body-management and gymnastics skills well, you should be aware of some research on teaching and the study of how content knowledge of gymnastics combined with pedagogical knowledge of teaching interact (Graham

2008; Shulman 1987). If you want children to become skilled gymnasts with positive attitudes toward managing their bodies well, you must adhere to the following practices.

Begin With Knowledge of Skill Components

Although you needn't be an expert performer to teach a skill, there is no substitute for knowing how it is performed. Otherwise you have no idea what to look for, what performance cues to give, how to evaluate a child's performance, or what to correct. Imagine a teacher trying to teach the cartwheel. She says, "You put your hands down, then your feet." An inaccurate demonstration by the teacher or a selected child follows. Children begin practicing. Some succeed. Others crash to the floor with arms and legs bent and out of control. "Try again; you can do better," the teacher encourages. But poor form continues.

The children obviously need a better model. Because the cartwheel is sequential, spoken performance cues like these are needed:

- Start in a wide stretch, with your arms and legs stretched like spokes in a wheel.
- Place hand, then hand, then foot, then foot on the floor.
- Start and finish facing the same direction.
- Keep your arms and legs straight.
- Try to get your shoulders over your hands and your hips over your shoulders when you are upside down.
- Push hard with your hands and arms as you return to your feet.
- Keep your body tight.
- Land softly on your feet.

Allow Considerable Practice Time

Children need lengthy and appropriate practice to learn such skills as a roll; a cartwheel; a balance; or a sequence involving a balance, a weight transfer, and a second balance. When you line students up and spot them one by one, they may get only one or two attempts before moving on to a new skill; the rest of the time they are waiting in line. This is not a good use of teaching time.

Let's examine a common format for teaching the forward roll, the backward roll, and the log roll. Children are lined up in squads at each of four mats. They listen to an explanation, watch a demonstration, and begin to practice. Each child takes a turn and returns to the end of the line. After three tries, they learn the next roll. Their total practice is only nine attempts—three times on three rolls.

Although each roll may be taught with an excellent explanation and demonstration, the children aren't getting enough practice to capitalize on the good instruction. These children could get in much more practice if you were to reorganize the class, perhaps by assigning partners to go back and forth across the mat or by having one mat for every two students or carpet squares for every child in open (scattered) formation (see figure 1.6).

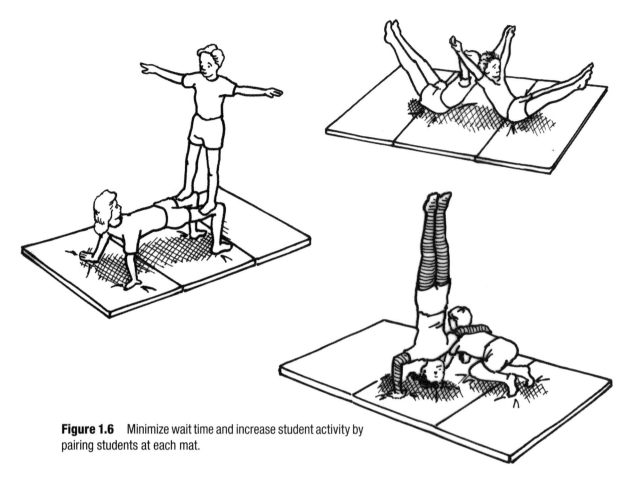

Figure 1.6   Minimize wait time and increase student activity by pairing students at each mat.

Use Developmentally Appropriate Activities

Children are not miniature adults; they have very different abilities, needs, and interests. Likewise, preschool children are not the same as elementary school children. The point is that programs need to be developed to meet the needs of children's various age and ability levels.

Activities in gymnastics for children should start out with basic skills and simple sequences. Gradually, more difficult skills can be added as children are ready for them, as well as sequences that are more complex and require higher levels of problem-solving ability. Children should progress from working by themselves on mats to working with small and large equipment and partners or small groups.

Students' satisfaction results from success. High success rates on tasks and a student's general achievement are positively correlated. When a task is too hard or above their ability level, children become frustrated, giving up or engaging in off-task behavior. You can design tasks or movement problems to allow for differences in the children's individual levels. When tasks are at appropriate levels, students will be challenged. Rather than require an entire class to do a headstand for 10 seconds or a handspring, it would be more appropriate to work on balances in inverted positions or the transfer of weight from the feet to the hands and back to the feet. For example, some students may do reasonably well learning backward rolls, whereas others have a great deal of difficulty because the arms are weak, the head gets in the way, they have limited abdominal strength, or they open up instead of staying tucked.

Consider modifying the task for students who have difficulty. For example, using a backward roll over the shoulder eases the move. Another alternative is to work on the concept of rolling in general, showing students how to transfer body weight from one adjacent body part to another. After they learn this concept, then children could

Elizabeth's Story

In a fourth grade class, a girl named Elizabeth had leukemia and was in a wheelchair. She was very bright, but physically she was quite weak. When it came time to perform rolls for other students, Elizabeth used her limited arm strength to turn her wheels to go forward and backward and to spin right and left. When we were doing balancing activities, Elizabeth would create symmetrical, asymmetrical, wide, and narrow shapes with her arms and upper body while she sat in her chair. We also worked on partner balances by allowing students to place their partial or complete weight on her chair.

As we concluded our unit on gymnastics, we asked the students to perform a sequence with a partner or group of three. At first the group that Elizabeth was in seemed to be at a loss for what to do. But they worked out a series of rolls and balances in which two partners did symmetrical and asymmetrical balances connected by forward and backward rolls, and then a sit-spin. In the culmination of the sequence, the two partners assisted Elizabeth out of her chair and supported her complete weight in a lying-down position with her abdomen facing the ceiling. We practiced the sequences and performed them at a PTA meeting. Elizabeth was so proud. As reported by her parents, on the way home she said that was the best school day of her life.

roll choosing a direction and style that they can accomplish successfully. Once a roll is mastered, challenge the children to link a roll with a balance or a traveling action, taking the skill to a higher level of difficulty.

Consider also all children with special needs. Just because some children are more challenged than others does not mean that gymnastics is inappropriate or that children with special needs are unable to perform gymnastics. Be willing to adapt or modify skills or alter your teaching style to accommodate the needs of each child. A person in a wheelchair can perform balances while in the chair or down on the floor. She can perform rolls or rotation movements by spinning wheels and rotating through a vertical axis. Some children who use a wheelchair might have very strong arms but weaker and more atrophied lower bodies. Such students may actually have an advantage when it comes to supporting weight with the arms. Students who have intellectual disabilities or are autistic may need a peer helper, special verbal or visual directions, or passive manipulation through a skill.

Encourage Cognitive and Affective Development

Rich learning environments engage children both cognitively and affectively. Children need to learn good body mechanics and understand why one balance is better than another. To challenge their minds, children need tasks that require resolution. They need to examine which movements link together well. Children need to work together with peers, giving and receiving feedback on form, suggesting alternatives to movements, and helping each other perform new skills (see figure 1.7).

Often teachers ask children to do predesigned skills or sequences without allowing them input in the matter. Instead of specifying a scale into a forward roll or a round-off into a backward roll, try designing open-ended movement tasks. For example, you could say to the children, "Perform a balance of your choice and hold it for three seconds. Move smoothly into a rolling action. Finish with a second balance." Or, "Take weight momentarily on your hands and, as you return to your feet, perform a roll of

Figure 1.7   Children can assist each other, cooperate, and give suggestions on improving form.

your choice." As children choose which skills link together more smoothly and which skills look and feel more aesthetically pleasing, and as they give and receive feedback from partners, they gain an appreciation for, and begin to value, what it takes to be a quality gymnast. This is the essence of affective development. They can work alone or with a partner to develop good responses to this instruction.

Offer a Structured Environment

A structured and focused learning environment helps children understand goals. When teachers set goals, children know what is expected. The children know what to do and how to do it. Goals also make children accountable when the time comes for assessment.

Some teachers assign several balance positions in no apparent order and for no apparent reason. Children learn a scale, stork stand, tip-up, and tripod. They practice a hodgepodge of animal walks, such as the crab walk, bear walk, and mule kicks. By putting balances and movements into logical sets, you help your students understand why they are learning them.

At the beginning of the gymnastics unit or lesson, give students a brief orientation. Tell them what to expect: "Gymnastics is about putting balances together with traveling actions, weight transfers, and rotations." You might add a demonstration. This way the students receive a clear picture of the goal for the day or the unit.

WHERE ARE WE NOW?

Gymnastics, as traditionally defined, is almost dead in many schools throughout the United States. Children learn the same forward roll, backward roll, and cartwheel in every grade level from K to 12. As they repeat these skills each year, some children get increasingly bored. Others never master the simpler skills to standard and feel they are no good. Some students fall and get injured attempting skills they have no business trying. These children become fearful and refuse to continue.

It is no wonder we find educators asking whether gymnastics should have a prominent place in the school curriculum and what its benefits are. How can we present gymnastics to maintain children's enthusiasm and motivate high levels of participation?

Some of the reasons people question the validity of gymnastics—despite its rich history in medicine, fitness, Olympic sports, body management, problem solving, and acrobatics—trace back to college curricula. Over the last 30 years physical education programs have added such courses as sport psychology, motor learning, exercise physiology, and biomechanics. The total number of overall hours, however, has not increased proportionally. As a result, students have time to take only one content course in gymnastics, perhaps neglecting stunts and tumbling, apparatus, and rhythmic or educational training. It is difficult, then, for teachers to present a content area confidently and well, having very little background in that area. Teachers are confused. Should they teach Olympic gymnastics? Should they teach educational gymnastics? Should they use direct methods while teaching? Should they use indirect methods while teaching?

In fact, there are excellent aspects of each approach to gymnastics. The strength of Olympic gymnastics is the progressive development of skill. Educational gymnastics allows for individual differences, focusing on problem solving and developing body-management skills. We can teach Olympic gymnastics with both direct and indirect teaching styles. The same is true of educational gymnastics. Because of time constraints, gymnastics at the elementary school level should focus on entry-level body-management skills rather than more tangential pursuits such as acrobatics and modern rhythmic gymnastics. Sound basic skills are more important than an exposure to several gymnastics systems without enough time to do any of them justice.

A LOOK TO THE FUTURE

These are exciting times to be teaching and particularly to be involved in teaching gymnastics. Standards-based education has provided a blueprint to students' learning. Once you assess what your students know, are able to do, and value, then, using state or national physical education content standards, you can determine what your students should know, do, and value at each grade range. The final result will be physically educated students.

The *2008 Physical Activity Guidelines for Americans* (U.S. Department of Health and Human Services 2008) have recognized the need for muscle- and bone-strengthening activities highlighting gymnastics as a critical curriculum component for achieving these goals. To allow for this strengthening of muscles and bones to take place, programs such as gymnastics must take place more than once per week and for more than one unit per year for four to six weeks. Gymnastics is an important component of the physical education program and must be treated as such.

At the international level, there is a movement to link gymnastics with healthy living and active lifestyles (Physical Education Association of Great Britain and Northern Ireland 1991). British educators are debating the concept of gymnastics as health-related fitness for life. In many European countries, gymnastics has become a leisure and fitness activity. German gymnastics clubs consist of large recreational sport complexes, centers for self-improvement with a strong emphasis on the physical well-being of members. In other European countries, rhythmic gymnastics (work to music) is the most common type of fitness class. National festivals display various techniques such as *Lingiades, Turnfests, Spartakiades,* and *Gymnaestrades.*

Let's bring this festival spirit to the local level. Imagine in your school gymnasium a fitness night for parents and children, a field day with gymnastics in the spotlight. This occasion would focus on a holistic approach to gymnastics, incorporating movement criteria; natural activities; concepts of dynamic, static, and flow; and a stimulating environment with apparatus and music. It might be the impetus to help gymnastics regain prominence in the school curriculum.

SUMMARY

Gymnastics is at a crossroads in public school education. It has a rich history of contributing to healthy lifestyles, yet because of numerous factors it has not figured significantly in the physical education curriculum for several decades. Recently educators have called for reforms to redefine quality in daily physical education. Gymnastics has much to contribute to children's development of skills as well as in physical fitness, aesthetic, creative, psychological, and cognitive areas. Gymnastics should be an integral part of every elementary school physical education.

QUESTIONS FOR REFLECTION

- What experiences did you have during your early years that contributed to your positive or negative feelings toward yourself as a gymnast?
- Relate how different cultures over time have contributed to the development of gymnastics.
- Based on experiences you have had in gymnastics, how would you define gymnastics?
- Provide examples of the branches of gymnastics. Based on your knowledge of schools, teachers, and students, how should gymnastics be taught in the schools today? Why?
- Review the sample performance outcomes for a physically educated person related to gymnastics for two elementary grade ranges. What are some practical gymnastics experiences that could be done to achieve the outcomes?
- Based on your own experiences in gymnastics in school physical education, how did gymnastics contribute to your own development in each of the three domains?
- Visit a local school when a gymnastics lesson is taught. What was the main objective of the lesson? Based on what you saw taught, how did the lesson contribute to the achievement of selected performance outcomes at the appropriate grade range?

CHAPTER 2

Tailoring Gymnastics to Fit Your Teaching Situation

After reading and understanding this chapter, you will be able to

- discuss factors that are similar in teaching school physical education no matter where or in what school you teach;
- discuss factors that are different and unique to each school and teaching situation;
- discuss ideas that guide decision making when planning to teach gymnastics; and
- apply knowledge about content, pedagogy, and pedagogical content knowledge in order to effectively implement a gymnastics program.

Teaching would be much easier if all schools and all grade levels were identical. Then a standardized curriculum with detailed lesson plans would work everywhere. The fact is, however, that our teaching situations have some similarities—and some definite differences! Similarities include the need to plan; to establish equipment protocols; to provide ample practice; to develop a positive learning environment; to promote a safe environment; to provide for a broad range of ages, abilities, and special needs within the same class of children; and to serve as an advocate for gymnastics. Differences include class size, class frequency and length of class period, facilities, and types of equipment.

In developing a gymnastics program, you should have a set of practices that guide and direct your decisions. Some of the practices might relate directly to the *Appropriate Instructional Practice Guidelines for Elementary School Physical Education* (NASPE 2010). Other practices relate just to effective teaching techniques. While all circumstances cannot be covered, the practices should provide a basis for decisions about developing a sound program in body management. This chapter describes some ways the content in this book can be adapted to various teaching situations to best meet the needs of the children and also to heighten their enjoyment and learning.

PLANNING

Planning for gymnastics should be part of the process used to develop the whole physical education curriculum from kindergarten through grades 5 and 6 (Graham 2008). Units on gymnastics should be a part of the overall planning process for school physical education. Specific learning experiences for lessons in gymnastics should be planned in detail as well. Planning for both units and learning experiences in gymnastics should be tied into meeting benchmarks (i.e., assessment standards) outlined in chapter 1 (figure 1.5, pages 9-13). More specific suggestions for planning of scope and sequence for units of gymnastics work are discussed in chapter 3. Examples of specific learning experiences appear in part II of this book in chapters 5 through 7.

With preschool and kindergarten gymnastics, large-group or whole-class instruction works well for short periods, much the same as the opening circle or story time works in the classroom. Having an opening activity in which everyone participates is a good routine, providing the regularity that gives children the confidence and security they need to be successful in the gymnasium. Most of the time that very young children spend in gymnastics should be structured for small groups or individual work. A thematic learning environment, created as one of several learning centers that children can choose to visit as interest comes and goes, can be helpful. For example, set out mats with hoops in vertical or horizontal alignment and ask the children to find various ways to go over and under or in and out of them as a theme for the day. Another theme is setting up mats and benches to use in exploring ways to move forward and backward. Have the children try different ways of moving on the hands and feet. Over time you can structure learning centers to ensure that children explore and develop movement patterns based on body and spatial awareness, effort actions, and relationships (BSER). Although the instruction may not seem formal, young children will learn an enormous amount that prepares them to succeed in later, more formal schooling.

During the early primary years, children should acquire a sound foundation of traveling actions, balancing skills, and rotation work. They should learn to do all of this work on the floor or a mat by themselves. Good body management is essential. They need to develop good control and efficient movement. Design sequences that progress in a developmentally appropriate way. Build on the children's successes. As it is appropriate, add equipment such as boxes and benches, hoops, ropes, and hurdles. In the intermediate years, children progress toward more difficult skills, so add larger equipment; introduce partner work; and develop more formal, complicated sequences.

Another planning factor is the length of time you have taught the children. Your plans will (and should) be different for the 1st year of a program than for the 10th year. When you have worked with fifth- and sixth-graders from the time they started school, they will be able to do, and will know, different things than the fifth- and sixth-graders did your first year at that school.

Class Size

To ensure that students both receive individual attention and work in safe environments, keep class sizes as small as possible. A class size of about 25 students (which is normal for most classrooms) is a good number to work with. Some schools and districts, however, schedule two or three physical education classes at the same time, which means one physical education teacher must teach 60 or more children simultaneously. Although this makes your job difficult, you can find ways to develop content that provides children with positive (albeit far from ideal) learning experiences. For example, the use of stations, or learning centers, is an efficient way to organize large groups of children. (Ideas for station task cards, balance puzzles, gymnastics notation systems, and learning centers are provided in the appendix.) Using written directions can minimize the time spent talking about the activity to the children, who often seem less inclined to listen when they are in large groups. With larger class sizes or where children are divided into smaller groups for station work, parents and upper-level elementary children can be trained to help supervise, assist, or spot for selected skills. Regardless of class size, you must devote substantial time to teaching-management routines (Siedentop 1991) or protocols (Graham 2008) so that classes are run efficiently with minimal interruptions.

Equipment

Many physical educators equate gymnastics with an elaborate inventory of commercial equipment (e.g., vaulting boxes, parallel bars, balance beams). Consequently, they consider a lack of such equipment justification for excluding gymnastics from a program. These notions must be challenged. Students can readily practice and refine body-management skills with the use of mats, wooden benches, and a little resourcefulness. For example, skipping ropes, carpet squares, hula hoops, hurdles made from paper wands, and milk crates (common in most schools), along with mats and benches, are sufficient apparatus for motivating and challenging students (see table 2.1).

With these simple pieces of equipment, students can travel, balance, and rotate on, over, into, out of, under, along, and beside the apparatus. These tasks, in turn, help children practice linking actions. Children can learn to form a continuous sequence with smooth transitions—a component in body management. For example, children could create a standing balance of their choice inside a hoop. Then they could jump or hop out of the hoop, land smoothly, lower their bodies to the ground in a logical way, perform a roll of their choice, and finish in a balance at a low level. Or they might start with a balance in a symmetrical or asymmetrical position on a bench. After establishing control, they could perform a roll off the equipment and finish with a contrasting balance on the floor.

The key practices in using equipment are modification and innovation. Keeping in mind the skill themes of traveling, statics, and rotation, you decide which specific skills the children will practice and learn in sequence or linked together. These skills may be balancing, hanging, supporting, rolling, or steplike actions. After deciding to

Table 2.1 Alternative Equipment

Piece	Specifications	Suggested uses
Boxes from school cafeteria or office	• 12-18 in. (30-45 cm) high • 18-24 in. (45-60 cm) long and wide • Filled with newspaper • Ends sealed with masking tape	• Jump onto, off, over • Balance on completely or partially • Roll onto, off • Cartwheel over
Benches	• 12-18 in. (30-45 cm) high • 10-12 ft. (3-4 m) long • 10-12 in. (25-30 cm) wide • Wide, stable base to prevent tipping	• Travel along • Balance on • Jump onto, off, over • Roll along, onto, off • Cartwheel over, off
Tables	• 2-3 ft. (0.6-1 m) high • 24-36 in. (60-90 cm) wide • 6-8 ft. (2-2.4 m) long • Stable, sturdy, nonfolding	• Balance on completely or partially • Roll off • Jump off
Chairs	• Stable, sturdy • Four legs, back	• Balance on • Vault over • Jump onto, off
Plastic crates (milk, soft drink)	• 6-18 in. (15-45 cm) high • 18-24 in. (45-60 cm) long and wide • Place upside down on mats or other nonskid surfaces	• Balance on • Jump over, onto, off • Roll onto, off • Cartwheel over

develop a particular skill theme, you consider the type of equipment that might be useful and how to arrange it to enhance skill development in the particular area. If balancing is the chosen area, you then decide whether balancing will take place on the floor or on equipment. Likewise, traveling and rotation actions can be done on the floor or on equipment or as a means of approaching or dismounting the equipment.

What equipment is available on which to balance? You may be blessed with commercial 10-by-12-foot benches or nice vaulting boxes. Chances are, though, that you do not have enough benches and boxes to permit one piece for every one or two children. The focus of this gymnastics work is body management, however, and not the development of competitive gymnastics. Feeling encouraged to innovate and modify, perhaps you will come up with tables, chairs, milk crates, folded mats, or cardboard boxes filled with newspaper—all acceptable surfaces on which children can safely balance (see figure 2.1). (See the Safety Concerns and Safety Guidelines and Liability sections later in this chapter.)

Figure 2.1   Although some programs may have standard gymnastics equipment, you can also use hoops, boxes, benches, and chairs as equipment.

Figure 2.2   Equipment can be used in innovative ways.

In addition to using innovative objects such as tables and chairs for gymnastics, you can creatively modify the gymnastics apparatus you do have for developing body-management skills (see figure 2.2). For example, children can do forward hip circles around a balance beam or a singular parallel bar. They can work under a balance beam performing rotation actions, balance against the beam, hang under it, and rise up from the beam. In addition to performing a selection of vaulting actions, students can use horses to support their body weight while creating balance shapes and use rolls or sliding actions to approach or dismount the equipment.

The arrangement of equipment is another key to linking gymnastics actions together and developing sequence work. A mat placed at the end of or beside a bench can mark points of entry and exit. Placing the mat between a bench and the parallel bars encourages linking actions between these apparatus. You will first decide which skills to link or sequence and then arrange the equipment accordingly.

If you have a limited amount of commercially made gymnastics equipment available to you right now, you need to develop a plan. For example, if you have only three to five 4-by-6-foot mats to work with, you might buy one or two more each year, meanwhile substituting carpet squares or yoga mats. The school's parent–teacher organization may be willing to do a special fund-raiser or event for the purchase of mats or a piece of apparatus. You could also share equipment with the local parks and recreation department or other schools within the district. Try setting up a rotation schedule in the fall with each school contributing two or more mats; collectively there should be enough for one school's program at a time.

If you have no benches or boxes now, develop a plan to purchase one or two a year until you have sufficient equipment. Perhaps you can contract with the high school shop class to design and build the benches and boxes (see the plans for constructing boxes and benches in Graham, Holt/Hale, and Parker 2010). In the meantime, you can substitute tables and chairs, commercial milk crates, wooden boxes, and cardboard boxes filled with newspapers. Define your purpose. Perhaps you need equipment for balancing or jumping. Choose something that will allow you to accomplish the purpose safely.

After you have mats, benches, and boxes, you will want to expand the gymnastics program, eventually providing opportunities for children to hang, swing, support body weight, balance, spring, vault, and so on. Balance beams, parallel bars, horizontal bars, and minitrampolines (about 3 by 3 feet and about 18 inches high) support these gymnastics movement skills. Build toward this goal, but don't give up and say you can't teach gymnastics because you don't have an ideal situation. Do the best you can with what you have. As interest in the program grows, parents and school administrators will support it.

After you acquire gymnastics equipment, think about its organization and arrangement. It is tempting to put mats, benches, and boxes in nice straight rows and columns. Having everything neat and orderly helps you feel good as a teacher. There are more important goals to consider in placing equipment, however. You should arrange a natural flow from one piece of equipment to the next, setting the pieces to link actions between one activity or skill and another. One such arrangement is shown in figure 2.3.

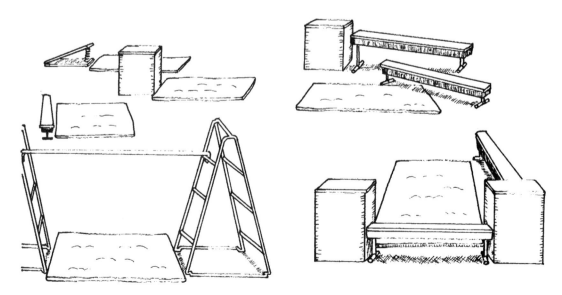

Figure 2.3   Arrange equipment to provide a natural flow from one piece to the next.

Equipment Protocols

When you are planning to teach a unit on gymnastics, it is best to do so for the whole school simultaneously. If you have sequential classes in games, gymnastics, games, dance, gymnastics, and so on, you have an equipment nightmare as well as a planning nightmare. It is best to put your equipment out in the morning and leave it up for the whole day or at least the whole morning before taking it down. Rather than do all of the work yourself, you can have children help you. One such way is to have upper-elementary children come to the gym as school starts in the morning and closes at the end of the day to help you set up and arrange the equipment and then put it away. Another option is to have the children in each class set up and take down the equipment.

Children enjoy being given responsibility for taking care of the equipment. They can also learn some lessons about lifting and carrying heavy equipment as well as working

with a partner. They should work with partners in lifting boxes, benches, mats, and other pieces of large equipment. They should also use the larger, stronger muscles of the body when lifting heavy equipment. This means that you should teach the children to bend from the knees, keep the back straight, and lift with the quadriceps muscles (figure 2.4). Each child should lift simultaneously with his or her partner, walk the equipment to where it is to be placed, and set it down gently.

Figure 2.4   Teach children the proper ways to carry equipment.

At the start of each class or any time instruction is given, the children should sit off the equipment, either on the floor or on a mat in an erect gymnastics-like sitting position. Children who sit on equipment or lie down are less likely to pay attention while you are talking. And there are always class clowns who will "fall" off the equipment just to get a laugh as well as their peers' attention. Don't even give them a chance to get hurt or cause a distraction.

Facilities

Although some teachers have adequate indoor and outdoor space, others are less fortunate. In fact, some teachers have no indoor space whatsoever. Others have no grassy areas. Following are some ideas and suggestions for adapting the content in this book for limited indoor or outdoor space.

Who wouldn't want to teach children in Bela Karolyi's gym and have all the best equipment money can buy? A large, open exercise space with the latest cushioned mats, multiple beams, bars, horses—wouldn't that be great? I recall a friend in graduate school who once declared, "A master fencer could teach fencing with broom handles better than I could with all of the latest models of foils." The point is that you need to make the best of your present situation but build toward the future.

An open space is critical to teaching gymnastics safely and successfully. Children need space to run, jump, land, roll, balance, and practice all the other gymnastics skills. There must be enough space between pieces of equipment for children to execute skills without bumping into the walls, classmates, or equipment. A large gymnasium or multipurpose room is the dream of gymnastics teachers. Gymnastics can be taught, however, on school stages, in empty classrooms, or in hallways, with some compromises. These kinds of spaces usually are small, so safety and participation levels become concerns. You have to judge how many children can safely participate at a time in a given area. If children are spending inordinate time in line waiting for their turn, you may wish to make alternative plans. One solution is to divide the class into groups, assigning two or more activities. One group might do a ball skill or jump rope outside while the other group is inside doing gymnastics. When a class is split into two or more groups, volunteers, parents, or teacher aides can supervise one activity. Another solution is to move gymnastics outdoors.

Teaching gymnastics outside is not ideal, but it is workable. In warmer climates, where many schools often do not have gyms, there may be no other choice. Practicing gymnastics on a blacktop surface (with or without the protection of a roof) on the playground, or in an open grassy area can be difficult. You need to be creative. Moving mats and equipment outside and back in every day is a management nightmare. Children can help, especially students who arrive at school early and take the late bus home, if they are taught how to carry mats in and out safely (see Equipment Protocols; Graham 2008). Large parachutes can be placed on grass or dirt surfaces to help protect skin and clothes. Organization is the key.

Class Frequency and Length

Schools and classes differ in both the number of days per week that the children attend physical education classes and the length of the classes. Children who have physical education every day for 30 minutes can be expected to learn more than children who have only 60 minutes of physical education each week. This is one reason that it is virtually impossible to suggest a standardized physical education curriculum. It is not unreasonable, however, to expect to teach gymnastics to children for one quarter of the yearly allotted curricular time for physical education. As an example, aim to organize and teach your classes so that if students have physical education twice a week for 30 minutes, they receive more than 8 hours of actual learning time each year in gymnastics (Kelly 1989).

Each of the gymnastics learning experiences includes suggested beginning or warm-up activities, new skills, and the integration of newly acquired skills with other skill themes for developing sequences, or routines. If children already have some background, such as knowing how to do simple rolls or individual balances well, they might accomplish a given learning experience in one class period. For other skills, such as taking weight on the hands or achieving partner balances, a learning experience may take several class periods or even constitute a short unit. It is important to develop quality movement and build skill. There is no sense in moving on before students master fundamental skills. This is a key to ensuring safety.

Ample Practice

Children need time to practice new skills and to combine skills into sequences so that they can gain mastery and develop feelings of success. You might question how to judge the number of practice trials it takes for a child to learn a skill. The answer is that no specific number of practice attempts applies to every situation. Every child is different; some take longer than others to learn. Certainly, just as no one learns to throw or dribble a ball or perform a dance in only a few tries, we cannot expect most people to learn gymnastics skills well with relatively few trials.

A given lesson should allow 10 to 20 appropriate practice tries for each task. Creating that many practice opportunities in varied ways dictates how you organize the lesson. It is not efficient to set up only one line so that you have to spot every child at every trial. One long relay line makes for very few practice attempts. In a class of 30 children, even having two to four gymnastics stations with students rotating among them would place 8 to 15 youngsters at each station. A child would have only one turn and then wait for 7 to 14 others to complete their turns. In a typical 30-minute lesson this arrangement would allow only two or three trials at each station. That is not enough practice for mastery.

You must organize the lessons and provide enough equipment to allow children to work as individuals, in partnerships, or in groups of three or four. With that low ratio, children are guaranteed more practice time and less waiting time (see figure 2.5).

Figure 2.5   Children should have ample opportunities for practice.

Take a realistic look at how many tasks you can present in a given lesson. To increase practice time, you will have to decrease instruction time. Using a goal of 10 to 20 practice trials per student for each task, there probably should be three to six tasks in a lesson (i.e., children could practice three tasks 20 times or six tasks 10 times each). That averages out to two practice attempts every minute, including instruction and waiting. By keeping instructions short and clear, you can accomplish this goal.

Children benefit from repetition. To prevent boredom, change tasks slightly within each lesson or at least between lessons. For example, if static work is the focus of the lesson and children are balancing on various bases of support, you might refine the work by making the children aware of extensions through the arms and legs or smooth curved lines through the back. You could vary a task by having children alter the height or shape of their balances or the relationship of the body parts. Likewise, you can change a sequence slightly to produce a new focus. Add a roll to the balance–travel–balance sequence. Require one of the balances in the sequence to be on a piece of equipment. In each instance, the children have a new focus or challenge. They will stay on task and benefit from variety in their practice.

DEVELOPING A POSITIVE LEARNING ENVIRONMENT

According to research about teacher education, you need to consider several factors when creating a positive and productive learning environment for children (Graham 2008; Rink 2010; Siedentop 1991). One factor is your expectations. It is up to you to design and build a positive atmosphere for the class. It is also up to you to establish rules and procedures that encourage all children to behave, stay on task, and work productively.

Rules for conduct in the gymnasium or on the playground should be clear and positive. They should also be posted. Specific rules related to gymnastics might include sitting like a gymnast off the equipment while you are providing instruction (see figure 2.6), staying on task, working safely, doing one's best, and encouraging others.

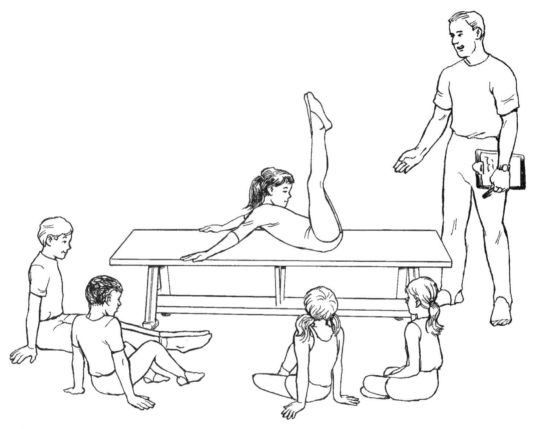

Figure 2.6   Students should sit attentively off the equipment when you are giving instructions.

Other factors that help to create a positive learning atmosphere are establishing procedures for how the children enter and exit the gym, having signals that indicate the beginning and end of activities, developing protocols for using equipment, and establishing procedures for selecting partners. You should also develop protocols that instruct children on what to do

- with their shoes and clothes when they enter the gym,
- when they bring valuables such as jewelry or money to class,
- when they need to go to the bathroom or get a drink during class, or
- when an injury or accident occurs in class.

Children's Ability Levels and Rates of Learning

Children entering gymnastics classes have various sizes, shapes, and ability levels. They come from different backgrounds and with varied experiences. These differences are evident even in the early grades (see figure 2.7). For some youngsters, gymnastics comes naturally. Their parents have been doing gymnastics-like activities with them, such as rolling on the floor and tossing them in the air, since they were toddlers. Some children may already have had a variety of experiences in preschool tumbling programs. Other children may not have had this experience but are blessed with the right kind of body—small, strong, and flexible. Some students will have all of the tools but are attracted to spectator sports or no sports at all because the family does not encourage active participation. A few simply are not gifted in gymnastics. Many of these children are large, verging on obese. They may have the desire to participate yet lack strength, flexibility, and body coordination. Perhaps they lack desire because they are embarrassed or self-conscious. They do not want to make fools of themselves in front of others. With older children, these differences often escalate. Some go on to become accomplished gymnasts, even at the Olympic level. Others may not progress at all, finding it difficult to control a forward roll or cartwheel.

Figure 2.7 Children should progress at their own developmental level and rate.

All of these children will enter your gymnastics classes. As a teacher, you should keep in mind these differences in ability and rates of learning. Unlike Olympic gymnastics, which is primarily concerned with content progressions from easy to more difficult, a system of body management should encompass individual needs. You need to be sensitive to and knowledgeable of how able children are. You need to understand content progressions (from easy to difficult) to modify and adapt tasks suitably to meet each child's needs.

Inclusion: Accommodating Individual Differences

Many classes today have children with special needs who are mainstreamed (i.e., they participate in classes and activities with children who don't have special needs). In some instances you can accommodate children with special needs (not only those who are mainstreamed) by using techniques such as *teaching by invitation* or *intratask variation*. In teaching by invitation, you provide children with two or more ways to perform an activity and allow the children to choose which one they will perform. In teaching with intratask variation, you make a decision to provide levels of difficulty within a task. Children who can't perform the task are given an easier way to complete the task. Children of high ability level have the task changed so that it is more challenging (Graham 2008; see figure 2.8). In other instances it may be necessary to make different adaptations to accommodate the needs of these students. In this section we discuss some accommodations that you can make for children when teaching gymnastics.

Figure 2.8 Intratask variations can accommodate individual differences in skill or ability. Compare *(a)* a child with low skill doing a simple forward roll with *(b)* a child with high skill doing a forward straddle roll.

If you have students with special needs in gymnastics, you should teach them in a specific way, using an individualized education plan (IEP). In many instances, a hearing- or vision-impaired child can partner with a nonimpaired child who will assist the impaired child in performing a skill or sequence. Visual demonstrations can show hearing-impaired children what to do. For example, if you want the child to perform a cartwheel, show the student what you want sequentially—arms and legs straight, X position, hand–hand–foot–foot, start and finish facing the same direction.

You can modify tasks in many ways to fit an individual student's needs. For example, a child in a wheelchair can make shapes with the arms and upper torso and do rotations with a spin of the chair. You can make tasks easier for low-skilled, obese, and nonambulatory children as well. Instead of doing rolls, cartwheels, or springing and vaulting actions, less-abled children can practice a seated roll or simple weight-bearing tasks with the arms. Children can create balances on patches or points, on different body parts, in various shapes, and so on according to their

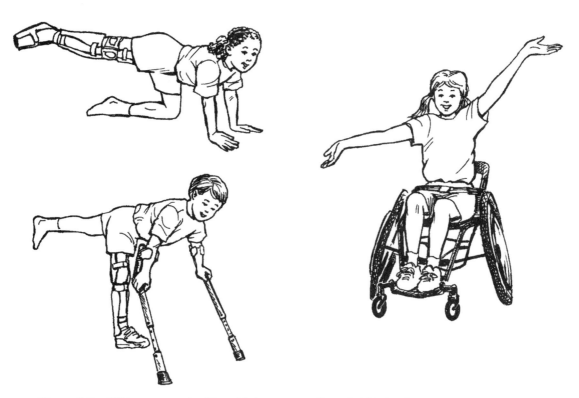

Figure 2.9   Children can create different balances regardless of ability level or special needs.

ability level, even if their activity includes the use of a crutch, a prosthetic device, or a wheelchair (figure 2.9).

Safety Concerns

Many public school administrators and physical educators hesitate to teach gymnastics because of their concern for legal liability and safety. Like other risk sports, such as rock climbing, whitewater canoeing, or kayaking, gymnastics presents challenges and some danger. That does not mean these sports should not be in a physical education program. When you exercise care by using good equipment and sound educational practices, risk sports have very good records for safety.

In promoting a strong body-management program in gymnastics, your concerns for safety should turn primarily to the areas of equipment and educational practices. Select equipment on the basis of quality. Mats should be durable and absorbent. Large equipment such as balance beams, benches, boxes, and bars should meet standards set by the industry. If tables, chairs, milk crates, and other multipurpose equipment are used, inspect each piece for sturdiness and carefully decide how to work with a given piece. Always monitor equipment to make sure it is being used in a suitable manner. In addition, make sure that the equipment will not skid or slide when taking the weight of students. Arrange equipment judiciously, leaving adequate room between pieces to permit the intended actions. As a rule, place mats beside or under equipment to provide absorbent landings and to cushion any falls that might occur.

Clothing and footwear are part of equipment considerations. Clothes should be loose enough to permit free, unrestricted movement, but not so baggy as to risk catching on something. Gym uniforms and stretchy nylon or spandex clothing intended for active movement are probably best. Indoors, children should go barefoot. Gymnasts have a much better feel for the floor and supporting surface when the feet directly contact the floor or equipment. Tactile-kinesthetic perception is more acute, giving the gymnast messages about the body and space. Outdoors, nonskid shoes are acceptable for safety.

Besides selecting and using equipment well, teaching must be based on other sound principles. Spotting, a primary concern, is a technique in which the teacher or another student provides the gymnast assistance in executing a skill. The spotter usually is in position to physically assist at the critical point in the student's performance of the skill. Although the spotter does not always directly assist the child, the spotter is there to catch the child in case she loses balance and falls. Spotting involves a range of invasiveness.

For example, on the lower end, the spotter can simply stand there with one hand held out near the gymnast's back and just be there so that the gymnast feels comfortable doing the skill without tactile help or so that the spotter can easily catch the gymnast in case the gymnast makes a mistake. Direct assistance would be the more invasive form of spotting—both hands on the body helping the gymnast through the skill. Olympic gymnastics programs typically use spotting. In this book, we advocate spotting only in selected circumstances (see figure 2.10). In general, spotting is used for developing new and more difficult skills and for combining previously learned skills. Use it on an individual basis as children need or request it. A program in body management teaches children to move under control.

Figure 2.10   Use spotting when teaching new and more difficult skills.

Do not permit crashing (falling to the floor out of control—on the back or shins—in a position where a person will readily get hurt); silly, off-task behavior; or foolish, daredevil tricks. Make sure children have mastered a skill at an easier level before allowing them to attempt it at a higher level. For example, a child should not attempt an actual handstand before having control over taking weight on the hands and coming down softly on the feet. Gradually a student will kick higher and get vertical alignment under control. Teach children to recover from any loss of control by twisting out into a cartwheel or tucking into a forward roll. With rolling, a child who controls a roll on the floor may next try to roll onto, along, or off equipment. The environment should be specially set for these occasions. Use extra raised or folded mats to reduce the impact of any possible fall. Encourage only those children who have mastered easier skills to perform them in a more challenging situation. All children should work within the limits of their ability. You can reduce risks by not requiring that all children try a given skill, instead allowing them to modify actions within a movement challenge.

Imagine an example in which a task is set and children are working, perhaps at transferring their weight from the feet to the hands and back to the feet. As the teacher, you observe for skill level and may call a few children over for specific instruction and spotting on a back walkover, front handspring, or back handspring. It is not important that everyone master these more advanced skills. Perhaps a child is working on a sequence, combining two skills, or trying to perform a skill in a new way or on a new piece of equipment. The child should feel free to ask for help (spotting) in these situations. Encourage children to take self-responsibility, to work within their ability level, and to develop movement based on sound mechanical principles.

D.W. Flips

When introducing a unit of instruction in gymnastics to children at the elementary level, I am usually bombarded with comments conveying excitement and sometimes trepidation. "Can we learn to do flips?" "Will we stand on our head?" "Are we going to swing on the bars?" "Are we going to hang upside down?" Some are sure they can do these skills already, and others hope they never have an opportunity because they are terrified. Over the years I have found that a children's fiction book helps with my introduction (set induction) of the unit. It is titled *D.W. Flips* by Marc Brown. I have learned that children have a wide variety of interpretations of what it means to flip. Flipping can mean a simple forward or backward roll. It can mean a dive roll through a hoop. It can mean a change of body positions. It can mean a somersault or handspring. As I read the story to the children, they become excited that they'll be doing gymnastics and comforted by the fact that in our gymnastics unit, flipping, standing, swinging, or hanging will be done in such a way that each child can feel comfortable and safe because what we do will be based on their comfort level.

Safety Guidelines and Liability

Gymnastics teachers are always concerned about providing a safe learning environment for children (see figure 2.11). No one would want to place children in an unsafe situation where they might get hurt. You should consider these guidelines in order to provide a safe environment.

- Teach the children how to use the equipment safely, and provide written guidelines. Written guidelines are appropriate even for young elementary students if you keep the guidelines simple, such as "Sit off the equipment" or "Be safe." Injuries usually occur when equipment is misused. For example, acceptable activities on a balance beam are walking across, balancing on, jumping onto and off of, and rolling off of it when the task is appropriate.

- Conduct a gymnastics class in a worklike environment. Many injuries occur when kids are fooling around, goofing off, or daring each other. Acceptable behaviors include staying focused and on task and working within one's ability level.

- Practice a skill first on the floor and then close to the floor on a wide base before taking it to a more difficult level. Mastery is the key.

- Provide enough room for children to move safely. In small areas such as classrooms, stages, and hallways, space is a critical issue. Make sure there is enough room for each child to complete a skill without bumping a wall, another child, or a piece of equipment. For example, have children roll from near a wall toward an open space, or cartwheel lengthwise if the space is long and narrow.

- Provide a safe surface. Place mats under and beside any large apparatus for proper padding. On an outdoor surface, use mats or large parachutes to protect children's skins and clothes. Remove all glass and sharp objects from the area.

- Inspect each apparatus regularly as a safety precaution. Is the surface free of splinters? Tighten any loose nuts or bolts, and remove protruding items such as nuts, bolts, dollies, and transporters.

- Make sure each piece of equipment is stable and set up on a nonskid surface. Equipment should not move when in use.

Figure 2.11 Providing a safe learning environment is always important in gymnastics. Students can spot each other when necessary, or you can spot for them.

Bad accidents in gymnastics have occurred, and some school districts have banned the use of specific pieces of equipment or even the teaching of gymnastics altogether. Any accident is unfortunate, and the job of reinstituting a full-blown gymnastics program into the school may be difficult. It is not impossible, however. Collect good literature on the benefits of gymnastics for children and present it to the principal, superintendent, or school board. Sell the program by developing safety measures and body management. Develop a program based on sound tumbling skills on the floor and through the use of wide benches and boxes close to the floor, perhaps naming it *body management* instead of *gymnastics.*

Advocacy

Advocacy is action aimed at promoting, maintaining, or defending a cause. In the case of gymnastics, many people, including administrators, teachers, and parents, do not understand the goals and outcomes of a well-taught program. Most people see gymnastics as a sport for cheerleaders, acrobats, and elite athletes. For safety reasons, they have concerns about teaching gymnastics to all children in the schools. It is your job to be an advocate for gymnastics and to show how gymnastics can contribute to the development of body and spatial awareness and fitness in all children. You need to promote the activity and educate people about the benefits of a well-taught gymnastics program. You have to show how gymnastics can be taught in a safe manner to all children.

Fortunately, over the last several years, several articles and books have been published that promote quality gymnastics programs (Coelho 2010; Graham, Holt/Hale, and Parker 2010; Mitchell, Davis, and Lopez 2002; Nilges 1997, 1999, 2000; Nilges-Charles 2008; Ravegno 1988; Rikard 1992). Gymnastics has also been included in the National Standards for Physical Education K-12 (NASPE 1995, 2004). Use this information to promote the cause. Share this information with school principals, parents, and others who have concerns about the teaching of gymnastics in schools. Share the information available to promote gymnastics. Over time, share with principals some of the articles cited here. Create one or more documents that promote the sport and inform people about gymnastics and send them home to parents. Present gymnastics as having a very positive outcome for children. As an advocate, you should engage in as many of the following practices as possible.

- Educate the principal, teachers, and parents you work with about gymnastics. Emphasize that it develops health-related fitness and body management. It is for all children, not just an elite few.

- Inform concerned people about the content of gymnastics—balancing, traveling, and rotation. Show them that gymnastics is about teaching skills that start out easy and progressively get more difficult.

- Emphasize that children at all times work within their own ability level and are not challenged to do things that they are not capable of doing.

- Found the program on sound and safe practices. Build skills and confidence on the floor before moving to equipment. Develop the children's self-control with good body mechanics. Gymnastics should not place children at risk.

- Sell the program. Invite parents to watch classes. Propose and carry out a program for the parent–teacher organization highlighting the skills and sequences that children learn. When parents see a good educational program, they are likely to support it.

SUMMARY

One of the most valid criticisms of physical education programs in the past has been that they were designed for athletes only and were a painful experience for those who were poorly skilled. Contemporary physical educators are moving away from this one-model-fits-all pattern of restrictive physical education; now they are moving toward programs that are adjusted, adapted, and designed specifically to match the characteristics of their schools and the abilities, interests, and needs of the children they teach. This chapter describes some of the considerations that contemporary teachers take into account when designing gymnastics programs for the children at their schools. Some similarities among teaching situations such as the need to plan, establish protocols with equipment, develop a positive and safe learning environment, provide for a wide range of student abilities, and serve as an advocate for gymnastics are discussed. Specific differences such as class size, class frequency, facilities, and types of equipment that make each teaching situation unique are also discussed.

QUESTIONS FOR REFLECTION

- Visit two or more schools similar to your school, or talk to two or more teachers at other schools. Compare the teaching situations at each of the schools with regard to the factors identified in this chapter. What similarities do you find among the school situations? What differences are evident? What suggestions would you recommend for handling each of the situations?

- Based on the benchmarks for each grade level identified in the national standards, how would you change the content of what you teach as children move from the beginning elementary school years to the intermediate elementary years?

- What strategies would you use in teaching children gymnastics in classes of 30 or more students?

- If you have a limited amount of gymnastics equipment in your school, what options do you have in using alternative equipment or in using equipment from other settings?

- Develop a long-term plan to acquire the gymnastics equipment you need in order to conduct your program. What are your immediate needs? What equipment would you sequentially purchase over a period of five years? Why?
- Develop a diagram of how you might place gymnastics equipment in your space to allow for safety yet encourage good flow from one piece to another to create good linking opportunities for children as they develop sequences.
- Identify the rules and equipment protocols you have in your gym when conducting a gymnastics unit. Are they the same as or different than when you teach games or dance? Why?
- With regard to facilities, how can you best use the spaces available to you to create a safe and productive learning environment?
- What changes in gymnastics content could you expect to teach in a one-day-a-week program as compared to a two- or three-day-a-week program?
- As you teach gymnastics, what ideas do you have that would promote ample practice time and increase children's chances of mastering gymnastics skills and concepts?
- All children in your school are unique. What can you do in your classes to modify your teaching to meet individual differences and rates of learning?
- How do you allow for accommodating children with special needs in your gymnastics program?
- What guidelines do you think are important in providing a safe environment for children in gymnastics?
- Develop an advocacy plan to promote gymnastics in your school. How would you go about convincing your principal or parents in your school that gymnastics, when conducted in a safe manner, can have a positive effect on the development of children?

CHAPTER 3

Incorporating Gymnastics Into Your Program

After reading and understanding this chapter, you will be able to

- develop your own scope and sequence table for gymnastics based on your knowledge of the national standards and performance outcomes for physical education and your own teaching situation;

- describe the stages of gymnastics and provide examples of each stage in your own words;

- choose an informing task or starting point for a learning experience in gymnastics and provide three extending, three refining, and three application tasks for developing content in gymnastics;

- discuss the skill themes for gymnastics with respect to categories within each skill theme, examples of each category, and principles of movement governing each category;

- describe how the process variables (body, space, effort, and relationships) can be used in developing content in gymnastics;

- list the components of a learning experience and provide an example of each; and

- explain what makes a learning experience developmentally appropriate.

The content areas of games, dance, and gymnastics include many skills. Rather than consider skills individually, it is convenient to group them into categories that can organize units of work. With gymnastics there are several ways to organize such frameworks. Some educators group gymnastics into stunts, tumbling, and apparatus. Others organize it around a framework of manipulative, stability, and locomotor actions. Still other teachers use the concepts of body, space, effort, and relationships (BSER) as frameworks.

Skill themes are the framework for the content in this book. Three skill themes form the framework: the body's traveling actions, static work, and rotation (figure 3.1).

Each skill theme can be thought of as a *set,* or group of activities, as in mathematics. Traveling actions include activities in which the intent is to move the body from one place to another. Static work includes those activities in which the focus is to achieve stillness or balance. Rotation includes activities in which the intent is to twist, turn, or roll around one of the three axes of the body.

As is evident in figure 3.1, each of the skill themes can function as a separate set. As these sets of skill themes interact with each other, overlapping and joining of the themes occur. This intersection of sets is a mathematical concept that applies to gymnastics work. For example, a skill such as rolling at times might be thought

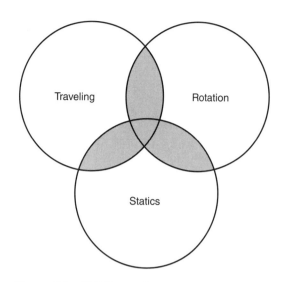

Figure 3.1   Skill themes for gymnastics.

of as turning around the body's horizontal or vertical axis. At other times a rolling action might function to transfer the body's weight from one place to another as a traveling action. While traveling through the air, a gymnast might rotate the body to create a particular shape or change directions. In many instances one skill set will be the main theme for a given lesson, although other skills will support, link, or combine with the main theme to unify gymnastics work.

The beauty of thinking about gymnastics as sets or units of work is that we can at times separate out single skills to teach developmentally by refining and extending tasks. Using sets of skills also allows us to combine work logically. In reality, we associate gymnastics floor exercise, the balance beam, or parallel bars with routines. Gymnasts continually strive to perfect individual skills and then combine them with other skills to develop sequences or routines. They piece actions together, or link one action to another, to use the momentum created by one action flowing into the next. This flow, this functional movement with complete body awareness and management, is what makes gymnastics aesthetic.

SCOPE AND SEQUENCE

As established in chapter 2, planning is a part of developing your gymnastics program and how it fits into your overall program in physical education. With respect to gymnastics, you must give careful consideration to the scope and sequence of possibilities (tables 3.1 and 3.2). *Scope* refers to what you will and will not include in your program. For example, if you have only mats or do not have an indoor facility, what you teach will be different from what someone with more extensive equipment and an indoor facility will teach. The order in which the content is taught and at what grade levels are called *sequence*. As the teacher, you are the one who must determine the scope and sequence in gymnastics for your specific teaching situation. In an effort to provide some models for you to follow, we have outlined the scope and sequence of gymnastics from grades K to 5 using the national standards (NASPE 2004) and a skill-theme and movement-concept approach (Graham, Holt/Hale, and Parker 2010). In general, simple skills in traveling, balancing, and rotation such as steplike actions of the feet, transferring weight to the hands, balancing on various body parts, and rolling in various directions are included in the early grades. In the area of movement concepts, children in the early grades concentrate on the development of spatial awareness, the use of time and force in the area of effort, and the relationships of body parts to one another and to objects such as hoops, wands, ropes, boxes, and benches. Combining skills is also part of gymnastics development in the early years. As children develop a sound foundation in gymnastics, the later elementary years focus on traveling using the feet, taking weight on the hands, transferring weight, balancing, and rolling in more sophisticated ways. Skills might include the flight phases of jumping and vaulting, handstands, cartwheels, round-offs, handsprings, straddle rolls, and so on. In the later elementary years children also use equipment to mount; balance; travel on, off, along; and establish work with partners and small groups. There is also a focus on sequence work.

Table 3.1 Scope and Sequence for Gymnastics Using the National Standards for Grades K to 5

	K-2	3-5
Travels in a variety of locomotor patterns (e.g., skips, hops, gallops, slides) using mature form.	X	
Demonstrates clear contrasts between slow and fast movements.	X	
Balances demonstrating momentary stillness in symmetrical and asymmetrical shapes on a variety of body parts and at different levels.	X	
Balances using various bases of support on low equipment.	X	
Rolls in different directions (sideways, forward), maintaining a round shape, without hesitating or stopping.	X	
Jumps and lands using a variety of takeoffs and landings in relation to various equipment.	X	
Momentarily transfers weight from feet to hands, making the legs land in various places around the body.	X	
Designs and performs simple sequences involving traveling, balancing, and rolling and incorporates change of level and shapes.	X	
Travels and then uses a spring takeoff, landing safely on an apparatus.		X
Jumps off equipment and rotates while in flight (quarter, half, three-quarter, or full turns).		X
Balances in inverted positions with the center of gravity over the head (frog stand, tripod, headstand).		X
Balances with a partner using principles of counterbalance and countertension.		X
Performs a variety of rolls demonstrating a mature pattern starting and landing on feet.		X
Uses a variety of body actions to move from feet to hands and return to feet using large extensions (cartwheel, round-off, twisting to different landing positions).		X
Designs and performs gymnastics sequences that combine traveling, rolling, balancing, and transferring weight with intentional changes in direction, speed, and flow.		X
Designs and performs a partner routine on and off equipment.		X

Based on Graham, Holt/Hale, and Parker 2010; and NASPE 2004.

Table 3.2 Scope and Sequence of Skill Theme and Movement Concept for Grades K to 5

Movement concept or skill theme	K	1	2	3	4	5
Spatial awareness						
Self-space and general space	X	X				
Levels, directions, pathways	X	X	X			
Extensions			X	X		
Effort						
Time and speed	X	X	X	X	X	
Force			X	X	X	X
Flow			X	X	X	X
Relationships						
One body part to another	X	X				
Body shapes	X	X	X			
With objects	X	X	X	X		
With people			X	X	X	X
Traveling						
Walking and running	X	X				
Hopping, skipping, galloping	X	X	X			
Leaping, sliding	X	X	X	X		
Jumping and landing	X	X	X	X	X	
Balancing	X	X	X	X	X	X
Transferring weight			X	X	X	X
Rotating	X	X	X	X	X	X

X denotes that the movement concept or skill theme is a major focus at this grade level. They may be a part of other grade levels as well.
Based on Graham, Holt/Hale, and Parker 2010; and NASPE 2004.

STAGES OF GYMNASTICS

Developing content in gymnastics is thought to be similar to the games stages developed by Rink (2010). In the stages of game play, children develop basic skills in stage I, then move on to combining skills in stage II. Next, they use the skills they have developed in simple modified games during stage III. In stage IV they play more complex games that move them toward playing by the official rules in a given sport. Nilges (1997, 1999) has a similar set of stages for the development of content in gymnastics. It also has four stages (table 3.3).

Stage I includes the exploration and variation of individual skills. It allows students to develop a broad base of foundational skills in each of the skill themes of gymnastics. Beginning skills in the area of traveling include steplike weight transfer using the feet only and using hands and feet, and other means of weight transfer including sliding, rocking, and rolling. During this stage children learn to explore the development of specific skills by varying the process characteristics (BSER; see table 3.8, page 57). Though a lot of stage I development occurs during the early elementary grades, children also learn stage I skills throughout gymnastics content development. Examples are when

Table 3.3   Examples of Stages of Content Development in Gymnastics

Stage I: Exploration and variation of individual skills
Beginning: Bunny hop, cartwheel, egg roll, pencil roll, forward roll, balance on patches and points with changes of level and base of support, flight with shape in air
Advanced: Round-off, back handspring, straddle roll, hip circle around bar or beam, vaulting, use of different shapes from hanging or support positions on equipment
Stage II: Combination of individual skills
Various steplike actions with the feet in and out of hoop
Jump onto equipment with a transition into a balance
Balance, roll, balance
Round-off, back handspring
Balance on equipment, then a dismount
Stage III: Beginning sequence work
Beginning shape, weight transfer with hands to arrive at bench, jump to mount the bench, low-level balance, roll to dismount, ending shape
Individual mirror balance with partner, steplike action to arrive together, partner balance, transition out of partner balance, different mirror balance with partner
Stage IV: Advanced sequence work
Beginning and ending shape
Use of two pieces of equipment
Work in groups of three
Steplike or rolling actions as transitions to and from equipment
Three to five similar or contrasting balances on equipment, or rotation around the beam, or both

From Nilges 1997.

older children learn to do difficult balances, straddle rolls, handstands, handsprings, hip circles around a bar, and more complex vaulting skills.

During stage II children learn to combine individual skills into logical order. By combining skills, children learn to link two or more actions together by using smooth transitions. At simple levels, combining skills may include balancing on patches or points and then choosing a logical rolling or sliding action into a different balance. Or it may include taking weight on the hands using a bunny hop, landing back softly on the feet, and finishing in a low-level balance. At higher levels of skill, stage II work may include a round-off into a back handspring, two partners starting away from each other and using a rolling or stepping action to create a smooth transition into a partner balance, or a balance on a piece of equipment followed by a dismounting action.

Beginning sequence work is the focus of stage III. Students learn to make choices and narrow their work into limited repeatable sequences. Each sequence must have a clear beginning and ending shape, good body awareness throughout the sequence, and a combination of actions from two or more of the skill themes. Because children already know how to do the given actions, the focus in stage III work is on how to use actions or put them together in an aesthetically pleasing way. There is also an emphasis on the flow of a sequence—the student establishes continuity from one action to another. Examples of stage III sequence work might include the following:

- Establish a clear beginning shape; transfer weight using the hands to arrive at a bench; mount the bench using a jumping action; lower the body into a balance position using selected patches, points, or both; use a rolling action to dismount the bench; and finish in an ending balance position on the floor.
- Partners start away from each other in a balance pose in which they mirror each other, use a steplike traveling action to arrive together, transition into a partner balance, and transition out of the partner balance into an ending mirrored balance pose that differs from the first one by a change in the base of support or level.

Advanced sequence work is the focus of stage IV. Once again, the students' sequence work must be repeatable, but the nature of the sequence work has fewer limitations. Stage IV includes work from multiple skill themes. Often the students select and arrange the equipment. They may also choose to work with a partner or small group. More specific attention is paid to the process characteristics (BSER) of movement. The following sequence would be appropriate at the stage IV level: While working in a group of three using a bench and a balance beam, develop a sequence that includes a clear beginning and ending shape; appropriate steplike or rolling actions as transitions from one piece of equipment to another; and the use of three to five actions that show similar or contrasting balances on each piece of equipment, rotation around the beam, or both.

TASK DEVELOPMENT IN GYMNASTICS

During the teaching of a lesson or learning experience in gymnastics as well as games or dance, a teacher performs four functions (Rink 2010). The first is called an *informing task* that usually takes place at the start of a lesson but can also be used at other times during a lesson when a teacher introduces a completely new focus or intent. During the informing task, the teacher clearly explains and describes what the children will be learning. Demonstrations are often given to help clarify the nature of the task. In the learning experiences in this book, the informing tasks are marked with the symbol (I).

A second function of the teacher is to extend tasks during the lesson. Once the children have been given a starting task, the teacher needs to step back and analyze the children's responses to determine whether the task is too easy, just right, or too difficult. The intent of *extending tasks* is to create variety so that the children have a range of options (harder, new challenge, or easier) in a progression or series of tasks. In the learning experiences each new extending task is marked with the symbol (E).

Third, a teacher can refine a task by getting the students to focus on the quality of their work. *Refining tasks* do not always have to follow an extending task but are used when a teacher thinks that the children can benefit from practice with a focus on performing the critical elements of a task. At this time the teacher will usually stop an ongoing task and point out any errors in performances and provide a cue so that students focus on what will improve the performance. Refining tasks in the learning experiences in this book are marked with the symbol (R).

Application tasks serve as the teacher's fourth function of task development. *Application tasks* provide children with a challenge to determine their progress in learning a skill. Application tasks serve to maintain students' interest in and determine their success rate at a task. Application tasks in the learning experiences in this book are marked with the symbol (A). To help you understand the process of task development in gymnastics, table 3.4 illustrates each of the four functions.

Although the example in table 3.4 does not include all the possibilities of extending, refining, and applying tasks, as a teacher you can see that if you start a lesson with a task of a specific roll or rolling as a generalized concept, you will have several choices to make based on the children's responses to the first task. If the children show you that they can perform the general task of rolling quite well (80 percent success rate), you can choose to extend the next task by introducing the idea of rolling while the body is in different shapes or rolling in different directions. If the children are having some problems with the quality of their rolls, you can stop to have them refocus on rolling from one adjacent body part to the next (round body in direction of movement) and keeping arms and legs straight or chin and knees tucked into the

Table 3.4   Task Development of a Rolling Action

Informing	Extending	Refining	Application
Today we will perform rolling actions. We will start with rolling in a sideways direction.		• Roll from one adjacent body part to another. • Make your body round and smooth.	Perform a roll of your choice with good form.
	Roll in a sideways direction: • In a stretched shape • In a curled shape • In a seated shape	• Tight body • Like a pencil—stretch • Like an egg—curl up • Reach with arms, legs straight	Can you roll in a sideways direction using two different shapes?
	• Roll in a forward or backward direction. • Use an incline to assist your roll.	• Tight body—knees and chin to chest • Start on feet, return to feet • Keep body round, not like a flat tire	• Perform a forward or backward roll with good form. • Can you do two rolls, one after the other?
	Change your body shape while rolling in different directions.	• Long and tall • Short and small • Forward, backward, or sideways	Make up a sequence by performing two different rolls with a change in direction.

chest. If you want to give the children a self-testing activity, you can give them one of the application tasks. There is no specific order to the tasks. All tasks are dependent on the children's responses to the previous task.

DIRECT AND INDIRECT TEACHING STYLES

As a teacher, you sometimes want to be very specific in what you assign children to learn. This is a good way to build skill and develop sound fundamentals. It gives children a solid foundation from which to build. This type of teaching style has been called *direct, invariant,* or *command oriented* (Graham 2008). Some examples are specifically teaching the forward roll, cartwheel, or front support position as skills as opposed to teaching the concepts of rolling, weight transfer, or balancing. In direct teaching, a specific skill or routine is presented. The teacher sets a standard of performance. Children attempt to conform to the standard, having little or no choice. This approach tends to work well at beginning levels of skill development and in a more formal Olympic gymnastics setting, which takes successful performers to ever-higher levels of progressive skills. At times it is appropriate to teach specific skills, principles for good body mechanics, and movement fundamentals or concepts directly. These aspects serve as a foundation, or set of building blocks, from which children can begin to make choices.

Direct teaching, however, often does not work well in a system that fosters body management. It may doom some children to failure and stifle creativity and thinking. Because children come into a gymnastics setting with different experiences and levels of ability, we promote a more *indirect* teaching style, one that is oriented to discovery, questioning, and problem solving (figure 3.2). This type of teaching is often called *inquiry* and features convergent and divergent thinking. In this book you will find ways to teach children about traveling, balancing, and rotating from a conceptual point of view. Children first learn the principles of traveling, balancing, and rotating and then are asked to make choices. For example, combine two steplike traveling actions; balance your body in a stretched, then curled, shape; or sequence a travel, a balance, and a roll.

You could easily tell the children to skip and then hop or to balance in a T position and then curl into a ball. Ultimately, is it more valuable to the child to copy you, parrotlike, or to become empowered to make decisions and create a resolution to a movement problem? We contend that encouraging children to make movement decisions gives them ownership of the material. They may work at their own level of ability. They are allowed to sequence work in their own unique ways.

Figure 3.2   Indirect teaching encourages children to solve movement problems.

WHEN TO ENCOURAGE STUDENT DEMONSTRATIONS

Many teachers choose only highly skilled students to demonstrate or perform the sequences. As a teacher of body management, you should think about the purposes of demonstrations as well as how you choose the children who will demonstrate.

Figure 3.3 Use demonstrations wisely as examples of movement possibilities.

Demonstrations are useful when the class is beginning a skill or sequence to present a model or show examples of possibilities (see figure 3.3). During the middle of a task, modeling gives hints and shows how to refine or expand movement options. Students may correct errors and exhibit work that is on track (see description of pinpointing in Graham 2008). Late in the learning process, students demonstrate their sequence work as a performance.

The question remains about whose work to show. In choosing only highly skilled students, you give children a message with far-reaching implications. The average and below-average students begin to think that you do not value their work. As a teacher, you should convey that you value the work of all students. By watching all the children for work that is mechanically correct, unique solutions to a movement problem, or hard work that is on task, you can include everyone at some time in the demonstrations. Catch children in the act of doing something well. Giving everyone an opportunity to be highlighted increases the chances of productive work, because all children know they have an equal chance to be called on.

Keep in mind some other factors about demonstrations. If one child demonstrates, the rest are watching. It may be useful on occasion to have all the children watch something specific, but doing so cuts down on activity time. Often it is just as valuable to show work to a partner or small group or to have each half of the class perform for the rest.

Giving demonstrations makes some children nervous and self-conscious. Children should have the right to decline. Perhaps they do not feel ready or are not at ease with what they are doing. Return to them at a later time.

ACCOUNTABILITY: THE GYMNASTICS WORK ETHIC

Hold children accountable for their actions. You will be just as happy and accepting with a low-skilled child performing a seated sideways roll in the sequence as with an advanced learner performing a dive roll over a bench. A child who fools around to cover insecurity or embarrassment is just as dangerous as an irresponsible daredevil showing off. If you set proper rules in the gymnasium and enforce them, children will know you mean business: Listen during instruction. Respect others. Take care of equipment. Work productively.

Gymnastics should present a pleasurable and challenging yet worklike environment. It is serious and not a place to fool around out of control. Fooling around is how people get hurt. All children should work productively at their ability level. Like the army slogan "Be all you can be," your attitude should convey that you care and expect their best effort.

STRESSING GOOD BODY MECHANICS AND AESTHETICS

With a thematic, or conceptual, approach to teaching, children are given choices about which skills they perform, how they perform them, and how they link one skill to another in a sequence or routine. It is tempting to step back and let anything and everything happen—whatever the child chooses is fine, and movement exploration all the way! Unfortunately, that attitude carries risks and is far from what should happen in practice.

Though we want children to have choices, as a teacher you are the guide and the expert. You recognize good execution and body mechanics. You know what is aesthetically pleasing in gymnastics (see figure 3.4). It is your job to guide and help children discover proper ways to perform skills and to create flowing transitions between movements. If you see a child rolling forward who needs to push up with the hands at the end of the roll to return to the feet, you should step in and teach that student to stay tucked and to initiate and use body momentum. If you see

Figure 3.4 Execution and aesthetics are always important in gymnastics.

children placing the hands or head on the floor improperly, you need to teach them a safe way to do it. If you see kids falling and crashing to the floor on their shins, backs, or other body parts, you should teach them soft, absorbent landings. For example, when children take weight on the hands and return to the feet, no crashing or falling should occur! Whether children do simple bunny hops or go into handstands, they should always return softly to their feet. Shoulders are always over the hands, with the arms straight and elbows locked.

Furthermore, you should teach children what is aesthetically pleasing (i.e., no saggy bodies; maintain good lines and tension). If the body or a body part is stretched, is it fully extended? If the intent is to curl, does the body or body part become round and smooth? If the intent is to focus attention on line or design, is there a commitment to it? Lines can be horizontal, vertical, and so on. Several lines from the arms or legs may converge, diverge, or be parallel. In a given balance, do the arms and legs have a clear focus? A gymnast is like an artist painting on a canvas. The gymnast strives to move the body in ways that are not only efficient but also pleasing to the eye. As a teacher, you can help children make these aesthetic choices.

SKILL THEMES FOR GYMNASTICS

Having considered the overall scope and sequence of gymnastics (tables 3.1 and 3.2), the stages of gymnastics (table 3.3), task development in gymnastics (table 3.4), and other factors that influence the teaching of gymnastics, it is now time to turn attention to a more detailed description of each of the skill themes that are a focus of work. These three skill themes consist of traveling actions, static work, and rotation actions.

Traveling Actions

In this book traveling actions of the body include all work in which the focus is to move the body from one place to another (see table 3.5). The intent of some traveling actions is to move the body to a new position on the floor or over a distance with reference to equipment. The intent of other traveling actions is to shift or transfer the body's weight to a new position, thus moving only a very short distance. Several major categories of traveling actions exist.

Table 3.5 Traveling Actions of the Body

Steplike—using feet	Steplike—using hands, feet, knees	Weight transfer	Flight
Walking	Crawling	Rocking, rolling	Takeoff
Running	Bear walk	Twisting, turning	Suspension
Hopping	Crab walk	Sliding	Landing
Jumping	Bunny hop		Minitramp work
Skipping	Mule kick		Vaulting
Galloping	Coffee grinder		
Sliding	Walkover (front, back)		
Leaping	Wheeling (cartwheel, round-off)		
	Springing (front and back handspring)		

Steplike Travel Using the Feet

All of the steplike actions of the feet are traveling actions. There are five ways to transfer weight using the feet: from one foot to the other (walk, run, leap), from one foot to the same foot (hop), from two feet to two feet (jump), from two feet to one foot, and from one foot to two feet. These basic stepping actions in combination produce skipping, galloping, sliding, and other more innovative ways of using the feet to travel across the floor. The use of the feet to produce traveling is called locomotion.

Steplike Travel Using the Hands, Feet, and Knees

Steplike actions also occur when a gymnast uses the hands and feet or hands and knees to travel. Some gymnastics teachers include these types of steplike actions in a category of weight transfer, but in this book we have chosen to separate them. When young children explore what their bodies can do to travel through space, they learn crawling, the bear walk, the crab walk, the bunny hop, animal walks of other sorts, the coffee grinder (a circular motion performed using a one-arm front support as the pivot point), and other stuntlike movements. These movement tasks, whether taught directly or indirectly (by challenging children to find various ways to move with their hands and feet), help children develop strength in the arms and legs and gain confidence in managing their bodies.

In this book, the words *gymnast* and *gymnastics-like* are used to set a tone, to establish a philosophy, or to set a frame of mind for teachers and children. Gymnastics is different from games and dance; it includes basic body-management skills as well as more formal gymnastics skills. This means that not everything is acceptable under the rubric of gymnastics. As children think like gymnasts, they will work more productively to link actions and skills into sequences and routines reflecting this attitude. What is not gymnastics-like are uncontrolled attempts at animal walks, silly sounds, racing about, and relays. To encourage the development of a gymnastics philosophy or attitude, always think of children as gymnasts.

As children develop these beginning skills using their hands and feet to transfer weight, consider the question of what work is gymnastics-like. What type of work in this category would you wish to continue and encourage, and what type would you try to eliminate? Beyond the early primary years, crawling, simple animal walks, and the like should be discouraged; they are no longer useful. They lead nowhere and are not gymnastics-like. As children develop readiness skills, arm and shoulder strength, and confidence, their steplike traveling gymnastics should include wheeling actions (the cartwheel or round-off), springing actions (the front or back handspring), and other actions in which weight is transferred from the feet to the hands and back to the feet. They might practice the walkover or use the hands to transfer weight over a bench, box, or horse.

Weight Transfer

The category of weight transfer as a traveling action includes all the movements that focus on the transfer of weight from one adjacent body part to another. Rocking forward and back on front or back body surfaces or from side to side, rolling actions of all types, and sliding are examples of work in this category. Though rolling presents some crossover of categories between traveling and rotation actions, this is not a problem if we keep in mind the idea of unified sets of work. Sometimes the focus of a roll involves principles of rotation. At other times a rolling action helps a student travel across a mat, arrive at a piece of equipment, or move off a piece of equipment to link with the next part in a sequence.

Twisting and turning actions of all types can also help the body travel a short distance and transfer body weight from one position to another. A person in a V-sit, with weight back on the hands, might effectively turn halfway over to the right or left into a push-up position. Another person might twist out of a shoulder stand to a position on two knees or a knee and a foot.

Sliding in this category is not to be confused with sliding sideways on the feet. As a means of weight transfer, sliding is a shift of body weight from one position to another in which the person chooses a particular body surface along which to slide. For example, a child lying on her belly on the floor or a bench might anchor the hands and slide along her belly or shins into a push-up (front support) position. Someone might slide on the belly over a horse, take weight on the hands, and finish with a roll to the feet. From a push-up position, a person could put his head on the floor, slide the feet toward his hands into a pike position, and press up into a headstand. In each instance the sliding action helped transfer body weight and is a functional part of the sequence.

Flight

Flight, the last category of traveling actions, includes such movements as the takeoff, suspension, travel through the air, and landing. Initial attempts at takeoff are exploratory in nature and should include steplike actions of the feet. Over time, children should learn specialized forms of the takeoff, such as the step into the two-foot hurdle action used in diving and vaulting in gymnastics. During the flight phase of the jump, the focus is on the body's shape—wide or narrow, extended or tucked, symmetrical or asymmetrical, and so on. Landings usually should be on the feet and controlled. Soft, squishy landings are key, in which children learn to absorb body weight smoothly by giving with the knees. More advanced students may learn landings on the hands, such as a dive roll, or even on other body parts; the principles are always the same. To receive weight, the body must give, or absorb the landing smoothly, under control. Under all conditions care must be taken to maximize safety through the protection of the head and other body parts.

Initial work on flight should be on the floor. Gradually takeoffs and landings can involve raised surfaces, such as jumping onto and off boxes and benches. As children gain skill and confidence, you can introduce special pieces of equipment, such as Reuter boards and minitrampolines, to emphasize the flight phase of the jump. Children can incorporate further work on the concept of flight into vaulting actions over a horse or by using one or more partners as a platform from which to vault, as in leapfrog. Specific vaults might include a courage vault, squat vault, straddle vault, and wolf vault. A variety of symmetrical, asymmetrical, stretched, curled, and twisted shapes and directional changes in the air should be the focus of the work. As always, the emphasis should also be on quality jumps, vaults, and flight through the air and soft, controlled landings.

Applying Principles of Traveling

For students to achieve quality movements, all traveling actions should focus on form and function. Gymnasts focus on the process characteristics of movement and try to make each action look good. When traveling on the feet, work should be predominantly light or soft, with students up on the balls of their feet. Occasionally, such as when vaulting, more force is used to generate flight. To get high in the air, students should reach their arms to the sky to propel the body upward. This might be called *resilient* or *rebound* jumping or hopping.

To make traveling actions look good, students must attend to the carriage of the torso, use of the arms, and position of the head. Gymnasts pay attention to detail.

Their bodies use good lines—straight, curved, twisted. They carry out extensions of the limbs through the pointing of hands and feet.

While in the air a gymnast tries to create quality shapes with an emphasis on good form. Once again, they should pay attention to what the whole body is doing. Depending on the shape (curled, twisted, straight, symmetrical, asymmetrical), a gymnast strives for perfect form. Because the period of flight is short in terms of time spent in the air, the gymnast must move quickly into the shape, create the good shape, and then quickly come out of the shape to prepare for landing.

Landings should be soft and absorbent. When landing from a height, the gymnast should bend at the hips, with knees and ankles under control to cushion the body's momentum. The arms should be used to help control or stabilize the body and stop its motion.

Static Work

Gymnastics work within the skill theme of statics includes those activities in which the focus is to achieve stillness or balance (see table 3.6). Initially, you are trying to help children achieve stillness in a controlled manner. Activities such as running and then stopping or freezing can help children differentiate between movement and no movement. They need to learn to feel the tightness of the muscles held in a static position. After learning to gain stillness on the feet, students may shift to creating balances on other body parts in a controlled manner. Emphasize control by counting to three or five. During early balance experiences, counting is helpful for focusing on mastery, but it should gradually receive less emphasis. In reality, gymnasts performing routines rarely hold positions for long periods. They hold balance positions just long enough to show control—almost as if to say, "I could stay here longer if I wanted to." The real beauty of gymnastics is not in the static balances but in the flow created when a gymnast links movements to and from those balances into a sequence or routine.

Types of Balance

Gymnastics includes many types of balance. Balances may be thought of as *upright,* with the head higher than the hips, or *inverted,* with the head lower than the hips. Balance positions may be *symmetrical* or *asymmetrical.* In symmetrical balances the left and right sides of the body mirror each other (i.e., they are the same). The headstand, handstand, V-sit, and other common balances are symmetrical. By changing one arm or leg position to a bend, stretch, or twist, thereby making the left side different from the right, a gymnast assumes an asymmetrical balance. There are countless variations

Table 3.6 Static Characteristics of the Body

Characteristics of balance	Principles of balance	Types of balance
Moments of stillness	Base of support	Upright or inverted
Tightness of body	Center of gravity	Symmetrical or asymmetrical
Control	Countertension/counterbalance	Hanging
	Linking actions	Supporting
	Movement into and out of balance	Relationship to equipment
		Individual or partner

of asymmetrical balances. Considered within the BSER framework, symmetrical and asymmetrical balances both are types of body shapes among the process variables (see table 3.8, page 57).

With the introduction of equipment such as a bench, box, beam, bar, or jungle gym, a gymnast can create still other balances from hanging or support positions. Additional relationships to equipment occur as gymnasts create balance positions, supporting their weight completely or partially on the equipment. Balances can be done individually or with a partner or small group.

Applying Principles of Balance

The main principles that govern balance stem from the base of support and center of gravity (see figure 3.5). In general, a wide base of support, with several body parts acting as bases, will be more stable than a narrow base with fewer body parts serving as supports. A low center of gravity is more stable than a high one. A key to choosing good balance positions is to keep the center of gravity over the base of support, then align the body parts that serve as bases. In a headstand, the head and hands must form a triangle, and the head and arms must distribute weight equally, with the hips and legs directly over the base to create a vertical column from the spine through the extended legs and feet. When the legs serve as a base, the knees and hips should be in vertical alignment with the feet. Good alignment produces strong balances.

Figure 3.5   Examples of balances with good bases and alignment.

At times a gymnast chooses to use the concepts of counterbalance and counter-tension to assume positions of balance (see figure 3.6). In a *counterbalance position,* the gymnast's center of gravity is outside the base of support, but by pushing against another gymnast or supporting his or her weight with or against a piece of equipment, the gymnast achieves a stable balance position. In a *countertension balance position,* two or more gymnasts are pulling away from each other with their center of gravity outside their base, but because they are countering each other's force in opposite directions through tension, they achieve a stable balance.

A gymnast may also use the concept of balance as a means of moving into or out of a balance position or from one balance position to another. When balancing in a given position, such as a scale, a gymnast might take the trunk forward and one

Figure 3.6 Examples of counterbalance and countertension with partners and equipment.

leg back. He or she could extend the arms sideways parallel to the floor for more stability. As long as the center of gravity remains over the support leg, the balance will be stable. Yet, by experimenting with a lean forward, backward, or sideways, a gymnast can find the point where loss of balance occurs. Once this loss of balance occurs, a gymnast can use the momentum generated to carry the body smoothly into the next balance. A twist, turn, roll, step, or other body action used under control is the common method of linking balances into sequences. Gymnasts continually seek ways to link balances smoothly and with control through actions of counterbalance: balance, then loss of balance, then balance regained. No falls. No crashes. No glitches. No unwanted or unnecessary steps. Gymnasts want the controlled use of momentum into and out of balances.

Rotation Actions

Rotary movement occurs around the three axes of the body—that is, the three planes (dimensions) of space. These are the vertical (longitudinal), horizontal, and transverse (medial) axes. If a rod were placed vertically from head to toe, rotation would occur in a vertical plane. Jumps with quarter, half, and full turns in the air and pencil rolls or log rolls are typical of rotation around a vertical axis. A rod placed horizontally from hip to hip (side to side) would allow for rotation around a horizontal axis. Forward rolls, backward rolls, somersaults, and front and back handsprings are typical examples of rotation around a horizontal axis. Front and back hip circles are examples of horizontal rotation when using equipment. A rod placed horizontally (front to back) would allow for rotation around a transverse axis. Wheeling actions such as a cartwheel or round-off, on the floor and onto and off equipment, are typical of rotation around a transverse axis.

Types of Rotation

Rotation in space occurs when the body moves around any of its three axes without equipment being involved, such as rolling actions on the mat, sitting spins, cartwheels, round-offs, springing actions, and jump turns in the air. Rotation around equipment occurs when a bar, beam, bench, or other piece of equipment acts as the radius of rotation.

Applying Principles of Rotation

Rotation work in gymnastics includes twisting, turning, and rolling activities around one of the body's three axes (see table 3.7). Movement around these three axes of the body is influenced by certain mechanical principles. The rate of rotation around a fixed point, or axis, increases as the radius (distance from axis to endpoint) decreases. Conversely, the rate of rotation around a fixed point is decreased if the radius is increased. This concept is important for gymnasts, divers, skaters, and other athletes who use turns and rolls in their sport. Staying tucked in a forward roll, hip circle, or somersault will help athletes spin quickly. It shortens or decreases the radius. Opening up or extending away from the center will slow or stop the rate of rotation; it lengthens or increases the radius. Gymnasts can use this principle to their advantage when they wish to accelerate, or speed up a movement, and to decelerate, or slow a movement. For example, gymnasts doing a headstand or handstand into a forward roll and finishing in a standing position would stay long, or extended, to begin the turn and generate momentum. They would then lower the body and quickly tuck, using that speed to complete the roll to the feet. Finally they would stand and extend to slow the action and stop the momentum. Think long and tall, short and small, or long and tall.

Learning to fix the eyes on a stationary point is another helpful principle for any athlete who turns, rolls, or spins about. Maintaining eye contact with a fixed spot gives a reference point to where the body is in space. Using this principle helps gymnasts maintain balance and overcome any tendencies toward dizziness.

Gymnasts should also strive to transfer body weight from one adjacent body part to another when rotating using rolling actions. This is true of rolls using the longitudinal axis as well as those using the horizontal axis. For example, when performing a log roll (also known as pencil roll), a gymnast should try to make the body roll smoothly from back to side to front to side and return to the starting position. The body needs to be long and stretched. Arms, elbows, or legs that are sticking out a bit make the gymnast

Table 3.7   Rotary Actions of the Body

Principles of rotation	Movement around three axes	Types of rotation
Radius of rotation	Vertical	In space
Eye focus	Spins	Around equipment
	Turns	
	Pencil (log) rolls	
	Horizontal	
	Forward rolls	
	Backward rolls	
	Handsprings	
	Somersaults	
	Hip circles	
	Transverse	
	Cartwheels or wheeling	
	Round-offs or springing	

roll like a flat tire—clunk, clunk, clunk. In a similar fashion, a gymnast accomplishes rolls in the horizontal axis by staying in a curled-up position, tucking the chin and knees to the chest. If the back is round, the roll proceeds smoothly. If the back is flat, the roll feels awkward. In a backward roll, as the body gets to an upside-down position, the gymnast places the hands on the floor with thumbs in toward the ears and elbows up. The arms can then do a quick upside-down push-up to create clearance for the head as the gymnast returns to the feet.

PROCESS VARIABLES

Each of the skill themes just described involves a continual awareness of concepts of body, space, effort, and relationships (BSER; see table 3.8). Rudolf Laban originally developed these process variables to provide a framework for dance. Superimposing Laban's process variables onto the travel, static, and rotation skill themes provides a

Table 3.8   BSER Framework of Human Movement

Body (what the body does)	Space (where the body moves)	Effort (how the body performs the movement)	Relationships (relationships that occur in movement)
Actions of the body	Areas	Time	Body parts
• Curl	• General	• Fast, accelerating, sudden	• Above, below
• Bend	• Personal	• Slow, decelerating, sustained	• Apart, together
• Twist	Directions	Force (weight)	• Behind, in front of
• Swing	• Forward	• Firm, strong	• Meeting, parting
Actions of body parts	• Backward	• Fine, light	• Near, far
• Support body weight	• Sideways	Space	Individuals and groups
• Lead action	• Upward	• Direct, straight	• Mirroring, matching
• Receive weight or force	• Downward	• Indirect, flexible	• Contrasting
• Apply force	• Diagonal	Flow	• Successive, alternating
Activities of the body	Levels	• Bound, stoppable, jerky	• Questioning, answering
• Locomotor	• Low	• Free, ongoing, smooth	• Acting, reacting
• Nonlocomotor	• Medium		• Leading, following
• Manipulative	• High		• Lifting, being lifted
Body shapes	Pathways		• Supporting, being supported
• Angular	• Straight		A person and equipment
• Straight	• Curved		• Around, along
• Round	• Zigzag		• Over, under
• Twisted	• Twisted		• Near, far
• Symmetrical, asymmetrical	Planes		• Above, below, alongside
	• Sagittal (wheel)		• Arriving on, dismounting
	• Frontal (door)		Other types
	• Horizontal (table)		• Goals, boundaries
	Extensions		• Music, sounds
	• Large		• Poems, stories, words
	• Small		• Beats, patterns
			• Art, artifacts

gymnastics movement vocabulary for students of all ages and skill levels. Each of these process variables can be interwoven with learning experiences on the skill themes of traveling, statics, and rotation at appropriate times. Although each is important in itself, they will become subthemes as we discuss the main skill themes.

Body

Focus for a moment on the body and what it can do: actions of the whole body and of specific body parts, activities of the body, and shapes that the body can assume. Actions of the body include curling, bending, twisting, and swinging movements. Actions of specific body parts include supporting weight, leading a movement, receiving force (or weight), and giving force. The body's activities include locomotion, nonlocomotion, and manipulation. In this book the traveling actions are locomotor activities, and static work is the equivalent in nonlocomotor activities. Manipulative activities are part of rhythmic gymnastics, but the skill themes of throwing, catching, and kicking (manipulative actions) lie outside the realm of this book (see Belka 1993; Buschner 1994; Graham, Holt/Hale, and Parker 2010). Finally, the body can assume such shapes as angular, straight, round, twisted, symmetrical, and asymmetrical.

Space

Directions, pathways, levels, planes, and extensions are the spatial elements gymnasts use most. Traveling and rotation skills move the body in forward, backward, sideways, up-and-down, and diagonal directions. By selecting a pathway in which to perform a sequence of actions, children can link together appropriate floor or air patterns for body movement. For example, "Jump, roll, then travel, taking weight on the hands" may lead to a zigzag, straight, circular, or twisted pathway. Practicing along straight lines during floor work helps children to transfer the skills and sequences later onto benches and the beam.

Although in traveling and rotation the body moves through general space, static work stays within one's personal space. The body can be held or moved through a range of levels, from very low to very high. Incorporating level changes into a sequence of actions gives a student the opportunity to create responses with more variety and aesthetic appeal. Changes in level also apply to body parts in relation to each other. For example, asking students to create a balance in which their feet are at a higher level than their hands may result in a shoulder balance, a headstand, or even a handstand.

The planes of space define the three dimensions of space, much the same as the three axes of rotation. The *table,* or *horizontal, plane* divides top from bottom. The *door,* or *frontal, plane* divides left from right. The *wheel,* or *sagittal, plane* divides front from back. Think of movement or balance positions as taking place in one or more of the planes of space. A headstand going from low to high takes place primarily in the horizontal plane. Sliding sideways on the feet across a bench emphasizes movement in the frontal plane. Movement of the body forward and then backward emphasizes the sagittal plane.

Large and small spatial extensions occur during gymnastics when the body is *extended* (body parts are far from the center) and when the body is *flexed* (body parts are close to the center). A second kind of extension occurs when a sequence takes a gymnast far away from a point of origin, covering a lot of space, or keeps the gymnast close to the point of origin.

Effort

Effort qualities consist of time, space, weight (or force), and flow. *Time* qualifies movement as occurring very quickly or in a slow, sustained fashion. A roll or a steplike traveling action may be executed quickly or slowly. Pressing up into a headstand might occur slowly, in a very controlled manner, and a roll out of a headstand might be done quickly to establish the momentum needed to move into the next action.

The variable of *space* refers to direct and indirect movement. A gymnast moving across the floor or moving to arrive at a piece of equipment may choose to travel directly to a chosen place or use an indirect pathway, such as a zigzag or curved pathway. As the arms, legs, or other body parts move through the air, they also move directly or indirectly through space.

The concept of *weight* (or *force)* refers to the amount of energy given to an action. Some gymnastics actions are soft and light; others require an extraordinary amount of heavy force. Skipping across the floor or hopping along a bench might be soft and delicate. A vaulting action or press into a handstand could use a lot of force.

Flow refers to whether a movement is free and smooth or bound and stoppable. Turning or spinning actions (rotation) are often free and flowing, whereas the balancing actions of static work are often bound and tense. Each of these effort qualities, although described separately, often interacts in combination with one or more of the others. Running across the floor may be quick, light, direct, and flowing. Balancing in a V-sit on a bench might be sustained, forceful, and bound. (For further information on the effort qualities of movement, see Buschner 1994.)

Relationships

Relationships involve interactions between body parts, between one person and another, between one person and a group, or between a person and equipment. Some of the relationships among body parts are above and below, apart and together, behind and in front, meeting and parting, and near and far. Working with a partner or small group, an individual may lead or follow; mirror, match, or contrast; lift or be lifted; and support or be supported. Within groups, we use the term *successive* to refer to an ordering (1, 2, 3) or taking turns in a small group and *alternating* to refer to taking turns in a partnership (you move, I move). Terms such as *questioning and answering* or *acting and reacting* are used mostly by dancers as they relate and interpret their expressive movements.

Working with equipment, whether large or small, a gymnast may move around, alongside, over, under, above, or below the apparatus. Gymnasts also move to arrive on the apparatus or to dismount the apparatus as well as moving near and far from the equipment. Music or sounds may accompany a gymnast who designs movement in a sequence to relate to the music. (Other types of relationships in the BSER framework are used with reference to games [goals, boundaries] and dance [poems, stories, words, beats, patterns, art, and artifacts].) Any of these general relationships can combine with the skill themes of traveling, statics, and rotation.

LEARNING EXPERIENCES

Earlier in this chapter we compared the skill themes of gymnastics to sets of actions. Each of the skill themes can be taught alone as a separate set, or they may be taught in combination so they overlap and interact with one another. In a similar manner, each of the learning experiences that follow in part II of this book can stand alone as a single lesson plan, or one learning experience may be developed into a series of related thematic lessons or a unit of work. For example, you might be able to develop two or more lessons from each learning experience, depending on your teaching situation. Realize, however, that in many instances if you were to teach an entire learning experience as a lesson, the children would no doubt finish confused, and probably frustrated, because learning experiences contain far more than can be reasonably taught, and learned, in one 30-minute experience. Most learning experiences contain several objectives. For most lessons you will want to select one, maybe two, objectives to concentrate on. In other words, you want to pick a "learnable piece" that children can truly understand and grasp rather than simply expose them to ideas that they can't possibly understand, much less learn, in the time allotted.

The decisions that you make as a teacher are unique because of your background level of understanding, the experiences of the children you teach, and your school setting and curriculum. For example, if you do not have a background of rich experiences in gymnastics or if the children you teach are absolute beginners, you may have to spend more time on each of the specific learning experiences. If you have worked on gymnastics with children over a number of years, you may choose at times to teach a given learning experience in a single lesson and at other times to expand a learning experience into a unit of work culminating in sequence development. In other instances the number of times a week you meet the students or the equipment you have available may regulate the development of your learning experiences. If you meet your students only once a week, you may not be able to have the luxury of extending a learning experience over several classes. If you meet your students three times a week, you may think you can stay on the same skill theme for several classes. A word to the wise, however: It is far better to cover less material and do a thorough job in an effort to develop a narrower range of skills than it is to brush over a lot of material and never give children the chance to become skillful or gain mastery.

To answer the question "What is a learning experience?" we would have to say that it is a *complete* experience. It has a series of objectives. It is intended for a specific age range and includes a complete description of how to teach the material. Again, a learning experience may be just one lesson, or it may be a series of related lessons.

Components of a Learning Experience

Each learning experience in this book is organized according to a consistent format. This format includes the following:

- The name of the learning experience.
- Objectives that explain the psychomotor, cognitive, and affective skills children will improve as a result of participating in this learning experience. When appropriate, the national standard that these objectives are helping students meet is referenced at the end of an objective in parentheses.
- A suggested grade range for the learning experience.
- The organization of the learning environment during the learning experience.
- The kinds and amounts of equipment needed for presenting this learning experience to children.
- A description of the total learning experience, explained as if you, the physical education teacher, were actually presenting the learning experience to children (additional information for teachers is set off in brackets). As the learning experience is developed, each new task for the children is identified regarding whether it is an informing (I), extending (E), refining (R), or applying (A) task.

- Ideas for Assessment, which give key points for you to keep in mind when informally observing and assessing children's progress in the learning experience. These are related to the objectives for the learning experience.
- How Can I Change This? allows you to either increase or decrease the difficulty level involved in the learning experience, thus allowing for all students to be challenged at their individual ability level.

In addition, although each of the following categories is not included in every learning experience, they are included where appropriate:

- Ideas for Teaching Fitness illustrates how components of physical fitness can be integrated into gymnastics.
- Ideas for Integrated Curriculum illustrates how concepts taught in gymnastics can be related to disciplinary learning in language arts, mathematics, science, social studies, or a combination of these.
- Ideas for Inclusion illustrates how you can meet the needs of special students by adapting tasks, equipment, or requirements for sequence work.

WHAT MAKES A LEARNING EXPERIENCE DEVELOPMENTALLY APPROPRIATE?

Learning experiences for children are appropriate when they meet the needs of all children in a class. You should teach learning experiences in such a way that children with low levels of ability as well as those with high levels of ability are appropriately challenged. You should also base learning experiences on children's previous experiences in gymnastics. As a result, you should present tasks and movement problems in such a way that there are multiple ways to respond. If the task is to balance on three body parts, one child may choose to balance on two hands and a foot. Another may choose to balance on a forearm, an elbow, and a knee. Another may choose to do a headstand. If the task is to perform a roll, children should have the choice of direction (backward, forward, sideways), shape (curled up, stretched out), time (fast, slow), and so on. If you ask the children to develop a balance, roll, balance for a movement sequence, each child should be allowed to solve the problem according to his or her ability level. It is your job as their teacher to know the children and to make sure that each child is challenging himself or herself in a meaningful way.

As referenced earlier, you should adhere to other components of *Appropriate Instructional Practice Guidelines for Elementary School Physical Education* (NASPE 2010) as well. For example, children should have frequent, meaningful, age-appropriate opportunities to develop a functional understanding of movement concepts. They should be provided experiences that encourage the development of their cognitive abilities. Social and cooperation skills should be developed through developmentally appropriate activities. All children should participate regularly in each class rather than sit and wait their turn for long periods. The learning environment should be structured for success. Children who fail regularly often stop trying and then fail to get any better. With respect to challenges, the learning environment should not be overly competitive, especially if you or parents impose the competition. Children should challenge themselves to do their own best work. The focus of competition should be on self-improvement. Ongoing individual assessment of children should be formative and reflect what children are learning physically, cognitively, and socially. Assessment should not be based on single test scores at the end of a unit of work. When you design learning experiences with these components in mind, chances are that they will be developmentally appropriate.

SUMMARY

This chapter serves as the foundation for the learning experiences in part II of this book. First, the scope and sequence of gymnastics are charted for the content of what should be taught, using the national standards as a guide over the elementary years. The next segment develops the four stages of gymnastics, and that is followed by how teachers commonly extend, refine, and apply tasks while teaching learning experiences. Following the discussion on task development, additional information on teaching styles, designing sequences, student demonstrations, a work ethic, and a focus on good body mechanics is presented.

This book is organized around the three skill themes of traveling, statics, and rotation. Each work unit (main skill theme) or chapter is further subdivided into lessons that use representative subsets, skills, or ideas. Laban's process variables of body, space, effort, and relationships support the development of content at both the unit and lesson plan level. Unlike in earlier books on gymnastics, which emphasize a single stunt or skill for a lesson (e.g., the forward roll or cartwheel) or a specific Laban theme (use of space, shape, time), our emphasis in skill theme work is on linking actions, or the transitions that flow from one action to another. The final segment of this chapter addresses the concept of a learning experience, the components of a learning experience, and what makes a learning experience developmentally appropriate.

QUESTIONS FOR REFLECTION

- Develop your own scope and sequence chart for content development in gymnastics during the elementary years. Based on your teaching situation, how does your chart vary from the one presented? Why?

- Choose three different concepts or skills in gymnastics (e.g., rolling actions, or more specifically, a pencil roll; traveling while taking weight on the hands, or more specifically, a cartwheel; balancing actions performed by oneself or with a partner) and illustrate the use of those concepts or skills at each of the four stages of gymnastics.

- Choose an initial task or skill theme in gymnastics and describe three ways that you could extend, refine, and apply that task or theme as you develop content in gymnastics.

- Choose a gymnastics skill or concept and discuss how you could teach it using both a direct and an indirect approach. Can you do this for five or more skills or concepts?

- After children learn a new gymnastics skill or concept at stage I, discuss how that skill or concept could be placed into a sequence with a beginning, a middle, and an end. Develop potential sequences for children working by themselves on a mat, working with a partner, and using a piece of equipment such as a box or bench.

- What considerations should you make when selecting students to perform demonstrations in gymnastics?

- What rules would you use in a gymnastics setting to hold children accountable for their work?

- As a teacher of gymnastics, how can you stress good body mechanics and aesthetic awareness and still provide children opportunities to make choices in their work? What are some of the important concepts to use to help children focus on detail and what is aesthetically pleasing?

- How can you use the process variables (BSER) to interact with the skill themes in gymnastics?
- What are the essential aspects of a learning experience? What other factors can influence the development of a learning experience when used appropriately?
- Choose a learning experience from one of the lessons in part II of this book and develop an observation sheet or checklist on process characteristics of skill development or a rubric on the inclusion of key components of a sequence. Why did you choose to include the factors you identified as relevant to that specific learning experience?
- Provide one example where a learning experience might take only one lesson and another where a learning experience might take a whole unit of work.
- What makes a learning experience developmentally appropriate? Why?

CHAPTER 4

Assessing Children's Progress in Gymnastics

After reading and understanding this chapter, you will be able to

- discuss why it may be important to assess children's progress in gymnastics;
- describe methods of alternative assessment and how you can use rubrics to measure progress;
- use the national standards and performance outcomes for selected grade levels to determine what to assess;
- describe types of alternative assessments;
- provide examples of informal assessments in the psychomotor, cognitive, and affective domains; and
- develop methods of reporting gymnastics assessments to parents and other interested parties.

Many physical educators teach 400 to 600 children a week, and each student averages two 30-minute lessons. The problems of short class times and large classes can make assessment seem like an insurmountable task. Yet there are many reasons to assess, including evaluating children's progress on achieving stated performance outcomes, evaluating the overall program, gaining credibility with administrators and parents, and checking what you, as a teacher, have taught.

NEW WAYS TO ASSESS

Since the first edition of this book was published in 1994, many changes have occurred in the process teachers use in assessing students. In these days of standards-based educational reform, teachers are increasingly being held accountable for what children learn or do not learn. Standards and performance outcomes identify what students should know and be able to do as they progress through school. Since standards provide consensus of what students should know and be able to do, they also provide a basis for assessment of achievement and program evaluation. Along with standards-based education come newer or alternative forms of assessment. *Alternative assessment* refers to any type of assessment that is different from traditional tests. There are other terms used to refer to alternative ways to assess, including *authentic assessment* and *performance-based assessment*. These terms are often used interchangeably. However, in physical education, *alternative assessment* refers to assessments such as projects, portfolios, event tasks, student logs and journals, checklists, rating scales, and rubrics. *Authentic assessment* describes assessment of performance that occurs in a realistic environment rather than one that is contrived.

Most alternative assessments include an assessment task and evaluative criteria for judging or scoring the performance of the task. For example, an assessment task may be to demonstrate a gymnastics sequence of a balance, a roll, and a different balance. Evaluative criteria for the assessment of the sequence include the following:

- Show a still beginning and ending by holding balances for three seconds.
- Balances must show at least two of these changes: shape, level, base of support.
- Roll should be performed smoothly with good technique and control.
- Smooth transitions should link the actions.

Student performance of an assessment task is typically evaluated using either an *analytic assessment* or a *holistic assessment*. It is considered an analytic assessment when a particular skill or a single component is evaluated. For example, an analytic assessment of the task described previously may evaluate the isolated skills of balancing and rolling. A holistic assessment of the performance would address the ability to perform the sequence, taking into account not only the performance of each individual skill but the actions or transitions that link the skills together in the performance of a quality sequence. Holistic assessment is considered more efficient and powerful because of the combination of components that create a more authentic assessment. Rubrics are commonly used in assessing student performance and may by analytic or holistic. Figure 4.1 depicts an example of an analytic rubric for assessing performance of a sequence of a balance, roll, and a different balance. Skills receiving a level 4 score would be considered proficient, level 3 scores would be deemed competent, and level 2 and 1 scores indicate that a level of competence has not been achieved. An overall score is determined by adding the score from each column or for each individual skill. An overall score using the sample rubric would range from 3 to 12.

Level	Beginning and ending	Balances	Roll
4	Beginning and ending balances are held still for 3 seconds.	Balances show clear and different shapes and a change in level or base of support.	Roll is performed with excellent technique.
3	Beginning and ending balances show momentary stillness.	Balances show different shapes and a change in level or base of support.	Roll is performed with good technique.
2	One balance is still.	Balances do not clearly show different shapes or a change in level or base of support.	Roll is performed with satisfactory technique.
1	Neither beginning nor ending balance is still.	Shapes are not clear or different.	Roll is performed with poor technique.

Figure 4.1 Example of an analytic rubric for a sequence of balance, roll, and different balance.
From P.H. Werner, L.H. Williams, T.J. Hall, 2012, *Teaching Children Gymnastics*, 3rd edition (Champaign, IL: Human Kinetics).

Figure 4.2 depicts an example of a holistic rubric. This rubric uses the categories of proficient, competent, and needs improvement in assessing performance. Other rubrics may use different categories, such as achieving, developing, and not yet developing, to describe performance. Additional assessments, including rubrics, are included in the appendix of this book. When used in the right way, alternative assessments help you assess the curriculum or program.

Proficient

- Balances are held for 3 seconds and show a clear beginning and ending.
- Balances show a change in at least 2 of the following: shape, level, base of support.
- Performs rolls smoothly with proficient technique and control.
- Consistently (75% of the time or more) shows smooth transitions linking the actions.

Competent

- Balances are held for at least 2 seconds and show a clear beginning and ending.
- Balances show a change in at least 2 of the following: shape, level, base of support.
- Performs rolls smoothly with good technique and control.
- Usually (50%-74% of the time) shows smooth transitions linking the actions.

Needs Improvement

- Balances are held for less than 2 seconds and show an unclear beginning and ending.
- Balances show only one change in the following: shape, level, base of support.
- Performs rolls with some technique and control.
- Sometimes (15%-49% of the time) shows smooth transitions.

Figure 4.2   Example of a holistic rubric for a sequence of balance, roll, and different balance.

From P.H. Werner, L.H. Williams, T.J. Hall, 2012, *Teaching Children Gymnastics*, 3rd edition (Champaign, IL: Human Kinetics).

With current changes in education, teachers are expected to show *that* students have learned and *what* students have learned as a result of participation in physical education. A few states are moving to mandated assessment of physical education programs. State education departments, administrators, and parents are provided information on how well students and programs are performing. Physical education is sharing the same level of accountability as other academic content areas. Assessment data can be used in demonstrating student achievement and support for physical education as a critical part of the school curriculum. A consequence of not assessing children and school programs is that authorities such as state education departments or school boards will select a test battery to administer to students. The result likely will be a physical fitness test. Although fitness is crucial to the success of a gymnastics program, it must not be the only criterion of assessment. Fitness batteries do not test all of the motor skills children learn in gymnastics, and they neglect the cognitive and affective components as well.

Assessment of children's work in gymnastics should evaluate their skills and their ability to combine skills into sequences or routines with smooth transitions. Cognitive development can be assessed verbally or in writing. It should involve the children's knowledge of cues for particular skills, proper use of mechanical principles, and selection of appropriate process variables (BSER) when they develop movement sequences. The children's work and the choices they make should reflect affective development. Accepting an appropriate level of challenge, working responsibly, choosing appropriate partners, and working cooperatively are just a few indicators of children's development of good attitudes and values. This chapter presents ideas on assessing children's gymnastics abilities in each of the three domains: psychomotor, cognitive, and affective.

WHAT TO ASSESS

An increasing number of excellent resources are available for physical educators who are making decisions about what might be taught and assessed in their programs. One such resource is the national standards document *Moving Into the Future: National Standards for Physical Education, Second Edition,* published by NASPE in 2004 (see chapter 1). The document describes six content standards along with key points for emphasis in grade ranges K-2, 3-5, 6-8, and 9-12. These points of emphasis are followed by sample performance outcomes. To help you review what you might teach and assess in gymnastics in grades K-2 and 3-5, figure 4.3 provides sample performance outcomes for standard 1. See chapter 1 for additional performance outcomes.

Grade range	Sample performance outcome
K-2	Travel (e.g., skip, hop, gallop, slide) using mature form.
	Travel in forward and sideways directions using a variety of locomotor patterns and change directions quickly in response to a signal or obstacle.
	Demonstrate clear contrasts between slow and fast movement while traveling.
	Balance, demonstrating momentary stillness, in symmetrical and asymmetrical shapes on a variety of body parts.
3-5	Balance with control on a variety of objects (balance board, large apparatus).
	Develop and refine a gymnastics sequence demonstrating smooth transitions.
	Jump and land for height and distance using mature form.

Figure 4.3   Sample performance outcomes for grade ranges K-2 and 3-5 for standard 1.
From P.H. Werner, L.H. Williams, T.J. Hall, 2012, *Teaching Children Gymnastics,* 3rd edition (Champaign, IL: Human Kinetics).

Using the national standards, state curriculum frameworks, curricula developed by school districts, or a combination of these serves as an excellent starting point for thinking about the purposes and goals of a physical education program. They answer the question "What outcomes do we want to accomplish in our physical education program?" This question is often recommended as the first step in the curriculum design process (Hopple 2005). Once you have decided on the overall program goals for gymnastics (K-5 for purposes of this book), the next step is to determine grade-level performance outcomes. When performance outcomes are determined, you have a guide or model from which to develop themes or units of instruction for the year, followed by specific lesson objectives that will lead to the accomplishment of these outcomes.

Once measureable instructional objectives have been clearly established, you can match each instructional objective to some form of assessment. It is essential for you to maintain *instructional alignment,* which refers to matching measureable objectives to an assessment that measures students' achievement of that objective. Simply stated, you must make sure you are assessing what you are teaching and teaching what you are assessing.

After you have decided what you are going to teach in gymnastics at various grade levels (see the sample gymnastics report card in the appendix), you also need to decide which outcomes to assess. Given the amount of time allocated for physical education, along with the scope of the curriculum, it is unrealistic for you to think that you can assess every performance outcome at each grade level. Perhaps it would be more realistic to choose to assess certain outcomes at particular grade levels. After you decide what to assess, the next step is to figure out how to best assess various learning outcomes.

HOW TO ASSESS

Today, physical educators have several alternative assessments to choose from. These assessments can be classified into projects, portfolios, event tasks, student logs and journals, and observation. Rubrics, checklists, and rating scales are typically used in evaluating these assessments.

Projects

Projects generated by students are assessments that may take the form of an exhibition or display. Examples of this type of assessment in gymnastics might include photography collections or exhibits using regular or digital cameras, videotapes of student performances, artwork, drawings, bulletin boards, posters, models, and collages. Projects can be completed as homework or in an integrated fashion with another class such as art, English, or science. Figure 4.4 is a sample rubric used for assessing a student project.

Score	Descriptor
4	All aspects of the assignment are completed in exemplary fashion. Information is organized and clearly communicated. All information is accurate.
3	Only one aspect of the assignment is missing or vaguely communicated. Most information is neatly presented. Most information is accurate.
2	Misses two significant portions of the assignment. Information is neatly presented with more than two exceptions. Most information is accurate.
1	Project is incomplete or not completed as assigned.

Figure 4.4   Sample rubric for assessing a student project.
From P.H. Werner, L.H. Williams, T.J. Hall, 2012, *Teaching Children Gymnastics*, 3rd edition (Champaign, IL: Human Kinetics).

Portfolios

Portfolios have become an increasingly popular means of assessing student progress and achievement. A portfolio may include a variety of objects that demonstrate student learning. According to Rink (2010), the intent of portfolios is to involve students in the assessment process and to establish student ownership of the portfolio. You or the student may decide what goes into the portfolio. Ideally, you would establish the learning goal and the student decides what evidence to put into the portfolio that best shows that the goal was achieved. You should establish clear criteria of how the portfolio will be assessed. The portfolio is typically assessed through the use of a rubric. The rubric should provide clear evaluative criteria yet allow for students' creativity.

Integrating Product Assessments

Each semester we supervise our physical education majors in their elementary school methods course. We place our students in local elementary schools. On one occasion during a unit on gymnastics, we worked with fourth- and fifth-grade students. In addition, we worked with the classroom teachers on an exemplary writing project. As the children worked through lessons on balancing, rolling, and traveling actions, we aimed toward the development of a partner sequence. The children tried to mirror or match each other when performing individual balances. They used rolling and traveling actions to move toward or away from each other or side by side. They took each other's weight partially or completely when performing partner countertension or counterbalance moves.

We videotaped and used a digital camera to capture the children's work. We downloaded pictures and gave them to the children to take back to their classroom teachers. In the classroom they were asked to observe their pictures and write about the quality of their work. What looked good (mechanics, good lines, stillness, partner cooperation)? What needed improvement? How did they feel about their experiences in gymnastics? How did they feel about themselves as gymnasts? Were they improving? Why? Here is what one student wrote about her experience:

I like our partner balance. What I like most about it is that all I had to do was hold Zola up. Luckily, she isn't very heavy. I would never be able to do what Zola is doing.

We are pretty much under control. In this part it doesn't look like I'm trying to kill her. Thank goodness Ms. Kirby cut out the ending part. In the end we really lost control. I guess in the end we had waited too long to get out of our balance. It looked as if I were throwing her down.

Zola and I are pretty straight. I'm not that straight, though. Zola is straight, but going at a diagonal.

We did a support balance. I was holding Zola up, but she wasn't supporting me.

I think we are stiff and straight. Zola's toes were pointed, her arms were straight, and my arms were straight.

Our balance was original. We looked at the sheet, chose it, and then tried it. We tried several balances. We did this one the best.

We had straightness in our balance too. I was straight, and Zola was at a diagonal but straight.

If I could change one thing, I would have me hold Zola straighter, and I would be standing straighter.

Reprinted, by permission, from P. Werner, 2003, "Clues to interdisciplinary learning: Check out the hallways," *Teaching Elementary Physical Education* 14 (1): 3-5. Created by Grant LeFever, 2-26-02.

Event Tasks

Event tasks are performance tasks that teachers ask students to complete during a single class period. Event tasks are often culminating experiences in which students are asked to apply or use what they have learned in meaningful ways. Examples of event tasks include gymnastics sequences, locomotor sequences, and gymnastics routines. Providing opportunities for students to create and perform a sequence or routine as part of a gymnastics lesson enables students to demonstrate their abilities specific to lesson objectives and the intent of the instruction. Event tasks also allow for flexibility and individuality in students' responses. Event tasks are commonly assessed with the use of a rubric, such as the one in figure 4.2. The rubric identifies the characteristics of the performance that are important for students to demonstrate. You may choose to assess the event task at the time of the performance or to videotape the task and assess it at a later time. A videotape of the event task also provides opportunity for self-assessment and peer assessment.

Student Logs and Journals

Student logs and journals provide additional types of alternative assessments in gymnastics. Student logs are used in recording events or behaviors that occur over time. Recorded information may show progress, change, participation patterns, or choices. Student journals are typically used in documenting students' feelings, attitudes, perceptions, and reflections regarding their experiences in physical education or in a gymnastics unit. Through journal writing, students become aware of the importance of expressing feelings, recognizing strengths and limitations of self and others, and identifying challenges and successes that result from participation in a physically and socially interactive environment. Recognizing and developing respect for individual similarities and differences and growing to value the challenges, fun, and social interaction that physical activity provides are part of the national standards for physical education.

Observation

The most common form of assessment used in physical education is observation. You observe students regularly as part of the instructional process. While observation may aid you in making decisions such as when to extend or refine a task, you would also use observation as a form of systematic assessment when collecting information on students' performance. Rubrics, checklists, and rating scales are often used in collecting and recording observational data. Students also may use observation in assessing themselves or assessing others. Self-assessments and peer assessments are often part of rich learning experiences for children. The use of evaluative criteria, such as that found in a rubric or checklist, allows students to focus on relevant information. When expectations for performance are clearly communicated, students can focus on improving their performance. A sample peer assessment can be found in figure 5.3 on page 93. You will need to teach students how to use self-assessments and peer assessments. As students become more experienced observers, they can become more involved in the assessment process.

PSYCHOMOTOR ASSESSMENT

As introduced earlier in this chapter, children should be assessed in the areas of psychomotor, cognitive, and affective development through their participation in gymnastics. The following sections illustrate how you might address each of the domains using alternative assessment ideas.

As a teacher, you should continuously ask questions such as "Are the children learning the concept I am teaching, and are they performing correctly with good form?" Questions such as these attempt to assess the progress of individuals or of an entire class. You can develop and use checklists for assessing critical components of skills (figure 4.5). Checklists are used in identifying the presence or absence of desired behaviors. Many checklists previously developed by teachers are accessible on the internet, such as those found at www.pecentral.org, or in books by Hopple (2005) and others.

When using checklists, you can observe one child at a time or scan the whole class. If you are concerned that you may miss one or more of the components of a particular

Behavior	Check if observed	Comments
Weight is transferred from feet to hands to feet.		
Arms are stretched like spokes on a wheel.		
Legs are stretched like spokes on a wheel.		
Starts and finishes facing same direction.		
Movements are controlled and smooth.		

Figure 4.5   Sample checklist for cartwheel.

From P.H. Werner, L.H. Williams, T.J. Hall, 2012, *Teaching Children Gymnastics*, 3rd edition (Champaign, IL: Human Kinetics).

skill, you can videotape practice attempts or performances and check at a later time. Whether using live observation or videotape, you can have children check themselves, peers check each other, an older child check younger ones, or a parent volunteer assist.

Assessing Critical Components

Testing of motor skills often provides a quantitative score: how many, how far, how high. This is particularly true in the areas of manipulative skills and games, where it is easy to keep score. In recent years there has been an increasing interest in assessing how children perform the qualitative components of a skill. This assessment is particularly suitable for gymnastics skills, in which process figures prominently.

The ultimate goal of qualitative assessment is to analyze whether a movement is mechanically correct. Often critical components, focal points, or developmental sequences of a given movement are analyzed for research purposes with the use of high-speed film or stop-action video. This is time consuming and impractical for most teachers. It is more practical to develop checklists of critical components (see figure 4.5) and use them as you give the children a task or movement sequence. Once the children start working, you can step back and observe one critical component (cue, refinement) at a time. For example, you assign the children the task of doing a cartwheel on the floor or with a piece of equipment. While the children are practicing, you check to see if they are keeping their arms and legs straight; a general estimate can be obtained and recorded on a class list in three to five minutes.

Some qualitative components are more easily observed for assessment than others. For example, it is easy to observe whether children can return to the feet at the end of a rolling action. It is more difficult to see whether the knees stay tucked to the chest during the roll. The use of stop-action videotapes can sharpen observation skills and obtain more reliable assessment. This method is not quick, but it is worth doing occasionally to get a more accurate idea of what help the children need so that they can refine skills.

You can get together with other teachers from area schools from time to time, perhaps once a month, to discuss the critical components of selected skills. You can compare checklists and discuss what is important to observe. Together, watch a videotape of some children doing the skill under discussion, seeing if you are in agreement about what you have or have not observed. This is another process that can sharpen observation skills.

Testing Routines and Sequences

Although the development of specific individual skills is important in gymnastics, the ability to link the skills and create smooth transitions from one action or balance to another is even more important. At a beginning level, you might want to use a checklist to *test for the presence of a desired behavior.* After calling for a sequence or routine at the end of a class period, you quickly assess whether the specified components are included. For example, when asking children to balance–travel–balance, you scan to see if students have selected a balance that they can hold for three seconds, an appropriate traveling action, and a second balance that they again hold for three seconds to show control. Most children will exhibit compliance with this type of task, and you will get a quick read on whether a child has understood your directions, a check for clarity.

A somewhat more complicated technique might be called *assessing for qualitative components and process variables.* Over time children should learn that variety, quality, contrast, and challenges are important parts of gymnastics sequences. Although assessing or judging gymnastics is subjective in nature, it is based on how well skills are executed and linked together. As a result, rating scales such as the one in figure 4.6 can help make the children aware of the array of process variables possible in their sequence. Rating scales are used in assessing the degree to which desired behaviors are demonstrated. Much like checklists and rubrics, rating scales can be used for communicating expectations of performance and encouraging and challenging children to include variety and contrast as they create routines. If the first balance is at a low level on two body parts, a patch and a point, perhaps the second balance will be at a higher level on three body parts. If the first balance is upright, perhaps the second will be inverted. If one is symmetrical, the second will be asymmetrical. The rolling action could be slow and sustained or very sudden and quick, focusing on the time element during transition. Variety in definitive lines (extension out through the toes and fingers), angles at the joints, shape (stretch, curl, twist), and eye focus can further contrast and improve the quality in a routine. Additional ideas for individual and partner sequences are provided in chapter 8.

Gymnastics routine: Rate each of the following characteristics on a 3-point scale:

3 = always   2 = sometimes   1 = never

_____ Holds balances for 5 seconds.

_____ Upright or inverted balances show clear shape and extensions.

_____ Demonstrates movements with good technique.

_____ Transitions between movements are smooth.

_____ Demonstrates controlled use of momentum and stillness.

_____ Gains height during flight or aerial movements.

Figure 4.6 Rating scale for gymnastics routine.

From P.H. Werner, L.H. Williams, T.J. Hall, 2012, *Teaching Children Gymnastics*, 3rd edition (Champaign, IL: Human Kinetics).

COGNITIVE ASSESSMENT

A wealth of information that children should know about body management, including critical elements of motor skills, movement concepts, and applying mechanical principles to gymnastics, is clarified in standard 2 of the National Physical Education Standards (NASPE 2004). Realistically, as a teacher you make several decisions about what, when, and how to test the children's cognitive development. First, test items should reflect what is taught in the gymnastics program, and second, testing needs to be manageable. Here are several ideas that are time efficient yet gather valuable information at the beginning or end of a class. As an alternative, create a testing station in a quiet corner of the gym that each child can visit briefly during the class. Either way, the test should not take more than 10 minutes to administer; it will give a quick assessment of a child's understanding of the given skill or principle (figures 4.7 and 4.8).

1. To run better, you should
    a. swing your arms from side to side
    b. stay on the balls of your feet
    c. bounce up and down
    d. get a good backward lean
2. A skip could be described as a
    a. jump, hop
    b. hop, jump
    c. step, hop
    d. hop, step
3. If you are trying to jump onto or over a bench, what should you do to help you jump higher?
    a. Keep your legs straight before you jump.
    b. Stand on your toes before you jump.
    c. Bend your knees before you jump.
    d. Keep your arms still.
4. Which of the following are forms of weight transfer?
    a. feet only
    b. hands and feet
    c. adjacent body parts
    d. all of these
5. Which of these is a pathway you could use while traveling on your feet?
    a. curved
    b. forward
    c. direct
    d. backward

Figure 4.7 Sample multiple-choice questions about traveling actions.

1. To increase your balance or stability in a chosen statue-like shape, you could lower your center of gravity by bending.

    ❏ true   ❏ false

2. To increase your balance or stability in a chosen statue-like shape, you could make your base narrower by pulling your supports closer together.

    ❏ true   ❏ false

3. You will remain balanced and still even if your center of gravity shifts outside your base of support.

    ❏ true   ❏ false

4. In general, you will have better balance if you have three body parts touching the ground than if you have only one part touching the ground while you are trying to stay still.

    ❏ true   ❏ false

5. You can balance only if you are in a symmetrical shape. If you are in an asymmetrical shape, you cannot balance.

    ❏ true   ❏ false

Figure 4.8   Sample true-or-false questions about the principles of balance.
From P.H. Werner, L.H. Williams, T.J. Hall, 2012, *Teaching Children Gymnastics*, 3rd edition (Champaign, IL: Human Kinetics).

Another way to check for understanding quickly is to have the children write out the major cues necessary for performing a given skill (see figure 4.9). A cue is a component critical to the successful execution of a skill. Before class, set out paper and pencils for the students in an area away from gymnastics activities. Three-by-five-inch (or five-by-eight-inch) cards work well if you are outdoors. At some point in the lesson, ask the children to go to this area and respond to a cue question about a skill. As soon as the children are finished, they can resume activity. This cognitive assessment takes less than five minutes of class time.

The most effective questions are those you design to assess what is being taught in your program (Graham 2008). Good questions take time to write. Often you will want to revise questions based on the children's responses and levels of understanding. In time, however, you can develop a battery of questions that indicate what children are learning in gymnastics. By asking only a few questions at a time, you will not feel

Your friend Trapezoid doesn't know how to do a forward roll very well. List five things that can help her become better at doing the forward roll.

    1. Hands on floor, thumbs pointed in

    2. Bottom up in air

    3. Look between legs

    4. Stay in a ball

    5. Return to feet

Figure 4.9   You can check for children's understanding with open-ended questions.
From P.H. Werner, L.H. Williams, T.J. Hall, 2012, *Teaching Children Gymnastics*, 3rd edition (Champaign, IL: Human Kinetics).

overburdened with scoring and record keeping. For example, by asking 5 to 10 questions three times a semester, you can accomplish testing and grading in manageable blocks of time. You can test different classes or grades at various times in the term. Rather than score several hundred tests of 30 questions in a single weekend, limit testing to a quick check for understanding during the unit of instruction.

Checking for Understanding

It is also possible to assess in a quick test how well children understand a concept. To check for understanding (Graham 2008), simply ask the children to demonstrate comprehension of a particular skill, concept, or process variable by stating the cues, focal points, or critical components. Besides verbalizing understanding, students can demonstrate the skill. For example, you might give the children these kinds of spoken instructions:

- Tell me the cues for doing the cartwheel properly.
- Show me where and how to place your hands on the floor when you do a backward roll.
- Tell me the proper cues for taking weight on your hands to transfer it into a handstand.
- Show me three ways to come out of a forward roll or to come out of a shoulder stand.

A scan will quickly let you know how well the children have understood the skill or concept. Of course, simply knowing how to do it doesn't mean they will always perform the skill correctly, but it is a necessary first step. This check for understanding is an excellent closure to a lesson; the class reviews the one or two cues (reminder words) that you have emphasized during the learning experience (see examples in the learning experiences in chapters 5 to 7).

Poker Chip Survey

Another way to survey the children to determine how well they understand a cognitive concept is to have them place different-colored poker chips, straws, Popsicle sticks, or other such items in a container. At the end of a class you demonstrate a roll incorrectly—for example, using the hands on the floor to help push up in returning to the feet. Ask the children, as they leave the class, to put a red chip, straw, or stick in the box if the roll was done correctly, and a blue chip, straw, or stick if the roll was done incorrectly. A quick survey of the colors placed in the container will tell you how well the children understand the concept.

AFFECTIVE ASSESSMENT

The affective domain includes characteristics associated with a person's feelings, attitudes, values, interests, and social behavior. Two of the six national standards for physical education are related to affective outcomes. The standards state that a physically educated person "exhibits responsible personal and social behavior that respects self and others in physical activity settings" (standard 5) and "values physical activity for health, enjoyment, challenge, self-expression, and/or social interaction" (standard 6).* Affective outcomes are frequently measured with the use of paper-and-pencil instruments. Children's attitudes and values can be barometers of their likelihood to develop active, healthy lifestyles in adulthood.

*Reprinted from National Association for Sport and Physical Education, 2004. *Moving into the future: National standards for physical education*, 2nd ed. (Reston, VA: NASPE), 11. This is referencing the two standards, not the entire text.

Paper-and-Pencil Instruments

Paper-and-pencil instruments include questionnaires, interest inventories, and rating scales. These instruments may ask students to identify likes and dislikes and interests, or they may ask for reflection on experiences or behavior. These self-assessments can provide you with insight into a child's perceptions or self-concept. The sample questionnaire in figure 4.10 suggests ways that you might assess the children's feelings and attitudes.

---

1. I like to roll, tumble, and do cartwheels at home and out on the playground.
   ❏ yes ❏ no
2. I like doing balance activities with a partner.
   ❏ yes ❏ no
3. I like making up sequences in gymnastics.
   ❏ yes ❏ no
4. If gymnastics is on television, I would watch it.
   ❏ yes ❏ no
5. I would like to get extra gymnastics lessons outside of school.
   ❏ yes ❏ no
6. How do you feel about your ability to jump onto and off of boxes or benches?
   ❏ ☺   ❏ ☺   ❏ ☹
7. How do you feel about your ability to roll on the floor or a mat?
   ❏ ☺   ❏ ☺   ❏ ☹
8. How do you feel about your ability to balance upside down?
   ❏ ☺   ❏ ☺   ❏ ☹
9. How do you feel about your ability to balance on a piece of equipment?
   ❏ ☺   ❏ ☺   ❏ ☹
10. How do you feel about your ability to vault over objects?
   ❏ ☺   ❏ ☺   ❏ ☹

Figure 4.10   Sample questions that evaluate children's feelings and attitudes toward gymnastics.

From P.H. Werner, L.H. Williams, T.J. Hall, 2012, *Teaching Children Gymnastics*, 3rd edition (Champaign, IL: Human Kinetics).

Smiley-Face Exit Poll

A simple way to learn how children feel is to survey them in a manner similar to that of the poker chip survey. This time, however, laminate cartoon faces: smiley, neutral, and frowny (Graham 2008). As children leave the gym, ask them to pick from one of the three boxes by the door the face that best represents their feelings about their skill in or enjoyment of the lesson and deposit it in the ballot box. Here are some sample questions and statements for the children to respond to:

- How do you feel about your ability to do rolls?
- How do you feel about your ability to balance?
- Gymnastics makes me feel stronger.
- Gymnastics makes me feel more flexible.
- How do you feel about designing your own sequence in the next gymnastics class?
- How do you feel about today's lesson?

REPORTING WHAT HAS BEEN ASSESSED

After you decide what to assess and select or devise an assessment task with a rubric, the next step is to develop a way to report to parents on the progress the children are making (Graham 2008). Alternative assessments of ongoing work during a unit of instruction or at the end of a unit of instruction can be used (see sample rubrics for selected grade levels in the appendix, pages 245-248). Most often they are easily understood, and parents appreciate being informed about what their children are learning and their mastery of those skills.

An example of a progress report given during a unit of work in gymnastics is provided in figure 4.11. The progress report specifies what the children are learning. In this case

---

What We Are Doing in Gymnastics

Name _____ Date _____

This week we learned about balance skills in physical education. We learned about some principles of balancing well and about different types of balance.

Principles of balance should include the following:

- Wide base of support
- Low center of gravity
- Stillness—hold for 3 seconds
- Tight body
- Use of eyes to focus

Types of balance include the following:

- Number of body parts touching the floor or equipment
- Shape—bend, stretch, twist
- Level—high, medium, low
- Symmetry and asymmetry, same and different
- Upright and inverted, head higher or lower than hips

Give your child some opportunities to practice balancing skills at home. Push some furniture out of the way on a carpeted surface in your home. Or go outside and have your child show you his or her balances on the grass or on a padded surface such as a sleeping mat for camping or a yoga mat.

Have your child try different balances chosen from the categories listed previously. Ask your child to tell you why some balances are stronger than others. Ask to see your child's favorite balances.

Your child has

- ❑ accomplished balancing the body in a variety of ways using good form.
- ❑ made good progress toward balancing the body in a variety of ways and sometimes uses good form.
- ❑ not yet developed good balancing skills.

Next week we will be working on moving from one balance position into another using smooth transitions. I continue to look forward to working with your child. Our goal is to have each child develop a sequence of a balance–weight transfer–balance.

Please discuss with your child what it might mean to put a sequence together, and return this sheet to me.

Parent's or guardian's signature_____

Figure 4.11 Example of a progress report to parents.

From P.H. Werner, L.H. Williams, T.J. Hall, 2012, *Teaching Children Gymnastics*, 3rd edition (Champaign, IL: Human Kinetics).

the children are learning about balance, including principles and types of balance. A scale depicting whether the child has achieved or mastered the skill, is making good progress, or has not yet developed the skill informs parents of their children's progress. You can send progress reports such as these home to parents; the reports can then be returned and placed in children's folders that are kept in physical education.

In addition to progress reports, you are likely asked to provide a letter grade or even a satisfactory or unsatisfactory rating for 400 to 600 children at least two times each year. This proves to be a challenging task, and the grade actually provides parents with very little information about their children's progress in physical education. Developing a physical education progress report, sent home as an insert with the child's regular report card one or more times per year, is perhaps a better system (in addition, see the sample report card in the appendix, pages 236-237). In gymnastics this progress report could include a checklist of the skills the child has learned during the year. A progress report might include a record of graded performances of sequences or routines at the end of a unit on gymnastics. This kind of progress report tells parents much more about what their children are learning in physical education than a mere letter grade does. Regardless of the type of report, it is important that student assessment be congruent with program objectives.

SUMMARY

This chapter presents numerous examples of ways to assess children in the psychomotor, cognitive, and affective domains, and some will be more attractive than others to you. Some assessment methods invite frequent use, and others may never be used. As a teacher, you select assessment tools that work for you, given the time and your class sizes. You need to be smart about assessment.

A well-thought-out assessment program has two advantages. First, it indicates the progress the children are making in developing skills, knowledge, and dispositions. Second, assessment allows you to share with parents, school boards, and administrators some relatively objective information about what children are learning in physical education. In this era of accountability, an assessment program provides a way to demonstrate the program's value for children.

QUESTIONS FOR REFLECTION

- What problems or conditions exist in your school that would make it a challenge to assess children's progress in a gymnastics setting? Why? How could you best address those problems to make assessment more realistic?
- Using the national standards and performance outcomes for selected grade ranges, what would you choose to assess in gymnastics?
- Using the examples provided in this chapter and in the appendix of this book, develop a minimum of two of your own assessment documents. What type of rubric do you find most helpful to you? If you gave this assessment to children or sent it home to parents, would they understand it?
- In addition to the use of skill tests and checklists, what are some alternative ways you could assess children's work in gymnastics? Within the categories of projects, portfolios, event tasks, student logs and journals, and observations, choose two and explain how you could use each as part of an ongoing assessment program in gymnastics.
- Using the sample informal assessments illustrated in this book in the psychomotor, cognitive, and affective domains, develop a sample assessment in each of the domains for your own use. What would you assess in each of the domains? Why?
- How would you report to parents the progress of the children you teach in gymnastics? Develop your own example of a progress report.

Teaching Developmentally Appropriate Learning Experiences in Gymnastics

Part II of this book presents four chapters that describe in detail how gymnastics can be developed for teaching children. Chapters 5 to 7 in part II are organized around one skill theme in educational gymnastics (see figure 3.1 on page 42): traveling, statics, or rotation. Within each chapter, work is further divided into categories. Categories of traveling in chapter 5 include steplike actions using the feet; steplike actions using the hands, feet, and knees; jumping and landing under control; weight transfer; flight; and traveling in relation to a partner. Characteristics, principles, and types of balance are the categories of statics in chapter 6. Chapter 7 focuses on the principles of rotation, movement around three axes, and rotation of the body. The process variables of human movement—body, space, effort, and relationships (see table 3.8 on page 57)—support all work. In this third edition of *Teaching Children Gymnastics*, chapter 8 has been added as a focus on sequence work. Principles of what makes a good sequence are discussed, and sample sequences are provided.

The learning experiences described do not develop in only one dimension. Although one skill theme is chosen as the primary focus in each learning experience, other skill themes are used to support the development of that concept through sequence work. The themes develop parallel to and dependent on one another. This means that a lesson will never be only about forward rolls, cartwheels, balances, or jumping and landing. Rather, after a warm-up period, the main focus of the lesson is developed. Children learn new material and refine it. Then they develop a sequence that integrates the main focus with other previously learned skills. For example, if the children work on rolling skills, by the end of the lesson they might integrate a jump, hop, land, and roll of their choice, finishing in a balance at a low level.

The concept behind the lessons is to focus on specific skill development and then to combine that skill with others in logical pieces of work. For example, students learning to perform rolls may link two different rolls together with a balance. Students focusing on traveling actions may jump, jump, jump with a turn or shape; land; and resolve the movement with a balance.

Chapters 5, 6, and 7 consist of 11 learning experiences each. Although each chapter focuses on one of the principal categories of the content, feel free to subdivide the learning experiences into more than one class as described in chapter 3. Use the ideas for changing an experience, emphasizing the integrated curriculum, fitness, or inclusive aspects of the learning experience to further enhance your teaching. Each learning experience may stand by itself or carry over into several sessions, perhaps comprising a mini-unit of instruction.

At the end of each of the skill theme chapters, you will find a section titled Additional Ideas for Learning Experiences. These are provided as guides for developing more lessons in gymnastics for children. You can use these ideas to initiate various ways of teaching the same content to children or to generate your own ideas for teaching lessons through divergent thinking.

Important to the idea of linking actions is the concept of a sequence. All gymnastics work should have a beginning, a middle, and an end. The beginning may be a held position of readiness or a balance pose that signals that the gymnast is about to begin. The middle consists of the action phase in which all work is linked together aesthetically, with an emphasis on good lines, smooth flow from one action to another, and a focus on the important aspects of the work. The ending position is a clear stop that signals that the work is completed.

The sample sequences provided in chapter 8 are divided into four categories. They are individual sequences on a mat, partner sequences on a mat, individual sequences with a piece of equipment on a mat, and partner sequences with a piece of equipment on a mat.

CHAPTER 5

Learning Experiences for Traveling

This chapter offers 11 learning experiences in the skill theme of traveling. We have developed learning experiences with a focus on various ways of traveling. These include steplike actions using the feet; steplike actions using the hands, feet, and knees; jumping and landing under control; weight transfer; flight; and traveling in relation to a partner.

The following chart provides a quick outline of the focus and suggested grade range for each learning experience. At the end of the chapter you will find additional suggestions to stimulate the development of further gymnastics experiences for children.

Mini-Index

Focus	Name	Suggested grade range
Steplike actions using feet: walking, running, hopping, jumping	And Away We Go	Pre-K-1
Jumping and landing under control	Landing Pad	Pre-K-1
Traveling, changing speed and pathways	Traveling Transformers	1-2
Steplike actions using hands, feet, knees: feet to hands to feet	Bunny Hop	1-2
Flight: hurdle or spring takeoffs	Ready for Takeoff	1-2
Weight transfer: rocking, rolling, sliding	Rock and Roll	2-3
Flight: shapes in air, vaulting	Fantasy Flight	2-3
Traveling into, over, along, and out of a small piece of equipment using the hands and feet	Cross at the Intersection	3-4
Steplike actions using hands, feet, knees: feet to hands to feet	Clock Face	4-5
Weight transfer: under equipment	Beam Me Up	5
Variety of traveling actions: relationships to a partner	Me and My Shadow	5

AND AWAY WE GO

Objectives

As a result of participating in this learning experience, children will improve their ability to

- use their feet to travel by exploring each of the five basic steplike actions (standard 1);
- combine steplike actions while changing directions, pathways, and speeds with smooth transitions between actions (standard 1); and
- describe fundamental differences between walking, running, hopping, and jumping (standard 2).

Suggested Grade Range

Primary (Pre-K to 1)

Organization

A large open space is needed. Children spread out in personal space.

Equipment Needed

Gather a variety of pieces of small equipment—hoops, ropes, paper or wooden wands supported by two milk crates. One piece of equipment for each child is appropriate.

Description

"As we begin I would like everyone sitting like a gymnast [long sit, pike position]. That's right—legs together, back straight, head up, toes pointed. This is our gymnast sit. See if you can bend over and reach for your toes when you're sitting like a gymnast. Let your knees bend a little bit. This time keep your head down close to your knees, and let's count together to 10. Good! Now sit up and rock back onto your shoulders with your legs up in the air [support hips with hands, elbows bent on floor]. This is called a shoulder stand. Straddle your legs wide apart side by side, just like a big V. Scissor your legs with one forward and one back. Change back to a V-straddle. Let's hold each position and count out loud to 10. Do you feel the muscles in your legs and back stretch? Sit back up, and straddle your legs apart on the floor in front of you. Now lean forward; see if you can move your chest and head close to the floor in front of you. OK, back to your gymnast sit—legs together in front. Put your hands by your hips and rise up into a back support position [tight body], just like I'm doing. Good! See if you can turn over into a front support position [push-up position]. Now, let your tummy sag down to the floor, then arch up like an angry cat. Try that again—sagging tummy, angry cat. Good stretching! Now, let's put all of this together. See if you can follow what I say. Ready? [Say each cue as students perform.] Gymnast sit, touch your toes, rock back to a shoulder stand, gymnast sit, rise into a back support, turn over to front support, turn again to a back support, now go into a gymnast sit. Did you feel your muscles stretch way out?

"See all of the equipment out on the floor? When I say go, I'd like all the girls to nicely get one piece, take it to your personal space, and sit down beside it. Go. Now, the boys . . . go. You did that very safely! This time, when I say go, we will begin running softly in, out, and around all of the equipment in general space (I). Visit all of the places in the gym, and be careful not to bump into other children or other equipment. This is not a race. I'll be looking for high knees and light, springy feet like this [demonstrate]. Go. Good! I like how you're picking your knees up and moving with light feet!

"Run a little faster [move feet quickly] (E). Now slower (E). I see a few people changing pathways so they don't run into other people. That's good! Now take long running steps (E). OK, now short quick steps (E). Can you run forward (E)? Backward (E)? Sideways (E)? How about running straight [curved, zigzag] (E)? Let's use walking steps this time and do the same things. Walk fast—now slow. Long steps! Short steps. Forward [backward, sideways, straight, curved, zigzag]. Good! Stop where you are.

"Walking and running involve transfer of weight from one foot to the other. What is it called when we step from one foot to the same foot? [Demonstrate.] That's right, Allan, it is a hop. Let's do what we just did, only this time, I'm looking for great hops (E). Don't forget to use both right and left feet. Go. Fast hops, slow hops (E). Let's see long hops (E). [Vary with short hops; hops forward, backward, sideways; and in straight, curved, zigzag pathways.] Use your arms to help you hop (R)! Stop; let's take a rest.

"Next we will try jumping (E). Do you know there are three ways we can use our feet when we jump? We can jump from one foot to two feet [demonstrate], two feet to two feet [demonstrate], and two feet to one foot [demonstrate]. See if you can do these in your own space. Try one foot to two [two to two, two to one; let children try each jump a few times]. Use all three of these jumps when you travel this time. Go! [Call out the different ways; vary speeds, length of jumps, directions, and pathways.]

"Remember, bend and explode to get super jumps (R)! Use light and springy feet like a bunny (R). Land softly on the front [balls] of your feet (R). Bend your knees when you land to make it soft (R). Stop.

"Now let's experiment with our feet as we travel about the space (E). Pick one of the steplike actions we've done. That means you can walk, hop, or jump. Watch me first. I'll pick jumping from two feet to two feet. [Demonstrate.] Now I'll jump up to and over a piece of equipment. See how I keep using this jump to go to the next piece of equipment? Now watch—I can jump close to, then into, and even over a hoop. Then I jump to the next piece of equipment. When I say go, you pick your favorite way to move. Make sure you go to all the open spaces and go to lots of equipment. Go! [Signal stop.]

"Go back home to your first piece of equipment. Do you remember where it was? It's OK if you don't—just find one! For our final task we are going to make a sequence (A). That means we will put the actions together. You will work only in your personal space and with your piece of equipment. Start a couple steps away from your equipment. See if you can use three different steplike actions—the hops, jumps, and walk—to move toward, over, and away from your equipment. Watch me. Instead of using all jumps this time, I'm going to try different steps. I can hop toward the rope, use one or two feet over the rope, and jump with both feet away from the rope. I used three different actions. Now you try it. I'm going to see if you can use three different actions, too. Good! Try it again, another way (A)! [Signal stop.] Now show me the one way you like best (A). Do it three times. Very good. I can see that you are really working hard and using your feet to travel in different ways. You are going into, out of, over, and around your piece of equipment. [Signal stop.]

"Who can tell me what you do with your feet when you walk and run? That's right— one foot to the other is walking and running. Hop? Yes, one foot to the same foot is hopping. Jump? Yes, there are three different jumps—two feet to two feet, two feet to one foot, and one foot to two feet. That is all for today. Show me one of the steplike actions as you safely line up to go back to your classroom."

Ideas for Assessment

- This is not a race. Emphasis should be on quality locomotor patterns. Soft feet; high knees; use of the arms to assist traveling actions; and erect posture, or body carriage (see figure 5.1), are all important. Choose one or two of these to emphasize and look for them on the assessment sheet.

- Focus on smooth transitions from one action to another. Encourage the children to move smoothly from a hop to a jump or to a step without stopping or taking extra stutter steps. Code whether or not each child makes a smooth transition from one locomotor action to another.

Figure 5.1 Children should use a variety of high-quality, steplike actions to travel about the equipment.

How Can I Change This?

- Introduce concepts of speed, direction, relationship of body parts, or pathways in the sequence work. For example, do long, powerful two-foot jumps with the feet wide apart on the approach; jump using two feet with a half turn in the air over equipment to a landing on one foot; or take quick steps away from a hurdle while running zigzag forward or backward.

- Add a roll, a balance, or both to the sequence. For example, hop toward the equipment, jump over it, land, roll, and finish in a balance.

Ideas for Teaching Fitness

- At the beginning of the learning experience, during the warm-up, talk to the children about the importance of stretching and having a flexible body. In a simple way, tell the children what muscle groups they are stretching during each exercise.

- When the children are doing the locomotor portion of the learning experience, from time to time have them stop and check how hard they are working. Traveling is a way to increase heart rate and get the benefit of cardiorespiratory fitness. In a simple way, have them feel their chests to feel their heart beating. Ask them if they notice that they are breathing harder or more rapidly ("huffing and puffing") and that their bodies are getting warmer.

Ideas for Integrated Curriculum

- Children can develop word cues for their sequences—for example, step, step, hop, turn, jump, jump, jump.

- Some children may be able to choreograph and notate the sequences (see the appendix)—for example, J2 to 1, J1 to 2, 3 3 F; J2 to 1, 1/4 T; 1H, 4 3 S to denote jump two feet to one, then one foot to two feet three times forward; jump two feet to one with a quarter turn over the hurdle; one foot hop four times sideways.

Ideas for Inclusion

- Children in wheelchairs can travel forward, backward, and sideways; turn around; and go faster and slower while others are hopping, jumping, sliding, and so on.
- Nonambulatory children can slide along the floor on their bellies or backs if they have the use of their arms. Others may rock or roll in a pencil shape or seated shape from side to side, faster and slower.

LANDING PAD

Objectives

As a result of participating in this learning experience, children will improve their ability to

- come to moments of stillness after traveling (standard 1),
- land from a jump under control (standard 1), and
- explain in their own words an understanding of mechanical principles necessary for controlled stopping and landing actions (base of support, center of gravity, receiving force) (standard 2).

Suggested Grade Range

Primary (Pre-K to 1)

Organization

A large, open space is needed. Spread out mats, benches, and boxes throughout the space, with adequate distance between pieces for safety. Place mats beside each bench or box for padding.

Equipment Needed

You will need one mat and one box or bench for each child or pair of children for this activity. A drum or tambourine is useful for starting and stopping signals.

Description

"As we begin today, we're going to play a little game. I want you to run about on the floor like a good gymnast (I). I want you to run softly, up on the balls of your feet (R). I want to see high knees (R). I also want to see your arms swinging (R). This isn't a race to see who is the fastest. I want to see your best run. [Demonstrate.] I want you to avoid all of the mats, equipment, and other people. No bumping. When you hear the drum beat, you must try to come to a complete stop [freeze] as quickly as you can (no extra steps). Ready, go. [Beat. Repeat several times.]

   "I notice that some of you are having some problems stopping. Some are taking extra steps. I've even seen one or two fall over. What do you think we can do to improve our stopping? Yes, we could run a little slower. We always need to be in control, but that really doesn't talk about stopping. What helps us better? We need to get lower and wider in the direction we are traveling (R). That means we should bend a little at the hips and knees when we're stopping. Keep your back and head up. Don't lean. Spread your arms out for balance, too. [Demonstrate.] Let's try again. Ready, go. [Beat. Repeat several times.] You're doing much better now. Let's try to stop now while you skip, hop, or jump (E). Let's try run, jump, land, freeze (E). Good, you're getting the idea. We need to bend and get wide [bend, balance] as we stop our movement.

"Now we're going to try something really hard. Everyone go to a box or bench. We're going to step up onto the equipment. Then, we're going to make one big jump down [demonstrate] (E). Swing your arms up and push hard with your legs to get high into the air when you jump. The important thing, though, is how well we land. Again, we have to bend [squash] and get wide [spread] (R). I want to see your feet spread apart—shoulder width (R). Reach for the floor with the balls of your feet (R). Bend at your hips and knees (R). Keep your back and head up (R). Hold your arms out for extra balance (R). [Add each of these factors, one at a time, to the task focus as children begin jumping off the boxes and benches.] Jump and land several times at your box. Stop and stay where you are at your bench or box. Get on the box, jump, land—be still. Try it again and again. I will come around to see who can land without moving their feet (A). [Use a checklist to determine whether each child is landing wide, bending and squashing to make a soft landing, keeping the back and head up, using arms to assist, and coming to a complete stop.]

"Now we're going to run to other boxes, jump onto and off the box, land still, and then move on [demonstrate] (E). Come to a complete stop [freeze] before moving on. No crashing to the floor or extra steps in the landing. Remember to land wide, bend, head up, use your arms (R). [Use the same checklist to determine whether the children can land from a moving jump (A).]

"OK, stop. Everyone come in and sit down in front of me. Good. I like how quickly you did that. Everyone is sitting and ready to answer some of my questions. Who can tell me the most important parts of our lesson today? Yes, stopping under control after traveling and landing under control after a jump. Let me show you a jump with a landing off a box. [Jump, land, crash, and fall to the floor.] That looked kind of funny, but was it a good landing? [Children: No!] Who can tell me what I would have to do to land better? [Let several children provide the class with one of the factors.] Yes, bend, squash, spread, get wide, keep my back and head up, freeze. You sure learned a lot about stopping and landing under control today. When I say go, everyone will get up and go back to a box or bench and make one last jump with your best landing ever. Then, you will line up at the door. Go!"

Ideas for Assessment

- Children will tend to attempt their stopping actions with a forward body lean because that is generally the direction in which they are moving. Deceleration is enhanced by sitting back a little. Watch the children and code whether they have a forward body lean when stopping their momentum or whether they sit back and decelerate properly.

- Children tend to jump out, not up. This establishes forward momentum, which is difficult to control when jumping from a height. Getting vertical lift in the jump (explode up with the legs, reach for the sky with the arms) helps the child to come down and stick the landing. Code whether the children explode up with the legs and swing the arms back and up to get a vertical lift in the jump.

- Although coming to a stop for 5 to 10 seconds defeats the purpose of flowing gymnastics actions, you need to hold the stop or landing long enough to establish control before linking into other actions. Look for controlled jumps and controlled stopping (1 to 3 seconds). There should be no crashing to the floor out of control. Develop a simple checklist and observe whether the children control their landing from a jump. Do children hold their position with stillness for 3 seconds? Do they stop and land on their feet?

- Encourage children to strive for making no noise with the feet while using the freeze, jump, and squash actions. Soft feet that give when landing are important. Bend and spread in the direction of movement. Balance is also a key to understanding the concept of a good landing (figure 5.2). Code good landings for each of the factors.

Figure 5.2 Land and freeze from a jump by bending the knees, giving with the feet, and getting wide.

How Can I Change This?

- For those children who are ready, add a change of focus in the jump. Make a shape in the air—stretched, curled, or twisted. Make a turn while in the air—a one-quarter, one-half, or full turn. Because the process of flight occurs for only a fraction of a second, the children must learn to get into and out of the shape or turn quickly and efficiently. The emphasis for this lesson should remain on quality landings.

- Put the jump with a landing into a sequence. Approach the equipment (bench or box) with a steplike action, jump onto the equipment, jump off, land, lower into a roll of your choice, and finish with a balance (run, jump, jump, squash, roll, balance).

Ideas for Teaching Fitness

- Traveling while using different steplike actions and jumping onto and off equipment help to build cardiorespiratory endurance. Help the children to recognize some of the signs that they are working hard and building strong hearts—heavy breathing (huffing and puffing), warm skin, heart beating faster (have child place hand on chest to feel the beat).

- Jumping for height and landing help build leg strength, especially in the quadriceps muscles.

Ideas for Integrated Curriculum

- Use signals when doing the freeze work. Make stop and go signs (red and green), or use a physical signal such as raising a hand or placing both hands on your head. Using signals helps children pay attention and use another sense (sight versus sound) when interpreting directions.

- Do simple science experiments to help children understand the process of stability or balance. Have the children stand with their legs together, then apart. In which position can they be pushed over more easily? Bring in models and different geometric shapes. Talk about which models are more stable. A wide base with a low center of gravity provides stability (bend, spread).

TRAVELING TRANSFORMERS

Objectives

As a result of participating in this learning experience, children will improve their ability to

- travel in a variety of locomotor patterns changing pathways (standard 1);
- demonstrate clear contrasts between slow and fast movement when traveling (standard 1);
- match a sequence of traveling actions on the floor (standard 1);
- demonstrate momentary stillness in a variety of shapes on a variety of body parts and at different levels (standard 1);
- jump and land using a variety of takeoffs and landings in relation to small equipment (standard 1);
- jump and land using various patterns (one foot to the same [hop], one foot to the opposite [leap], two to two, one to two, and two to one) (standard 1);
- design and perform a simple sequence involving traveling and balancing and incorporate changes of shape and speed or pathway (standards 1 and 2);
- identify the critical elements of locomotor skills (standard 2); and
- work cooperatively in a group setting and with a partner by sharing equipment and space (standard 5).

Suggested Grade Range

Primary (1 to 2)

Organization

A large, open space. Children spread out in personal space with jump ropes stretched out, or in random shapes, on the floor and scattered throughout the area.

Equipment Needed

You will need several jump ropes, approximately one for each child to avoid collisions.

Description

"As we begin today, you can see all of the jump ropes spread about on the floor. We are going to start by staying away from them and moving all around them. When I say go I would like for you to run like a gymnast, traveling all around the ropes. I want you to run softly on the balls of your feet (I). Remember to get your knees up high and to swing your arms. When I say freeze you must come to a complete stop on your feet beside a rope that is nearby. Remember to watch where you are going and enter empty space so you will not bump into anyone. Go! Make sure you are visiting all the areas of our work space (R). I see many of you traveling at the same speed. See if you can change that by moving slowly and then speeding up and then slowing down again (E). See how many pathways you can travel in: Try a curved pathway and zigzag pathway as you move between and around the equipment (A). Great! I like how you are using soft feet and getting your knees high. Freeze.

"Now we are going to work on traveling over the ropes. What do you need to watch out for when you arrive at a rope? Yes, other people. So if someone else is about to travel over a rope, you should move on to an empty space. When I say go I want you to continue to run like a gymnast; but when you come to a rope, instead of traveling around it, hop over it (E). Who remembers what a hop is? Yes, Bethany it is taking off on one foot and landing on that same foot. When I say freeze, remember to come to a complete stop beside a rope. Go! I see a lot of good hopping using a one-foot takeoff and a soft landing. Many of you are hopping on your favorite foot only. So make sure the other foot gets a turn to hop (E). Remember to include a change of speed (E). See if you can change your pathway to get to another rope (E). Freeze!

"Next let's try galloping. Continue to hop over the rope when you come to it. But before I say go, who can tell me what a gallop looks like? Yes, Charlie, it's step, together, step, together. Would you like to demonstrate that for us? Nice job remembering to lead with the same foot forward. When I say go, gallop, and when you come to a rope, hop over it (E). Go! Remember to face forward while you gallop (R). Remember to give the other foot a turn being the leader and the other foot a turn to hop (E). See how smoothly you can change the lead foot (R). Try using your lead foot to hop over the rope to make a smooth move from the gallop to the hop. Work to make your actions flow (R). Also see if you can show a change in speed while you travel (E). Freeze!

"Let's gallop and jump this time. What does a good jump look like? You are right; when you jump do you take off on two feet and land on two feet? Should I hear your two-foot landing? No. Remember to land softly on the balls of your feet while bending at your hips, knees, and ankles. On go, travel by galloping, and when you come to a rope, jump over it (E). Go! How can you move smoothly from the gallop to the jump (R)? Remember to give the other foot a chance to lead when you gallop (E). See if you can gallop in a zigzag pathway (E). Can you change speed (E)? Freeze!

"We are going to gallop and jump again. But before we do, I want you to change the shape of the jump rope you are standing beside. You can make the shape of a letter of the alphabet or a letter in your name, or you can make a heart shape or a square—any shape that you like. Now, when you come to a rope you can decide if you are going to jump over it or in and out of it. This time I want you to work on making your moves look really smooth as you connect your gallop and jump and landings. I will be watching for galloping that moves smoothly into a jump and soft landing and then back to a gallop (R). Go! Freeze!

"Let's add a leap this time. On go, I want you to run like a gymnast, traveling through open space, changing speed and pathways. When you come to a rope, leap over it (E). When you leap, remember to take off on one foot and land on the other foot. Pretend you are leaping over a big mud puddle. It looks like this (demonstrate) run, run, run, l-e-a-p. Now you try it: Run, run, run l-e-a-p! One more time: Run, run, run l-e-a-p! You've got it! So when I say go, you are going to run like a gymnast, changing speed and pathways. When you come to a piece of equipment, leap over it (E). Go! Nice work, Grace. That was a very smooth, controlled move from the run to the leap and back to the run. Everyone focus on that (R). You can pretend that the ropes are puddles and decide if you want to leap all the way over them or you can leap with the lead foot landing right in the middle of the space made by the rope (E). You can decide. Freeze.

"Now let's skip as you travel throughout space (E). Remember that a skip is a step and a hop. Chris, would you like to demonstrate a skip showing really smooth moves from the step to the hop? Great! Notice how Chris gets his knees up high and swings his opposite arm forward. When you arrive at a rope, jump over it using a one-foot takeoff and then land on two feet (E). Who remembers what to do to make your landings soft? Yes, Stephanie, bend your knees and land on the balls of the feet (R)! When you hear me say go, skip and then travel over the ropes by jumping with a one-foot take-off and a two-foot landing (E). Go! Great, Manny, you are light on your feet and skipping like a gymnast (R). Yes, you too, Carol. Freeze.

"You have been doing such great work. Now I would like for you to show me your favorite way to travel around and over the ropes (A). Go! I see several of you like to gallop and jump. Nice leap, Da'quan. Freeze!

"Let's begin again with your favorite travel. But this time, after you travel over a rope and land, change to a different travel and continue to a new rope and a new way to travel over it (E). So after each landing, change to a different way to travel. Remember to make your movements flow smoothly from one to the next (R). Go! Good, I see skipping, hopping, galloping, jumping from one foot to two feet. Tess, what a smooth gallop in a curved pathway. Remember to also change your speed (E).

"In a few minutes you are going to create a travel sequence. You are going to begin and end the sequence with a shape. These two shapes must be different. Before we continue on with the sequence, let's practice making some really nice shapes. Remember to hold the shape for three seconds, or three hippopotamuses. Count in your head, one hippopotamus, two hippopotamus, three hippopotamus. Let's start with a narrow shape (I). Have a plan for all of your body parts to be doing something, even your fingers and toes. Now, show me a different narrow shape with a different base of support (E). I see a lot shapes on two feet. See if you can change the base of support to one foot, or maybe one foot and one hand, or a knee and an elbow (E). How about a curved shape (E)? Make your body parts really curved and round. How about a curved shape at a low level (E)? Hold it while you count three hippopotamuses in your head. Good work. Show me a twisted shape (E). How many body parts can you twist (A)? Make it really twisted and remember to hold it really still. Make a wide shape at a low level (E). How about a wide shape at a medium level (E)? Great!

"Now you are ready to start working on your sequence (A). Who has ever seen a transformer? What does a transformer do? Yes, it starts out as one thing and then changes, or transforms, into something else. The beginning shape of the transformer is different from the ending shape, isn't it? Who remembers how the sequence will begin? Yes, Rachel, with a still shape. Next, you are going to move out of your still shape into a travel to your rope. Once you arrive at the rope, you are going to travel over the rope and move into a different travel and finally into an ending shape. Remember, the ending shape should be different from your beginning shape. So when I say go, find a jump rope, take it to your work space, and arrange it in a shape on the floor that you would like to travel over. Then begin working on your sequence. Start with a beginning shape, then a travel, travel over, different travel, and ending shape. Remember *shape, travel, over, travel, shape*. Go!

"Make your sequence interesting by changing speed or pathways (R). Practice the same sequence each time and make your actions flow smoothly from one to the next and make your shapes clear by using tight muscles (R). Your sequences are looking really nice. Practice it one more time and then come have a seat in front of me.

"It's time to share your travel sequence. When I say go, I would like for you to quickly go sit beside someone you can work with today. Go! Three, two, one. Nice job finding a partner quickly. Now you are going to perform the sequence for your partner. Everyone will have a turn to share their sequence with their partner. But first, decide with your partner who is going to be the blue transformer and who will be the red transformer. When I say go I want all blue transformers to go to your work space and stand in the spot where your sequence begins. Go! Now all red transformers go join your partner by standing behind them so you can watch them perform their sequence. Blue transformers will demonstrate their sequence first (A). Red transformers, I want you to watch your partner's sequence carefully and then copy the sequence. Blue transformers will be your coach if you need help. You may even ask them to repeat the sequence for you.

"OK, red transformers, it's your turn to invite the blue transformers over to your work space and teach them your sequence (A). Blue transformers, watch closely so you can copy the red transformers' sequence exactly."

Ideas for Assessment

- Children should be able to identify the critical elements (learning cues) for locomotor skills. For example, when asked to state the cues for skipping, children should identify step, hop, step, hop; arm swing; high knees.
- The emphasis should be on quality performance of locomotor skills. Choose one or two to assess using a rubric.
- Have students observe and assess their partners' or classmates' sequence using a peer assessment (see figure 5.3). One student can be the gymnastics coach or judge (evaluator), the other the gymnast (performer). Design a peer assessment that addresses the desired performance criteria, such as the following:
  - Are children's traveling actions gymnastics-like? Children should be encouraged to work to improve the quality of their traveling actions. Racing, speed contests, or traveling out of control should not be allowed.
  - Videotape the sequences and have children identify what was really good about the sequence and what parts may need more work. Children could also evaluate the videotaped performance using a checklist to identify specific components or qualities of the sequence.

Peer Assessment of Travel Sequence

Name of gymnast _____

Name of coach _____

+ I see it

− I do not see it

_____ Two different shapes

_____ A travel *over* equipment

_____ Two different travels

_____ Smooth moves from one action to the next

Figure 5.3   Example of peer assessment for a travel sequence.

From P.H. Werner, L.H. Williams, T.J. Hall, 2012, *Teaching Children Gymnastics,* 3rd edition (Champaign, IL: Human Kinetics).

How Can I Change This?

- When sharing a sequence with a partner, work to synchronize movements so they are moving simultaneously, at exactly the same pace and at exactly the same time.
- When traveling over a rope, jump, hop, or leap for distance. Jump, hop, or leap with an emphasis on height.
- Use large equipment such as boxes, benches, or balance beams to travel over. Mount the equipment, make a shape on the equipment, and then dismount.
- Introduce the concept of relationships. Use a variety of small and large equipment to travel over, under, beside, onto, off, along, and through.
- Explore different ways to travel; travel in ways other than steplike actions on feet.

- Add a roll.
- Change directions while traveling.
- Emphasize jumping for height, then distance. Jump over the ropes with an emphasis on jumping for height. Then emphasize jumping for distance by stretching the ropes out and jumping from one end of the rope to the other. See how many jumps it takes to get to the end of the rope.
- Add a hoop for a starting point for the beginning shape and another hoop for the ending shape.

Ideas for Teaching Fitness

- Traveling using steplike actions provides the opportunity for developing cardiorespiratory fitness. Children benefit from short bouts of moderate to vigorous physical activity.
- Hopping, jumping, and landing enhance muscular strength and endurance.
- Balancing and holding shapes in various positions require strength and flexibility.

Ideas for Integrated Curriculum

- Have students draw a movement map of their sequence. The map should show the location of the beginning balance and the various pathways (straight, curved, zigzag) used in getting to their destination for the ending shape. The movement map should also identify the location of the rope traveled over.
- Create cards with locomotor actions, such as Jump, Skip, Hop. Children can use them to create a sequence or put them in order to describe the sequence that was created.

Ideas for Inclusion

- Children in wheelchairs can travel forward and backward at different speeds and pathways while other children are galloping, skipping, or hopping.
- Allow children to move about on the floor, traveling about and over equipment in any way they are capable of moving. Children could push with their arms or slide on the side, back, or belly.
- When students work with a partner, they can be assigned to work with someone with a similar or a different ability level. By working cooperatively and responsibly together, they learn to recognize and accept the skills and abilities of others.

BUNNY HOP

Objectives

As a result of participating in this learning experience, children will improve their ability to

- use steplike weight-transfer actions of the hands, feet, and knees in a variety of conditions both on the floor and on equipment (standard 1);
- use steplike weight-transfer actions of the hands, feet, and knees as a primary means of linking with other traveling and balancing actions (standard 1); and
- identify steplike weight-transfer actions of the hands, feet, and knees as a type of traveling action (standard 2).

Suggested Grade Range

Primary (1 to 2)

Organization

A large, open space is needed. Spread out a variety of small equipment (such as hula hoops, wands, and ropes) and large equipment (such as benches and boxes) with adequate distance between pieces for safety.

Equipment Needed

A piece of small equipment, such as a hula hoop, wand, or rope, is needed for each child. A box or bench is needed for every two children. Place mats or carpet squares beside the boxes and benches for padding.

Description

"See all of the equipment out on the floor? We'll start today by staying away from it. When we travel around the equipment, let's not touch any of it. Let's start with running. Remember, high knees, light feet. Go! [Signal stop.] Use a straight pathway now [then zigzag and curved pathways]. Let's change directions. Try forward. OK. Now go sideways. Good! When I say go, run backward. First move to open spaces, away from others. Go! [Signal stop.] Now let's skip. I want good skips, with high knees and swinging arms. [Signal stop.] Let's change pathways and directions. [Call out.] Now slide—go sideways one way. [Stop.] Now move in the other direction. Use light feet; glide across the floor.

"Stop. Sit down in a personal space. We have been using our feet to travel all around the room. There are other ways we can move, too. Today we are going to use our hands and feet to help us go somewhere (I). Let's see how many ways there are. Who can travel about the floor using two hands and one foot? Try this with your back to the ceiling, then belly to the ceiling. Good! How about using two feet and one hand (E)? Try two feet and two hands (E). Travel slowly; this is not a race (R)! [Try changing directions—forward, backward, sideways—and pathways—straight, curved, zigzag (E).] What about hands and knees (E)? I see two hands, two knees. Two hands, one knee. Two knees, one hand. Change directions and pathways. Excellent.

"Next, put your tummy up, facing the ceiling (E). Now show me different ways you can walk on your hands and feet. I see two hands and one foot . . . two feet and one hand . . . two hands and two feet. Take a rest! There sure are a lot of ways to move using our hands, feet, and knees.

"Find a small piece of equipment to sit beside—a hoop, a wand, or a rope. Go! We are going to experiment with ways we can move into, out of, over, and around your piece of equipment using hands and feet (E). First, let's alternate, or change from hand to foot. Hand, foot, hand, foot. [Demonstrate.] That's like walking. Use the alternating pattern to move into, out of, over, or around your equipment several times. Stop and rest. Next, we'll try twos (E). Move your hand and foot on one side, then on the other side [demonstrate alternating sides] to travel about your piece of equipment. Stop.

"Now let's try twos a different way (E). We will use two hands and two feet [belly down; demonstrate]. We call that a bunny hop. That's it. Two hands, then two feet. Use the bunny hop to move into, out of, over, and around your equipment. You can go forward and backward. Good! Now twist your body and put the hands down, feet to the right; now hands down, feet to the left (E). OK, stop and sit down.

"We're going to start using the large equipment next—the boxes and benches (E). I want you to use a steplike action to travel on your feet. You can hop, jump, or skip on the floor. [Demonstrate and talk children through.] When you get to a box or bench, use your hands and feet to travel onto, off, along, and from side to side around your equipment. Then jump, hop, or skip to another box or bench. Got it? OK, go. [As they practice, give cues.] Use your hands and feet in different ways. Remember, you can use two hands and one foot, alternate, use twos, or bunny hops. Stop. Did you find that some of these ways work better than others? For now, let's just do bunny hops onto the boxes and benches. Put both hands on the box or bench. Keep your fingers spread and arms straight (R). That's important. Your shoulders are over your hands (R). Kick up with two feet (R). Come down softly onto the bench or box on your two feet (R). Take turns, or alternate, using your hands and feet. Travel over the box or bench, along it, and side to side.

"To end this class, we'll make up a sequence (A). We will link together different actions. First, travel on the floor using only your feet. You can hop, jump, or skip. You can change directions and pathways as you move. When you get to a box or bench, do bunny hops over and along it, side to side. Move to the floor and safely lower your body to a mat or carpet square and do a roll of your choice, then return to your feet. Do all of that again. So, you travel, bunny hop, roll, then begin all over again. Any questions? Go.

"Stop. Everyone come in. Who can tell me some of the ways we used our hands, feet, and knees to move or transfer our weight as we traveled around the room today? That's right, Tomiko, two hands and a foot. Yes, Matt, two hands and two feet. There sure are a lot of ways we can use our body parts to travel along the floor and on equipment. You are getting very good at traveling while using different steplike actions. That's it for now. See you soon."

Ideas for Assessment

- The arms must be strong enough to completely support a child's body weight; the arms must be straight with elbows locked and shoulders over the wrists. Use a checklist to observe each child for these factors.

- Weight must be transferred from feet to hands and back to the feet (figure 5.4). There must be no flopping or crashing with landings on the shins, back, side, or any other body part. Check each student for this.

- Children must make good transitions (linking actions) when moving from floor to equipment. They must keep their momentum going. One action should lead into the next. Watch and check for any breaks in action, glitches, or unnecessary movement. Check each child during sequence work for these factors.

Figure 5.4　Children should use their hands and feet to travel on the large equipment.

How Can I Change This?

- Include small equipment in the sequence. Travel on the hands and feet onto, out of, over, or along the small equipment to arrive at the large equipment. Travel on hands and feet over, along, around, onto, and off the box or bench. Roll. Move on to another piece of equipment and continue.
- Add a balance (e.g., travel, bunny hop, roll, balance).
- Stay in one place. Place a piece of small equipment near a box or bench. Develop a repeatable sequence using feet, hand, feet weight transfer in one station rather than travel around the gym.

Ideas for Teaching Fitness

- Taking weight on the hands requires strength in the arm muscles.
- Traveling about the room while transferring weight using the hands, feet, and knees with and without equipment builds cardiorespiratory endurance.

Ideas for Integrated Curriculum

- Question the children about traveling. What is traveling? What body parts can they use to travel? How is using both hands and feet similar to using only the feet? (It is steplike.) How is using both the hands and feet similar to weight transfer? (When placed next to each other, hands and feet are adjacent.) Weight transfer and steplike actions form a category, type, or set of actions that help our bodies travel from one place to another.
- Have children observe how insects and animals move. Inchworms, caterpillars, snails, spiders, snakes, bears, horses, and monkeys use their bodies in different ways. Compare these with possible human movements.

Ideas for Inclusion

- Depending on individual ability levels, physical restrictions, or both, allow children to move about on the floor and onto, off, or along the equipment in any way they are capable of moving. For example, children could slide on their bellies or backs by pushing or pulling with their arms or legs.
- A child in a wheelchair could wheel up and down an inclined plane (wedge) or move the wheelchair along a line.

READY FOR TAKEOFF

Objectives

As a result of participating in this learning experience, children will improve their ability to

- develop a one- or two-foot takeoff as a powerful, explosive means of propelling the body into the air (standard 1);
- attempt a variety of stretched, curled, and twisted shapes in the air during flight (standard 1); and
- identify powerful, thrusting actions of the arms and legs in a vertical direction as a requirement for gaining lift (standard 2).

Suggested Grade Range

Primary (1 to 2)

Organization

A large, open space is needed. Children should spread out with one or two to a box, bench, or minitramp.

Equipment Needed

Use available mats. Children need a place to jump from; a 12- to 15-inch-high box (30-38 cm), milk crate, bench, stacked newspapers in a cardboard box, or a minitramp are all acceptable. Hula hoops or ropes are useful.

Description

"Today we're going to be jumping up high into the air. While we're in the air, we will make shapes. Let's begin now by jogging about on the floor—not too fast. Lift your knees high, and jog with a light spring up on the balls of your feet. Jog to open spaces. Be careful not to bump! Stop! Watch me quickly! This time, as you run toward someone, eyeball them. Look at them like this. [Demonstrate.] As you get close to them, change directions, and fade slowly away. [Fade.] Move quickly toward someone, but fade slowly away. Think of the speeds you're using. Go. [Let them repeat several times.] Stop!

"Now we're going to work on a specific type of jumping (I). It's called a hurdle jump or spring takeoff, and it looks like this. [Demonstrate.] Have you ever seen people do this? What were they doing? Yes, Jenna, divers and gymnasts jump this way to vault and get high into the air. As you can see, there are hula hoops in different places on the floor. I'd like you to jog toward a hoop, like this. [Demonstrate.] Take one last step outside the hoop and land on two feet in the hoop. Land softly and bend down in a crouch. Then, move on and repeat this jump several times. Practice this. Go. Good, you're landing nice and softly, balanced on two feet. Stop. Now, this time, from your crouch, I want you to use your arms and legs to explode high into the air and still land with both feet in the hoop (R). So, you'll jog, land, crouch, explode, and land again (R). Try that. Go! [As the children practice, talk them through the sequence.] Push hard with your legs. Swing your arms up high. Look toward the ceiling and reach for the sky! [Repeat several times.] I'm looking for good jumps and soft, balanced landings on two feet. [Signal stop.]

"Let's go back to running toward people. As you approach someone, use your hurdle jump and give your friend a double high five (E). Push with your legs hard and swing your arms up to get high (R). Land, then move on to another friend. Any questions? Go! [Students run, approach, high five, land, move away. Stop.]

"Think now about what you can do with your body while it is in the air. What shapes can it make? Wide? Narrow? Stretched? Bent? Twisted? Symmetrical or asymmetrical? What are your arms and legs doing while you are in the air? [Show pictures as examples.] Using the hula hoops again, you'll run, approach, hurdle, jump, make a shape, and land (E). Who would like to demonstrate this for us? OK, Rina. Notice how she runs, approaches the hoop, hurdles and jumps into it, makes a shape, lands, and then moves on. Let's see you practice this. Go! [During practice, give cues.] Try several shapes. Make your shape when you're high up in the air. Bend your knees quickly to land under control. Stop.

"Next, we will take our jumping to the equipment (E). Remember to use your arms and legs to help you explode up and out high (R). You'll jog, approach the equipment, hurdle onto it, jump off [or make a rebound], make a shape, and land. [Demonstrate or have a student demonstrate.] Jump onto and off the bench in one fluid movement; that's called a rebound. Use the momentum from landing on the bench to carry you high into the air as you rebound and jump off the bench. Reach for the sky. Go! [As children practice, give them reminders.] See if you can do the same shapes in the air jumping off the bench as you did when you jumped from the floor. Keep moving, or traveling, around the floor and visit each bench or box as you try making several different shapes in the air. [Signal stop.]

"For the last activity today, I want you to stay at one box or bench. Do the same sequence [jog, approach, jump on, rebound off, shape, land]. This time, however, I want you to choose one shape for when you are in the air (A). It may be your best or your favorite shape. Practice it several times. Show your sequence to a partner near you. Go! [Signal stop.]

"Come in quickly. Who can tell me the name of the jump we were working on today? Yes, Latasha, a hurdle jump. What body parts help us get high in the air? Yes, Zachary, the arms reach for the sky, and the legs help us to crouch and explode. What kinds of shapes did you make during flight? Yes, Ryan, a stretch, curl, twist. Very good. See you next time."

Ideas for Assessment

- Good timing is the key for successful jumps with a shape in the air. Children will tend to start the shape too early while still on the floor. It is essential to get a good jump first. The key is the explosive power in the legs and a powerful arm thrust up (crouch, explode, reach). The shape should occur at the peak of suspension and be done quickly: in and out of the shape, prepare to land. Create an observation sheet that helps you, as the teacher, watch for each of these factors sequentially: good jump; crouch; explode; reach; then a good, well-defined shape.

- Proper landings are also important. Children must recover from their shapes in the air quickly to land on the feet. Control is important: No crashing allowed. Either add to the observation sheet used previously or create a separate sheet to check for children recovering and landing softly on their feet.

- As you observe the children, watch for a variety of body shapes. Children should try different shapes: stretched, bent, twisted, wide, narrow, symmetrical, and asymmetrical (see figure 5.5). Use an observation sheet that lists a variety of shape possibilities, and check to see if indeed the children are trying different shapes while in the air.

Figure 5.5 Children should jump high and create different body shapes during flight.

How Can I Change This?

- Children create a similar sequence on the floor using a hula hoop or rope, but add a weight-transfer action and a balance. An example might be to jog, approach, jump, shape in the air, land on the feet in a hoop, use a weight-transfer action out of the hoop (cartwheel, roll, rock), and finish in a balance. Children should stay at their own hoops or ropes. Repeat the sequence several times and then they choose their best work and show it to a partner.

- Repeat the same sequence at their box, bench, or minitramp, but add a balance at the end: jog, approach, jump, rebound, shape in air, land, resolve, and balance. Resolve means to make a smooth transition of your choice from landing on two feet into a balance position. Balances may be on the feet or the weight transferred into balanced positions on other body parts.

Ideas for Teaching Fitness

The hurdle jump requires strong, powerful leg muscles to gain height in the air. Jumping onto and off equipment requires even more strength.

Ideas for Integrated Curriculum

- Bring pictures of athletes, dancers, and gymnasts into class to illustrate the use of body shapes during flight. Point out the relationships and transfer from one sport to another.

- Relate shapes in the air to different balance positions (e.g., pike, straddle, squat). Compare body shapes with geometric shapes from math class—wide, narrow; symmetrical, asymmetrical; stretched, bent; tall, short; big, little.

Ideas for Inclusion

Children who are in wheelchairs can move their chairs up or down ramps to develop arm strength. Others with limited mobility can use simple rolling or sliding movements to change their body positions followed by a shape to represent a shape in the air.

ROCK AND ROLL

Objectives

As a result of participating in this learning experience, children will improve their ability to

- use rocking, rolling, and sliding actions as a means of traveling from one body position to another (standard 1);

- identify a traveling action, including weight transfer, as one that can move the body a very short distance as well as a long distance across the floor (standard 2); and

- use weight-transfer actions to approach, mount, travel on, or dismount a piece of equipment (standard 1).

Suggested Grade Range

Primary (2 to 3)

Organization

A large, open space is needed with mats, benches, and boxes spread out at a safe distance from each other. Place mats beside each bench or box.

Equipment Needed

One mat and bench or box for each student are needed for this activity.

Description

"Let's start today with everyone on a mat or the floor in a gymnast sit, or long sitting position. Bend over and reach for your toes. Hold and count to 10 [or 15]. OK. Sit back up and place your hands on the floor. Press up into a back support position with your tummy and bottom tight. You should have a good, long, straight body. See if you can lift one arm up and turn your body into a push-up [front support] position. Good! Let's start with the back support position and do this all again, only this time you'll jump your feet toward your hands into a squat position. Then, lean forward and place your forehead on the floor. [Demonstrate tripod position.] Then you can place your knees on your elbows, and if you want to try it, you can then slowly raise your legs into a headstand. [Demonstrate.] Practice this a few times. [Signal start and stop.] This time, when your legs are back down, tuck your chin to your chest and go into a forward roll; finish in a long sitting position. Tuck in your chin. We'll do the whole thing five times: sit and reach, now back support position. Turn to a front support. Now, jump into a squat position with your forehead on the floor in a tripod. Press up into a headstand, and down. Tuck, and roll. Any questions? [Repeat several times.]

"OK. Everyone up. Let's see some good jogging between the mats, with your knees high, soft landings, and when you get to a mat, make a nice high jump (I). Make a shape in the air, land, and do a roll of your choice; then return to your feet. Keep doing this—run, jump, shape, land, roll. Make different shapes each time in the air and use different rolls. [Signal stop.]

"Now, we'll add the benches or boxes (E). Who would like to demonstrate? OK, Brian and Marta. Start with good running on the floor. Jump onto the equipment. Jump off high, making a shape in the air. Swing your arms up. Land softly—squash! Roll on the mat, return to your feet, and continue. Good, you two! Everyone, try to visit each piece of equipment, and travel to open spaces, so you don't have to wait. [Signal start and stop.]

"Everyone sit beside a mat near a piece of equipment. Remember the sequence when we first warmed up today? Gymnast sit, back support, front support, tripod, press, tuck, and roll? Yes? Good thinking. When you did that sequence, did your body end up in the same place on the mat or floor as when you started the sequence? No. It moved just a little distance away, didn't it? When we move from one body part to another we call that weight transfer. Weight transfer occurs when we do a rock, roll, or slide action. Let's look for it.

"Everyone kneel on your hands and knees (E). Get your hips over your knees. Begin to let yourself down, moving to one side or the other, to the right or left. Feel your weight on your thigh, then the hip, then back, and press up into a shoulder stand (R). (See And Away We Go in this chapter [page 84] and Shoulder Stand in chapter 6 [page 137] for a complete description of a shoulder stand.) Round your body. Make the weight transfer smooth. Watch me. [Demonstrate.] Use this nice, rocking action to transfer your weight from a kneeling balance to a shoulder-stand balance. Practice this a few times.

"From your shoulder stand, go right into a backward shoulder roll to a knee and a foot balance (E). [Demonstrate and give children time to practice it.] Can you do it without putting your hands down on the floor in the beginning (R)? Make your body round. You want smooth weight transfers. OK. Stop.

"Let's try a long pencil position on your tummy (E). Pull your body forward, sliding it into a push-up or front support position. Sliding is also a way to transfer weight. Try this a couple of times. Pull your body forward! Good. [Signal stop.] I want you to experiment now (E). Choose one body position and think of how you could use a slide, rock, or roll to help you travel from it smoothly into a new body position. Use different body parts and surfaces, and transfer your weight in different directions. Practice as many ways as you can. Good. I see Li in a seated straddle with a turn over onto one thigh into a straddle push-up position. Sonny's doing a shoulder stand to a rock onto two knees. Keep it up. Try several new ways (E)!

"OK. Finally, we can use these weight-transfer actions to help us travel to and get on or off equipment (E). For example, we can use a roll to arrive at a box or bench. If we are really crafty, we can even use a roll to mount or get up on the box or bench. The key is to figure out just how far away from the bench to start (R). You want your seat to make contact with the bench and to end the roll in a V-sit on the bench. [Demonstrate.] From a V-sit on the bench, you can roll halfway over onto the tummy. From there you can place your hands on the floor, slide your tummy and thighs off the bench, transfer your weight into a roll, and finish on the floor. Begin by experimenting with three ways to use a slide, rock, or roll to approach, mount, travel on, and dismount the bench or box. If you need to, use the mat to provide cushioning on the benches. If you are trying something new or something you are not sure about, ask me or a partner to spot for your safety. [Introduce the idea of spotting early in gymnastics. It is a way to help someone who is doing a new or difficult skill. Teach children how to spot for different skills so they can help each other.] Let's finish our class by making a short sequence: balance position, weight transfer, and new balance (A). Here are your choices:

- Balance off the equipment, weight transfer to arrive, balance on the equipment.
- Balance on the equipment, weight transfer to dismount, balance off the equipment.
- Balance on the equipment, weight transfer on the equipment, balance on the equipment.

"Work hard at developing your sequence. Practice it several times until you can remember it exactly. You want to eliminate all the bugs or glitches. There should be no extra hand movements, weight shifts, or extra steps. After you've practiced, show your sequence to a partner. Watch your partner's sequence, and then tell her one thing you really liked about her work. See if the rock, roll, or slide was fast or slow. Did she make a smooth transition from one balance to the next? Did she transfer weight onto or off the equipment smoothly? After sharing, put away the equipment and line up at the door."

Ideas for Assessment

- To move the body short distances or to change positions, weight should be transferred from one adjacent body part to the next (see figure 5.6). Observe each child to check whether weight is being transferred to adjacent body parts.
- When executing rocking and rolling actions, children should focus their attention on making the body parts smooth and rounded. Check to see if rocking and rolling actions are smooth and rounded or flat and clunky.

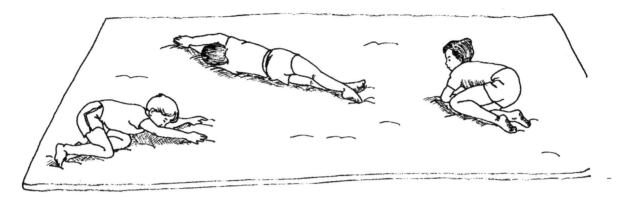

Figure 5.6   Rocking, rolling, twisting, and other weight-transfer actions are a means of traveling into new body positions.

- Weight-transfer actions from one balance to another should be completed with smooth transitions. Check to see if each child has eliminated unneeded steps, extra arm or leg gestures (glitches), pauses, and stops in the sequence.

How Can I Change This?

- Make up the weight-transfer sequence entirely on the floor (e.g., balance, weight transfer, balance, weight transfer, balance).
- Use weight transfer as traveling to make a longer, more complete sequence (e.g., balance, move to arrive, mount, balance, move on, balance, move to dismount, balance).
- Make up a simple weight transfer sequence performed with a partner either on or off the equipment.
- More able children might try a handstand with a lowering, rocking action onto the chest, tummy, and thighs into a front support position (fish flop). Using the same fish flop, they could move out of a backward exit to a shoulder stand. The key is in timing and arching the back to get a nicely curved (concave) surface on which to rock.

Ideas for Teaching Fitness

Rocking, rolling, and sliding are forms of weight transfer. The body requires strong muscles to execute these movements in a controlled manner.

Ideas for Integrated Curriculum

- Show the children the inside workings of a clock or simple machine. Point out how cogs mesh and pistons slide. Movement is smooth. Weight transfer from one adjacent part to the next helps the performance of the machine. In the same way, weight transfer helps the body travel from one position to another.
- Talk about dance fads, such as break dancing, the moon walk, or the body wave, as examples of ways people transfer weight. Except for the element of spinning on the head, which is too dangerous for children to try, break dancing is an excellent example of smooth, continuous weight transfer from one body part to another.

Ideas for Inclusion

Children of all abilities need to use weight-transfer actions in a variety of ways. Rolling over, sliding into or out of a seat, and shifting weight from side to side are a few examples of how all people need to use weight transfer in their everyday lives. Special-needs children can perform weight-transfer actions on the floor, in their chairs, using crutches, by pushing or pulling with their arms or legs only, or using other variations as appropriate.

FANTASY FLIGHT

Objectives

As a result of participating in this learning experience, children will improve their ability to

- vault onto and off selected equipment (standard 1);
- demonstrate a variety of shapes in the air and land safely (standard 1);
- experience flight through the air by gaining height and using good form (standard 1); and
- perform a linked movement sequence that includes a vault, a roll, and a balance (standard 1).

Suggested Grade Range

Primary (2 to 3)

Organization

Scatter benches and boxes around a large, open space. Arrange mats around the equipment for safety.

Equipment Needed

One hoop is needed for each student for the warm-up; one mat and a box, bench, or vaulting box are also needed for every two or three students.

Description

"Let's start moving! Start running slowly around the mats. Be careful not to run into anyone. Pick up the speed. OK, when you hear me clap, change your speed, choosing slow, medium, or fast as you travel around the gym. [Clap . . . clap . . . clap.] Now, everyone run at medium speed, and when you come near someone, jump up and give that person a double high five. Keep going; find a new partner and give a double high five. Use your arms and legs to jump as high as you can. Stop.

"Find a hoop on the floor, pick it up, and use it to stretch your body different ways. I like the way Ashley and Davey are moving in and out of their hoops to stretch their bodies. Really stretch your muscles and enjoy the feeling. Yes, Kelly, you can also sit or lie on the floor as you stretch with the hoop.

"Today, the main part of our lesson is to work on flight and vaulting. You'll travel around the room, and when you come to a bench or a box, jump onto and then off it (I). Use a hurdle or spring takeoff to jump onto the bench. [Demonstrate.] Swing your arms up to jump as high as you can on your rebound jump off the bench (R); land and keep going. Any questions? OK, go! [Give reminders during practice.] Keep your body tall. Good jump. Reach higher. Can you jump one body length high? Very good. And stop.

"Now when you jump off a bench, make a neat shape in the air, and still land on two feet (E). Try to make as many different shapes as you can. Go. Nice! I see a tuck with knees to the chest. Nicki's doing a star with her arms and legs stretched out. Jeremy's doing a pike with straight legs forward. Good, I see a straddle with legs spread out, and even symmetrical and asymmetrical shapes. Stop.

"Let's work on making better landings (R). Squash as you land, bending your hips, knees, and ankles. This will help you keep a soft, balanced landing. [Demonstrate.] Go. [Give reminders while children practice.] Keep your hands off the floor when you land. Land on the balls of your feet, not your heels. Much better. Squash! [Pinpoint several examples of good jumps and landings.] Stop. This time, move into a roll as you land from each jump (E). Roll in whatever direction your landing takes you. [Signal start and stop.]

"Now, we are going to learn how to vault onto and off apparatus in a variety of ways (E). [The ideal height for apparatus is at about the children's waist level. Using a hurdle or spring takeoff, the children should be able to land on the apparatus with the feet together between the hands, and then jump off.] For vaulting, hands arrive on the apparatus before the legs. [Be prepared to spot at the shoulders for the children, or teach them to spot for each other. Demonstrate.] So, you run, vault on, land, jump off, and squash.

"Some secrets to a good vault are to get good height off the first jump and get your weight up over your hands. Keep your arms straight, your hips high, and your head up (R). Think of these as you practice. Go! Now, try to vault without your feet landing on the vaulting box. Bring your feet through the middle without touching the apparatus [squat vault] (E). Great. After you take your turn vaulting over the box, turn and move to the bench (E). Jump onto the bench and make a shape. Then jump off, create a shape in the air, land, and roll. By the time you finish that, it will be your turn again to vault. Try to vault with your feet outside your hands in a straddle position [straddle vault] (E). Again, land on the vaulting box first, and when you feel confident, try to straddle vault over the vaulting box. [Demonstrate. Be prepared to spot for the children or to teach them to spot for each other.]

"Finally, let's take these vaults and link them to other actions we know. Our movement sequence today will be vault, roll, balance (A). Decide what movements you will use for your sequence and then practice the sequence over and over. Stop. Select a partner and show your sequence to your partner.

"Stop. Everyone come in. Who can tell me the names of two vaults we learned today? What is important to do when trying to vault well? Yes, Rinji. Good hurdle jumps, with the arms straight and shoulders over the hands, and good landings. What did you like best about the sequences you saw? Good, Matt—exciting vaults, shapes in the air. Yes, Marta, smooth transitions. Right, Tonya, different rolls, variety, and stillness in the final balances. You all worked hard today. That's it."

Ideas for Assessment

- A powerful, explosive leg thrust and an upward arm swing are keys to jumping in the air. Check to see if the children jump up and reach for the sky with their arms.
- During flights in the air, children should display clear, crisp shapes and proper timing into and out of shapes before landing. Watch for good lines in the arms and legs and good extension through the fingers and toes.

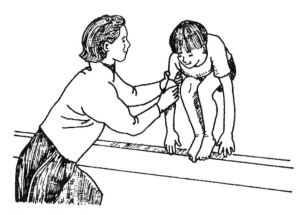

Figure 5.7   Children should vault onto and off the equipment by jumping high and keeping their hips high while the shoulders, hands, and arms are aligned with one another.

- Vaulting well requires a good two-foot takeoff. Check each student for this, as well as for good hand placement on the vaulting box. In addition, children should keep their arms straight, get their shoulders over their hands, and get their hips high (see figure 5.7). With the majority of weight placed over the arms, the legs are left free to do their work.

How Can I Change This?

- Try additional types of vaults: both legs over the same side (flank vault); one leg through the middle and one to the side (wolf vault); vault with a one-quarter or one-half turn to face a new direction.

- In the absence of a vaulting box, travel to a bench or smaller box. Jump onto the box and rebound (jump) into the air. Make a shape in the air, land, roll, and balance.

Ideas for Teaching Fitness

- Getting good height on a jump off the floor or a bench requires explosive leg strength. Becoming a good vaulter on various types of apparatus requires very strong arms to support and propel the body upward.

- Creating shapes while in flight requires good body flexibility.

Ideas for Integrated Curriculum

- Vaulting over objects is key to being a versatile mover. Vaults can be used in jumping over a bicycle rack, a fence, a fallen tree, or over other children, as in leapfrog. Have the children write a paragraph or short story about how they could use a type of vault to go over an object or person. The story can be about a real-life game or activity or a made-up situation, such as being chased by a bear in the woods.

- Vaulting and jumping actions are used in a variety of sports, including pole vault, high jump, hurdles, football (jumping over a potential tackler), basketball (jumping for a rebound), and volleyball (jumping for a spike). What shape does the body create while it is in the air? A stretch, bend, pike, or twist? Compare body shapes to shapes in mathematics.

CROSS AT THE INTERSECTION

Objectives

As a result of participating in this learning experience, children will improve their ability to

- use steplike actions of the feet and hands to transfer their body weight into, over, along, and out of a small piece of equipment (standard 1);

- identify line segments, line intersections, and adjacent quadrants (standard 2); and

- develop and perform a movement sequence that includes steplike actions using the feet and hands in relationship to the small equipment (standards 1 and 2).

Suggested Grade Range

Intermediate (3 to 4)

Organization

A large, open space is needed. Spread out equipment to permit free-flowing movement from one piece of equipment to another.

Equipment Needed

This learning experience requires two jump ropes and a mat for each pair of children, plus a variety of other small equipment such as hoops and wands.

Description

"As you come into the gym today you'll see that I have placed a set of two jump ropes on the floor for each pair of you. Each pair of jump ropes is in the shape of a cross, with a vertical line and a horizontal line. Be careful not to touch the ropes—we want them to stay exactly where they are. When I say go, I want each of you to get a partner and go to one set of ropes and stand in an open space [quadrant] between a horizontal line and a vertical line. When everybody has a place, stand still, look at me, and wait for further directions. Go. Good, you did that quickly. At your set of ropes I want you to do one-foot hops or two-foot jumps and travel from one open space [quadrant] to another (I). You can go side to side or diagonally. [Demonstrate going side to side and diagonally into different quadrants.] Go. Keep it going—side to side to side; diagonal, side, diagonal, side. Hops, jumps. What type of pattern can you make? Stop. This time keep your feet moving in the same way, using hops and jumps, but travel from open space [quadrant] to open space at your set of ropes while changing directions (E). Jump or hop sometimes forward, sometimes backward, sometimes sideways. Go. Remember—jumps and hops, forward, backward, and sideways. Keep it going. Try different ways. Develop a pattern that you can keep repeating. Show your patterns to your partner. Take turns with your partner. Stop.

"The next task is to travel from your jump ropes to another set of jump ropes with your partner. (E). When you're traveling between sets of jump ropes, you can skip, slide, or gallop. When you arrive at a new set of jump ropes, I want you to use hops or jumps to move into each space [quadrant]. Then, move on to another, and another. [Demonstrate.] What are we going to do this time? Yes, Susan. We're going to skip, slide, or gallop between ropes with our partner. We're going to jump or hop into each of the spaces at the ropes and then move on. Ready, go. Good! I saw Marvin and Steve skipping between ropes and backward jumping into each space [quadrant] at the ropes. Great! Matilda and her partner are galloping between ropes and hopping into each space at the ropes. Stop.

"Everyone walk here to this pair of ropes. Sit down. Next we're going to use our hands and feet to go from one space [quadrant] to another (E). Again, we will take turns with our partner. You will have several choices. I've set the jump ropes up in this way for a reason. In mathematics you're learning that when two lines cross, the point where they meet is called what? Right, Kalila. The point is called an intersection. When two lines intersect and make right angles, how do we describe the relationship of the lines to each other? Yes, Gertrude, perpendicular is correct. That's how I've arranged the jump ropes today. When two ropes cross, we have an intersection, creating four open spaces. See, like here—one, two, three, four. [Demonstrate.] Next we're going to stand in one open space facing one of the segments of rope. From a standing position, we'll put our hands down, both at the same time, onto the rope and kick our legs up into the air under control [stretch, topple, lunge; see Clock Face, page 110]. Then, we'll come back down to the floor softly on our feet [demonstrate] (R). You end up in the same space you started, in a standing position. I don't want to see any crashing to the ground. You can land on one or two feet. Start on your feet and end on your feet. Is everyone ready to try? Remember you will take turns with your partner at your mat. Walk back to your set of ropes. Begin. Good. Remember to put your two hands down at the same time. Make sure you land softly. That was excellent, Mark. I didn't even hear your feet when you landed! [Allow each set of partners several practice attempts.] Stop. Sit down.

"Next, we're going to use the ropes to try something different (E). Watch me. I'm going to start in one open space and face one of the rope segments. This time you'll put one hand down in the space where your feet started. Place our other hand down into a new adjacent space. What does adjacent mean? Yes, next to. Watch me. Kick your feet up in the air and bring them down in the new adjacent space (figure 5.8). Land on one foot and then the other. [Demonstrate.] Right. Like a cartwheel. Does everyone understand? Good. Begin. Remember to take turns with your partner. [Allow for several practice attempts.] Stop. Now, I want you to put both hands down, together or one at a time, and go from one open space to another diagonally [demonstrate] (E). Try to keep your legs as straight as you can (R). Keep your arms locked and straight, and try to get your shoulders over your hands (R). If you're bringing one foot down at a time, try to make it smooth—hand, hand, foot, foot—like a cartwheel (R). If you are bringing both feet down together, keep your legs together, pike, and snap both feet down together—like a round-off (R). Again, take turns with your partner. Begin. [Allow for several practice attempts.] Stop.

Figure 5.8 Travel from one space to another while using steplike actions that transfer weight from feet to hands to feet.

"That was very good! Now you may keep using the ropes, or you may replace your ropes with a hoop or a wand. We are going to work toward developing a sequence. You will work with your partner but develop your own individual sequence. When it is your turn to watch, you could help by giving your partner suggestions on how he could improve his form. We'll start by using our small piece of equipment. As we've been doing, I want you to start by transferring your weight from your feet to your hands to your feet. However, this time I want you to experiment by using the small piece of equipment to travel into and out of, over, or along [demonstrate] (E). Be sure that you tighten your bottom and legs as you land softly with control on your feet (R). Spread your fingers and place your whole palm on the floor as you take weight on your hands (R). Keep your arms straight—shoulders over wrists (R). Go. [Allow for several practice attempts.] Stop. This time do the same activity, but change the speed of your movements (E). For example, do several fast bunny hops and then slow bunny hops as you travel into, out of, over, or along your piece of equipment. Or, you could do one slow cartwheel over the equipment and return by doing a fast round-off. Think up your own way to solve the problem. It should be clear to me which of your movements are slow and which are fast. Go. [Allow for each partner to have several practice attempts.] Stop. [Pinpoint several students' examples and then let students continue to work.] Begin again. [Allow for several practice attempts.] Stop.

"Let's use this idea of transferring weight from feet to hands to feet while we move to different pieces of equipment (E). This time we will work as individuals. But, as you are traveling to a new piece of equipment, be aware of where others are located. I do not want to see more than two people at one piece of equipment at the same time (no long lines waiting turns). Use skips, slides, and gallops to travel from one piece of equipment to another. As you arrive at a new piece of equipment, use your feet-to-hands-to-feet movements to travel into, out of, over, or along. [Demonstrate.] Try new and challenging ways. Go. Remember to travel on your feet between equipment. Use your hands and feet to travel into, out of, over, or along. Try new and challenging ways. Stop. Come in and sit down.

"OK. We'll finish our class by developing a sequence (A). You're going to create a movement sequence using the skills you have just practiced. You will each select one piece of equipment and stay there. Begin in a balance away from the equipment. Use steplike actions on the feet to approach the equipment. Using feet to hands to feet, travel into, out of, over, or along the equipment. Finish in a balance. Also consider varying your speed as you develop your sequence. For example, I could balance at a low level to begin. After being still to show I have control, I could move slowly, rising to my feet in a standing position. Then, I could skip quickly to arrive at my piece of equipment. I could finish my sequence by cartwheeling into and out of my hoop, ending in a balance using two hands and a foot on the floor. My free leg could be straight, pointing up to the sky. [Demonstrate.] Try several ways to do this. Go. [Allow several practice attempts.] To end the class, I would like you to choose the sequence you like best. Practice it several times. Go. [Allow several practice attempts.] Stop. Now it's show time! I'd like this half of the class to perform her sequence twice. If it's your turn to watch, pick someone out and watch for her beginning balance, the approach, the transfer of weight from feet to hands to feet, and the finishing balance. When she's finished, tell her what you liked about the sequence. Then, it'll be your turn to perform while the first half watches."

Ideas for Assessment

- When transferring weight to the hands, children should keep their arms about shoulder-width apart. Their arms should also be straight, with elbows locked (shoulders over hands). Check to see if the children's arms are like spokes in a wheel and if their arms are straight, elbows locked.

- After transferring weight to the hands, children should return softly to their feet under control. Check to see if the children are landing softly or if they are crashing to the floor with a thud.

- Children should show variety in the way they transfer their weight from feet to hands and back to feet as they relate to their equipment (hand, hand; both hands together; foot, foot; both feet together). Observe whether the children show a variety of ways to transfer weight from the hands and back to the feet. Can they also lead from both sides—left and right?

- Children should show changes of speed as they transfer weight from feet to hands and back to feet—fast, slow. Can the children perform these weight-transfer actions slowly under control and with more speed?

How Can I Change This?

- Add benches, boxes, or a combination of these to make the transfer of weight more challenging. Use a feet-to-hands-to-feet weight transfer to move over, along, onto, and off the equipment.
- Do the final sequence to two different pieces of music—one fast and percussive, one slower and flowing—to elicit the same sequence showing changes in speed.

Ideas for Teaching Fitness

Transferring weight from feet to hands and back to feet requires the development of arm and shoulder girdle strength. Kicking the feet into the air requires children to support their entire body weight with their arms. Because arms may tire quickly at first, make sure to watch for fatigue, and give the children short rest periods so they can recover.

Ideas for Integrated Curriculum

Relate the use of the jump ropes during this lesson to mathematics concepts that children are learning in the classroom. These concepts could include line segments; intersection of lines; perpendicular lines; properties of adjacent and diagonal angles; and the use of flips, turns, and slides. In the case of flips, turns, and slides, the children could start in a balance shape in one of the quadrants, transfer their weight from feet to hands to feet into a new quadrant, and finish in a balance that is the same as the first (slide) or a mirror of it (flip).

Ideas for Inclusion

Because this lesson is about developing arm and shoulder strength, think about the children's developmental abilities. Children who are in a wheelchair could move from one quadrant to another through wheeling actions. Children on crutches could take weight on their crutches and then transfer their weight to another quadrant as they move from one place to another. Children who are nonambulatory could use their arms to push or pull (slide) themselves along the floor from quadrant to quadrant.

CLOCK FACE

Objectives

As a result of participating in this learning experience, children will improve their ability to

- use steplike actions to transfer body weight from the feet to the hands and back to the feet in a variety of ways (standard 1),
- develop strength in the arms and shoulder girdle (standard 4), and
- work cooperatively with a partner in individual tasks and in the development of a partner sequence (standard 5).

Suggested Grade Range

Intermediate (4 to 5)

Organization

A large, open area such as a gym floor, a stage, or a parachute on the grass is essential. Mats can be arranged in rows or columns or placed in scattered formation with adequate space between them.

Equipment Needed

One hula hoop, a piece of chalk, and one mat (4 by 6 feet, or 1.2 by 1.8 m) for every two children. Background music may also be used to provide an aesthetic worklike environment.

Description

"As we get started today, let's begin by using steplike actions around the floor. Stay off the mats. Yes, I see some of you running, others hopping, jumping, or skipping. Remember, I want good form, like a gymnast, not racing—high knees, light feet. Use the arms for lift and think of good posture through your trunk and head. Good. I also see you're remembering to go backward and sideways, use long and short steps, and sometimes go faster or slower. Stop!

"OK. This time when you travel, approach a mat. When you get to one, lower your body and put your hands down on the mat. Transfer your weight, changing from feet to hands to feet to hands as you travel across the mat. Then move away from the mat and travel on to another mat, using your feet and hands in a different traveling pattern to keep on going. Any questions? Go!

[After some practice] "Each time you come to a new mat, remember to do different things with your body and feet as you take weight on your hands. Stay tucked up and do bunny hops. [Demonstrate.] Stretch out and do mule kicks. Land on one foot, the other foot, both feet. Allow your feet to come down where they started. Take your feet to your left and right sides as you twist your body. Remember, you are traveling across the mat, so your hand and foot placements should take you somewhere. I also should see you land softly each time on your feet—no crashing! Try it one more time. [Signal start and stop.] Come on over to me.

"Good warm-up! Now we're ready for the main part of the lesson: taking weight on our hands using a clock face (I). Everyone will have a partner to work with cooperatively. When you're at your mat, use a piece of chalk or the hula hoop to create a clock face. Draw numbers on the mat from 1 to 12. Then you'll be ready to start. I'll explain what you'll be doing after I have a volunteer to help me demonstrate. [Choose student.]

"You and your partner will take turns. One will be the performer while the other is the observer. The observer will call out times and positions for the performer to start and finish in. [Post the progressions on a bulletin board, if you wish.] The observer also will give the performer some hints to help him or her do better.

"Start each movement with a long, thin [pencil] stretch, standing on a number at the edge of the clock (R). You'll all begin at the number 6. [Student demonstrates the following movements.] Your arms should be extended straight over the head; from here, lean or topple forward (R). This will throw your center of gravity outside your base of support, and you'll begin to lose your balance. So, take a small step or lunge forward; bend forward and place your hands on the ground in the center of the clock (R) (see figure 5.9). The trail leg—the one in the back—kicks up with the leg straight and tight, then lands softly back on the same foot, in this case on the number six again (R). So, the sequence goes stretch, topple, lunge, kick up. Let's watch Jenny do this all together. She starts at number 6, stretches, topples, lunges, kicks up. Notice she kicked up with

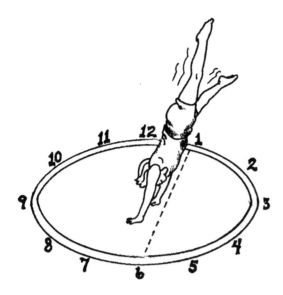

Figure 5.9   Take weight on the hands using the clock face.

only a small amount of force. Do this sequence until you can control your kick. If you kick up high and control it for a long time, what do you think you're doing? Yes, Zachary, a handstand!

"The observer should be looking for two hints (R). Are your partner's arms always straight, and when she lunges, is the knee right over the front foot? As Jenny tries it one more time, everyone notice if her arms are straight and where her knee is when she lunges. If she needed some help, the observer could tell her which of those things she needs to work on. Remember, while you're the observer, you will also give the different numbers to start and finish on. After two tries at each number, switch roles. OK? Any questions? If not, go ahead. Get a partner, go to a mat, and begin.

[During practice] "Remember that as you are using the clock face, you are developing arm strength and body control and using steplike actions to transfer weight from feet to hands to feet. Observers, check to see if your partner's arms are straight and if the knee is over the foot.

"Do these progressions (E):

• Start at 6, take weight on hands, return to 6. Start at 6, return to 5 or 7.

• Start at 6, return to 4 or 8, increasing the angle of rotation.

• Start at 6, return to 6 after changing the landing leg (scissors in air). Come down on both feet.

• Partner calls position: 6 to 8, 8 to 5, 4 to 7.

• Move the hand positions around the center to allow greater rotation: 6 to 10, 6 to 2, 6 to 11, 6 to 1, 6 to 12.

• For the very able who can pirouette, reduce the radius of the clock face. Get the feet close to the hands.

"Stop. Everyone gather around and sit down. Today we worked very hard at using several ways to transfer body weight from feet to hands to feet using various steplike actions. This helps develop arm strength and control. As we get better and better, we should be able to use these actions to build sequences individually, or with a partner. We'll work on that in future lessons. That's it for now."

Ideas for Assessment

• During the second part of the warm-up, children should use mats and floor spaces interchangeably. Move to open spaces and take turns rather than wait in long lines. Stop the class periodically to check for good use of space. Are the children spread out rather than bunched up?

• Stress good mechanics and control during practice. Focus children's efforts on straight arms, knee over foot, and tight bodies. Careful work now pays dividends later in more sophisticated sequence work.

How Can I Change This?

- For developing arm strength, an interesting variation on the clock face is to put the feet in the center and walk the hands around the clock while in push-up position.
- Once children develop control in taking weight on their hands, encourage them to use these steplike actions of transferring weight from feet to hands to feet in sequence work. Two examples follow that include a partner. During these two partner sequences, play music in the background. Children enjoy choreographing their work to music.
- Add sequence work with a partner:
  - *Lead, follow.* One partner puts together a short sequence that the other partner copies or repeats. For example, jump or hop three times to arrive at the mat (considering the direction, turns, and time), stretch, topple, lunge, return to one foot or two feet, lower into a rolling action of your choice, and finish in a balance of your choice.
  - *Partners moving simultaneously.* Perform a sequence similar to the previous one (in Lead, follow), with an emphasis on partner relationships. Partners mirror or match each other while moving face to face or side by side.

Ideas for Teaching Fitness

This lesson requires children to develop good arm and shoulder girdle strength. This could be a focus of work over time, because arm and shoulder strength cannot develop in one lesson. As a teacher, be sensitive to students as their arms and shoulders become fatigued. As students tire, move them into sequence work and come back to this practice over several lessons.

Ideas for Integrated Curriculum

Partner work may start with students calling out clock face position. Begin to place an emphasis on partners giving feedback to each other on performance. Have them talk to their partner about what they observe in arm and leg positions, soft landings, and hand placement, if necessary. This gives them responsibility for assisting with instruction, improving their speaking abilities, becoming more aware of the critical cues for good performance, and increasing their aesthetic perception. By having partners use checklists and make suggestions to each other, you are helping them develop their speaking and writing skills.

Ideas for Inclusion

This lesson has a focus on the development of arm strength and endurance. Children could participate in a variety of ways depending on individual abilities. For example, children who use crutches could use the arms with the crutches to support their body weight momentarily while swinging to various numbers on the clock face. If they are using wheelchairs, they could use their arms to move themselves up and down inclines. Children who are nonambulatory could use their arms to slide or push themselves forward, backward, or around in a circle (clock face) along the surface of the floor.

BEAM ME UP

Objectives

As a result of participating in this learning experience, children will improve their ability to

- demonstrate proper use of undergrip, overgrip, and mixed grip (standard 1); and
- perform a movement sequence that involves a rising action, a roll, and a balance starting under a large piece of apparatus (standard 1).

Suggested Grade Range

Intermediate (5)

Organization

A large, open space is needed, with mats arranged under each piece of apparatus for safety. Add mats so children can create movement sequences away from the equipment.

Equipment Needed

This learning experience requires one or more of the following large pieces of apparatus: balance beams, horizontal bars, or parallel bars. In this lesson, students will be working under the equipment, so as many as four children can use a piece of equipment at the same time. At least three pieces of equipment would be ideal, but you can adapt to whatever situation you have. In addition to placing mats under the equipment, use at least two mats leading to and away from each piece of apparatus to provide space for sequence work, maximize safety, and give multiple opportunities for practice.

Description

"As you can see, today we're going to be using large equipment. It's going to be a challenging class! But before we start working on the equipment, we need to warm up properly. Find a space on a mat and lie down in your space. Make yourself as long as you can. Really stretch. Pretend one person is pulling your arms and another person is pulling your legs at the same time. Now make your body as wide as you can; imagine that there is one person on each arm and leg pulling sideways out from your body at the same time. Next, curl your body into a tight ball. Relax into a long stretch again. Repeat these in a sequence three times very slowly on your own: long, wide, curl.

[When finished] "Now, start in a long sit and reach your arms toward your toes. Hold this position and count 10 to 15 seconds. Enjoy the stretch in your lower back and feel it in your hamstrings. Now rock back into a shoulder stand and stretch your legs wide like scissors. Come down into a straddle-sit position, place one hand behind your back, and lift your body into the air, stretching the free arm into the air. Your body weight should be on the one hand behind your back and your feet. Relax. Now, link these three actions together three times using a slow speed: long sit, shoulder stand, straddle. Try this on your own. [Signal stop.]

"Now, when I say go, move over to the beams, parallel bars, or horizontal bar. There should be no more than four of you to a balance beam or two to a set of parallel bars or horizontal bar. If necessary, you can double up and take turns with a partner. Go. [When situated] Wherever you are, sit directly under the equipment, so the beam or bar is over your head (I). Using the adjustment knobs, set the beam or bar at a height where each of your arms can reach up to grasp it as you stretch comfortably. Sit in alternating directions so that you are facing opposite the person next to you. This will allow you to move in opposite directions without interfering with each other.

"First we'll go over grip positions with our hands. You should all be able to do this at the same time. Reach up and grasp the bar or beam with both palms facing back to you [thumbs out] (R). This is called an undergrip. Reach up and grasp the bar or beam with both palms facing away from you [thumbs in] (R). This is called an overgrip. Reach up and grasp the beam or bar with one palm facing toward you and one facing away (R). This is called a mixed grip [demonstrate] (see figure 5.10) (R). Ready? Show me mixed . . . over . . . under. Right! You've got them.

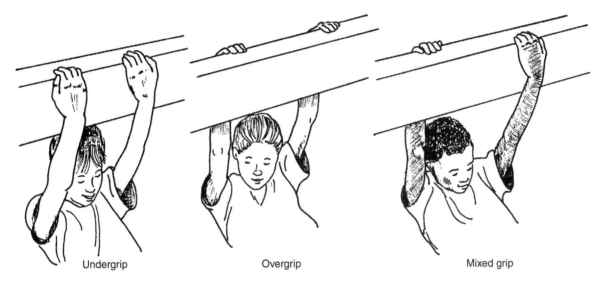

Undergrip   Overgrip   Mixed grip

Figure 5.10   The bars can be grasped with the hands in three different ways.

"Now we want to do something with these grips (E). Watch me demonstrate. Sitting directly under your equipment, you'll use a mixed grip. Pull, then push your body with a twist as you make a quarter turn and rise up to two knees [demonstrate] (R). Your arms end up crossing as you rise to a kneeling position (R). The sequence is pull, twist, knees. You can go in only one direction to make this work; see if you can figure it out. Take turns if you need to. Also, try the opposite mixed grip and rise to your knees facing the opposite direction (E). [After repeated practice] Try the same move, but make a half turn as you rise to your knees (E). Try it in the opposite direction, too (E).

"Next, I want you to use the mixed grip with a quarter or half turn and rise up to a knee and a foot (E). Now use an undergrip, and try to pull through and rise to a standing position facing away from the bar or beam (E). This is called a body wave. Pull through, wave, feet. As the arms thrust up and back, the chest should lead the body into an erect, standing position over the feet. [Demonstrate; allow repeated practice.]

"All of these rising actions are the same as when you resolve the shoulder stand. They put you in a position to decide what comes next. Rising to two knees allows you to rock back into a shoulder stand. Rising to one knee and foot gives you an easy exit into a cartwheel. A rise to two feet allows movement into steplike actions. With any of this work you can move either away from or back toward the bar or beam for continuous actions and sequence work. Let's try some of these combinations, starting with the rise to two knees, then rocking back into a shoulder stand (E). Practice this on your own as I travel around to watch and help. [Follow with other combinations.]

"Let's end the class by developing a short sequence (A). Perform a rising action of your choice. Take that into a shoulder stand, roll, cartwheel, or steplike action—away from or back toward the bar or beam. Finish in a balance position on the floor or on the bar or beam. Practice your sequence over and over until you can do it smoothly. Show your sequence to a partner.

"Stop. Everyone come in. Who can tell me the names of the three hand positions on the equipment that we learned today? When you started those positions, where were you? Right, Bill, sitting under the bar or beam in a long sitting position. As you moved out of the gymnast sit, what did you do? Yes, Li, you transferred your body weight to two feet, a knee and a foot, or to two knees. That movement created a smooth transition so you could go on and link one action to another to create a sequence. This is difficult work, and you are doing very well."

Ideas for Assessment

- Are the children using the proper grip (as in figure 5.10)?
- Are the children using good body lines? Rising actions should bring the body to erect positions (figure 5.11). Watch for tight bodies. A rise to two knees should have the hips over the knees, for example, and there should be no sagging bottoms. See that a rise to a knee and a foot includes the hips over the kneeling leg, with the leading knee over the foot. A rise using the body wave action should start from a long sitting position with the body erect and directly under the bar or beam, ending with body over feet.

Figure 5.11   Children can also rise from the bars or beam in various ways.

- Are the actions in the sequence linked together smoothly, with one action leading into the next? Using good body mechanics helps the flow in all actions. The pull-up in the rising actions raises the center of gravity over a new base (knees and feet). The rise can lead into a shoulder stand, steplike action, or wheeling action. Just like the pendulum of a clock, the rising action on one end of a swing is used to establish the momentum for the following downward action. One movement leads to the next smooth transition.

How Can I Change This?

- Add work to the sequence, such as a support position on top of the beam, a straddle over the beam, or a rotation around the beam.
- Combine work on top of and around the beam with work under the beam to create movement sequences.
- Add equipment such as benches or boxes to use for travel away from the beam and toward other pieces.

Ideas for Teaching Fitness

- Because the work of this lesson takes place primarily under the bars or beam, the children are developing arm strength as they use the different grips to push or pull their bodies into various positions in relation to the apparatus.

- The children can use the various grips to pull up and suspend their bodies in the air. Have a contest to see if they can hang for 10, 20, or 30 seconds.

- Have the children keep their heels on the floor in a long sitting position under the apparatus. Rise up to a hanging position under the apparatus with the body in a long, straight position. Then ask them to pull up into a modified chin-up position while keeping their bodies straight as a board—bent arms, straight body, heels on the floor in front.

Ideas for Integrated Curriculum

- Every routine has a beginning, a middle, and an end—a mount, some actions, and a dismount. The children do a rise, an action, and a balance. Compare a routine or sequence to a sentence. A sentence has a beginning, a middle, and an end—a noun, a verb, and a punctuation or end mark.

- Use videotapes taken in your previous classes or those of Olympic gymnasts. Show the children some gymnastics routines on beams or bars. Relate the taped sequencing to their routines. As a language assignment, have them write out their own sequences using words, checklist items, or diagrams.

- Emphasize the science concept of using good body mechanics to help the flow of all actions. The pull-up in the rising actions raises the center of gravity over a new base (knees and feet). The rise can lead into a shoulder stand, steplike action, or wheeling action. Just like the pendulum of a clock, the rising action on one end of a swing is used to establish the momentum for the following downward action. One movement leads in smooth transition to the next.

Ideas for Inclusion

Children who have at least the use of their arms can hang beneath the beam or bars for a specified time. They could also do vertical turns or twists (quarter, half) using the same grips as other children to reposition their bodies under the apparatus. These children could also support their body weight using over- and undergrips while creating different shapes (wide, narrow; symmetrical, asymmetrical; stretched, tucked).

ME AND MY SHADOW

Objectives

As a result of participating in this learning experience, children will improve their ability to

- explore the relationships of meeting and parting, leading and following, and mirroring and matching (standards 1 and 2);

- work responsibly with another person by making necessary adaptations (standard 5); and

- develop and perform a linked sequence of travel, balance, travel with a partner (standards 1, 2, and 5).

Suggested Grade Range

Intermediate (5)

Organization

A large, open space is needed with mats spread out so that children can travel between them.

Equipment Needed

One mat for every two children is ideal. You will also need a three-by-five-inch index card and a pencil for each student.

Description

"Today, you'll be working with a partner. Quickly sit next to someone by the time I count to five. One, two, three, four, five. We're going to work especially hard at different relationships you can have with your partner (I). We'll start by playing follow the leader to warm up. Which partner will lead? Follow? You choose. The leader may choose to run, jump, hop, skip, or whatever on the floor. The follower must do everything the leader does. When you arrive at a mat, choose a roll, a cartwheel, or some other action. Go.

[During warm-up] "Remember to change pathways and directions (E). Start rather slowly so your follower can remember what you do. A good leader watches out of the corner of the eye to make sure the follower can keep up (R). If you're ready, you can speed up; slow down; try turns, spins, and jumps with a shape in the air; or whatever you choose (E). Keep working hard. Good! I see people doing jumps with quarter and half turns, skips, pencil rolls, even a shoulder roll to a knee and a foot rise. Stop. Now, whoever was the follower becomes the leader. Work hard at staying with your partner. Stay close to your partner and anticipate any changes in his or her traveling. For example, try a skip forward, then slide sideways. Yes, Felipe! You were very alert that time. Stop; move to a mat with your partner.

"Next, you are going to work at mirroring your partner's movement while you're both moving (E). Mirroring means that you copy someone exactly, as though there is a reflection (as in a mirror). [Explain right to left.] Right now, decide who will be the leader and who will be the mirror. [When done] OK, you'll start in a stationary position, face to face with your partner. The leader will slowly change arm and leg positions to create different body shapes (E). Make some shapes symmetrical and some asymmetrical (E). Some should be at high levels, others at lower levels (E). Work at changing shapes so well together that I can't tell who is leading and who is following (R). Go. [After some practice] Try some traveling actions while you mirror each other (E). Use hops and jumps. While you're still mirroring each other, move to meet and part (E). Be sure to switch roles. Stop.

"Now, we're going to work at matching our partner's movement (E). Matching means that you are doing the exact same thing as your partner. This is the opposite of mirroring; it is right side to right side. We'll try this by working on a sequence I give you with a specific number of counts. First, let's see if we can all do four counts together. I'll lead. The counts will be hop left, hop left, jump forward to a two-foot straddle, turn halfway around clockwise. Ready? Do it with me: Hop, hop, jump, turn. Again! Hop, hop, jump, turn. Make sure we're all together. Again. Hop, hop, jump, turn. Great. You're getting the idea. Now, with your partner at a mat, create your own eight-count sequence (E). You may choose to be front to back or side by side. You may choose any combination of locomotor actions or even use a roll or cartwheel. Experiment for two minutes to choose the eight actions you want to sequence. [During practice] Now work hard at your timing. Make sure you are together. You should look like moving shadows. Good work! [Signal stop.]

"For the final challenge today we're going to build a sequence, adding some new choices (A). The sequence will be an eight-count travel, a balance, and another eight-count travel with your partner. Your new choices can include meeting and parting, mirroring, and matching. For example, as partners you could start away from each other, off the mat. You could use the first eight counts to hop, hop, jump turn a quarter clockwise, slide, slide, slide, jump turn a quarter counterclockwise, and jump straddle. During these eight counts you might be moving together to arrive on the mat; you'd be meeting. [Demonstrate.] Next, you could choose a symmetrical or an asymmetrical balance. [Demonstrate.] Finally, you could use eight more counts to travel away from each other, so you'd be parting. During this whole sequence you will choose to either mirror, right to left, or match, right to right, your partner's movements.

"The key is choosing traveling actions and a balance you can do with your partner. You and your partner will have to make a lot of decisions. This will challenge you to work hard. Remember, travel, balance, travel. Once you have decided on the actions and order of the sequence, practice it over and over until you're ready to present it to another set of partners.

[After repeated practice] "As we end today let's pretend we're at the Olympics. You're going to perform your partner sequence for another set of partners who haven't seen your routine yet. You will judge their partner sequence, and they will judge yours. I will give you an index card; you are to judge the sequence you watch on a six-point scale. Judges will give two points for choice of traveling actions. Everyone must show variety: steplike traveling and a roll or cartwheel, for example. Two points will be for choice of balance position. Two points will be for how well each person mirrors or matches their partner. In addition, you must write on your card one sentence that tells something that you liked about the sequence you judged."

Ideas for Assessment

- Accurate timing of the partner actions is important (see figure 5.12). Moving with someone while mirroring or matching is hard. Check to see if partners are using a silent count, a blink, or another signal to start, change direction, or move into a balance.

- Children should perform challenging tasks. Are the children working at an appropriate level of difficulty?

- Are the children exhibiting good quality in performing their actions, including good extensions through the arms and legs, good eye focus, and good awareness of all body parts?

How Can I Change This?

- Use simple equipment such as ropes, hoops, or wands to develop partner sequences.

Figure 5.12 Children should create a traveling sequence in which they mirror or match a partner's movements.

Figure 5.13 To change this learning experience, children can create a traveling sequence that mirrors or matches a partner's movements on equipment.

- Use a piece of apparatus to develop more complex partner sequences (see figure 5.13). Move to the apparatus, balance on it, and travel away from it. Use other choices for the ending sequence, such as starting away from the mat but moving sideways to meet at the mat, or starting side by side and moving together to arrive at the mat.

Ideas for Integrated Curriculum

- At this age, students are learning about graphic organizers such as sequencing and the use of Venn diagrams. As children build their sequences, they can diagram each of the parts in order.
- Children are also learning to compare and contrast as language skills. The use of mirror and matching images in this lesson helps them to develop these skills.
- Watching a partner routine, using a checklist, and writing a response help students with analyzing skills as well as note-taking skills.
- In mathematics, students are learning about reflections, rotations, and translations. These terms are similar to mirroring and matching and can be used during the traveling and balancing parts of the sequence to design travels that show translations of body position and body shapes that show reflections and rotations.

Ideas for Inclusion

As students work with partners, they can be assigned to work with someone of similar or different ability level. As they work on mirroring and matching in their traveling and balancing, they can adapt their responses to what each person is capable of doing. By working cooperatively and responsibly together, they are learning to accept the skills and abilities of others (standard 5).

ADDITIONAL IDEAS FOR LEARNING EXPERIENCES

STEPLIKE ACTIONS

About Face

- Run among each other while changing directions and pathways in open space, changing the way you face as you travel—skips backward, slide sideways, and so forth. Run and jump into the air with a one- or two-foot takeoff. Perform a quarter, half, or three-quarter turn in the air and land under control. (Help the children use the walls of the gym to identify the degree of turn.) Run, jump with a change of direction, then travel away in that new direction. Run, jump with a change of direction, land under control, roll, and finish in a balance.

- Run and perform a turning jump to land facing a different direction from where you started, and then do a different traveling action away from that new direction.

- Travel toward a box or bench from one angle. Use the equipment by balancing on it or going over it. Leave the equipment, traveling in a new direction.

Which Way Are You Going?

- Focus a learning experience on traveling in different pathways. Have the children travel in a straight, direct pathway for a short distance (5 yards or meters maximum). Travel in a flexible, curving pathway for a short distance. Try traveling in geometric pathways—triangle, square, circle, angular (acute, right, obtuse). Travel in one pathway (direct, indirect), jump, turn, roll, return to feet. Start the sequence all over again by traveling in a different pathway.

- Use pieces of large equipment such as boxes or benches. Travel in flexible, curved pathways on the floor between pieces of apparatus and in direct, straight pathways over or along them. Then travel in direct, straight pathways on the floor between pieces and in flexible, curved pathways over or along the equipment.

- Add the concepts of time and level while traveling in different pathways on the floor. While traveling on the floor for a short distance (no more than 5 yards or meters), develop a sequence using steplike actions using the feet, hands, and feet, or other body parts. Practice the sequence at a high speed, then in slow motion. Practice the same sequence by accelerating and decelerating. Make up a sequence that follows a straight pathway and a curved pathway, with changes of speed and level.

- Using the floor and a piece of apparatus, follow different pathways while using steplike actions of choice. Accelerate and decelerate as appropriate. Show changes of level.

- While working with a partner, work out a sequence that can be performed simultaneously and follows a definite pathway. Show changes in level and speed.

Play Fish

Make an assortment of three different types of cards similar to playing cards. Bigger sizes (four-by-six-inch or six-by-nine-inch cards) are better. One type of card should contain different steplike traveling actions—hopping, jumping, skipping, sliding, galloping, two hands and a foot, two feet and a hand. The second set should include different levels—high, medium, and low. The third set should include a choice of different directions—forward, backward, and sideways. You can also include additional sets of cards, such as pathway cards and speed cards. Have the children pull one card from each of the stacks. The combination they end up with determines the way they must travel toward or away from a hoop, approach or depart from a piece of large equipment such as a bench or a box, and so on.

Hoop-La

- Place hoops out on the floor in general space (one for each child). Have the children approach their own hoop with a steplike traveling action using the feet, such as running, hopping, skipping, or jumping. Upon arriving at the hoop, they should jump over or into the hoop and land under control. After landing, they add a balance at a high, medium, or low level.

- Use the same hoop and do the same sequence (travel, jump, land, balance), but travel from hoop to hoop doing a different form of traveling each time.

Wheeling and Dealing

- Have each child place two beanbags on the floor in a line, about two feet (shoulder-width) apart. The child does a cartwheel by placing each hand on a beanbag, picking the beanbag up, and then returning to the feet. Build the cartwheel work into a sequence of your choice—for example, cartwheel, balance at a high level, squat down and do a roll of your choice, finish in a balance.

- Have students stand toward the end of a bench, folded mat, or balance beam with enough room to initiate a cartwheel or round-off. Start the movement by placing the hands on the equipment—hand–hand or two hands simultaneously. Rotate the feet into the air and land on the floor. Although it may seem scary at first to be at a height of about a foot (30 cm) off the ground, the extra time for rotation in the air before the feet land actually simplifies the performance of the cartwheel or round-off. Build the cartwheel or round-off from the equipment into a sequence.

- Use a folded mat or stacked mats to provide a wide surface. Have the children do a cartwheel or round-off on the mat—stick it, no falling off. Perform a cartwheel only on a 10- to 12-foot (3-4 m) bench. Start on the bench, end on the bench. Build the cartwheel or round-off on the equipment into a sequence.

WEIGHT TRANSFER

Rock and Roll—or Slide, for That Matter

- Move around the room on body parts other than your feet—knees, back, front, and so on. For example, slide on your tummy, back, or side with changes of direction.

- Come off a piece of apparatus, such as a box or bench, with different body parts leading. For example, slide down onto your hands and into a forward roll.

- Get onto the apparatus with different parts of your body leading, approaching the apparatus from different angles.

- Slide along the apparatus with different parts of your body leading.

- Choose a balance on selected parts of your body. Can you move to another balance, taking weight on different body parts? Join together three different balancing or traveling movements, taking weight on different body parts. Look for a smooth joining of the sequence.

- Find as many ways as possible of getting on and off the box or bench, using different parts of the body to take weight. Approach the apparatus traveling forward and leave it traveling backward. Approach the apparatus with a stretched action and leave the apparatus tightly curled.

- Move over the floor using different body parts close together, then far apart. Approach a piece of apparatus with feet and hands close together. Leave the apparatus with feet and hands far apart. Find different ways of moving along the apparatus using different parts of your body close together and far apart.

- Travel around the room with one or two feet higher than your head. Travel over or along a box or bench with one or both feet higher than the other parts of your body. Look for sliding, balancing, rolling, and the like. On your box or bench, join three movements together, showing body parts together or apart. One of these movements must show your feet higher than your head.

Stretch, Curl

- Run and then stop in a still-stretched shape. Run and then stop in a still-curled shape. Move into a curled shape and hold it for a moment. Then move into a stretched shape and hold it. Can you travel along the floor in this way—curled, stretched, curled, stretched, and so forth?

- Travel over the floor with your body in a curled-up position. Show different curled-up positions while traveling across the floor. Take weight on your back, shoulders, and side. Travel backward, sideways, and forward while in a curled-up position. Run and then jump or leap into the air, creating a curled shape during flight. Now run and jump or leap, creating a stretched shape during flight.

- Approach a piece of equipment moving quickly, using small, curled-up movements, and leave it moving slowly in a stretched-out manner. Find a curled-up or stretched-out way of getting onto a piece of equipment. Then do the opposite in getting off the equipment.

Traveling Shape

Using steplike actions with the feet or weight-transfer actions with other body parts, travel about the room in a symmetrical or asymmetrical shape. Travel symmetrically by using bounces on two feet, jumps on two feet, hops on one foot, slides with one foot leading, or slides on the belly or back. Travel symmetrically at a high level, balance, travel symmetrically at a low level. Do just the opposite: travel asymmetrically at a low level, balance, travel asymmetrically at a high level.

FLIGHT

Leapin' Lizards!

Travel around the room with your feet wide apart—straddle jump, slide, gallop. Now run, run, run, and leap. In a leap, you take off on one foot and land on the other, trying to stay in the air as long as possible. Run, run, run, and leap over a jump rope, hoop, wand (6-12 inches, or 15-30 cm, off the floor). Put the leap into a sequence—run, run, run, leap, land, roll, balance.

Hopscotch

- Practice the five steplike weight transfers with your feet: one foot to the same foot (1 to the same), 1 foot to the other (1 to the other), one foot to two feet (1 to 2), two feet to one foot (2 to 1), and two feet to two feet (2 to 2). Travel around the room, putting them into a sequence. Join two of these jumps together: one foot to two feet and two feet to two feet (1 to 2 to 2 to 2) = height; one foot to the other foot (1 to other) = length. Join three together and see how far you can get: hop, step, jump. Join three together and see how high you can get: 1 to other, 2 to 2.

- Spring onto a box or bench using one of the steplike weight transfers. Spring off the apparatus using one of the steplike weight transfers. Always land on two feet and give at the knees for control. Put the combination together. Spring onto, spring off, land. Add a roll and a balance to finish a sequence.

How Buoyant Are You?

- Perform single small jumps on the floor on the same spot, landing on two feet (bouncing). Try several in a row, concentrating on buoyant landings. Try springing up and down using different combinations of feet: two feet to one foot, one foot to the other, one foot to two feet. The jumps should continue consecutively to concentrate on *give* (absorb or land softly) and *push* (explode upward with the legs and reach for the sky with your arms).

- Perform buoyant jumps in forward, backward, and sideways directions. Concentrate on body lean and arm swing. To jump forward, the body leans forward with the head up, and the arms swing up. To jump sideways, the body leans sideways with the head up, and the arms swing up and to the side. To jump backward, the body leans forward with the head up, but the emphasis is on the backward-and-up arm swing with a push back with the legs. To attempt a longer jump, run and jump to land over a mark on the floor. To attempt a higher jump, run and jump to land on a mark on the floor. Spring onto a box or bench and then off again in one continuous movement. Remember to execute a two-foot landing. Spring onto a piece of apparatus in one direction and off in another direction—forward, then sideways, and so forth. Build this into a sequence: spring on, spring off (direction change), land, roll, balance.

Sky

- Run to jump, and land on two feet. Try not to fall over or take extra steps once you have landed. Notice that keeping two feet together gives you a smaller base on which to balance, so you must control the body more, both in the air and upon landing. Jump up for height rather than forward, keep good body tension while in the air, and use your "shock absorbers" upon landing. Travel on your feet in different directions, then end with a jump onto two feet to land in a balanced way.

- Find a place on a piece of equipment where you can jump forward and sideways from it to land, two feet together, in a balanced way. After landing on two feet, use a transition such as bending down low or falling into a front support and finish in a balanced position on patches or points.

Flying Through the Air

- Find a way to spring onto a piece of apparatus (bench, beam, horse), using the hands and arms to arrive at and jump onto the apparatus. Land on both feet. Use a spotter for safety. Then jump off, land on the floor on two feet, and finish a sequence by traveling away from the apparatus.

- Spring onto a piece of apparatus using your hands and arms. Lower yourself onto the apparatus and slide off into a roll. Finish in a balance.

- Approach a piece of equipment such as a box or bench; jump onto and then off it using an explosive action. In the air during the flight phase, create different shapes—wide, narrow; symmetrical, asymmetrical; angular, curved.

- Work with a partner or in groups of three to perform vaults such as the ones shown in figure 5.14.

Face vault

Leapfrog

Through vault

Figure 5.14   Work with a partner or in groups of three to develop different types of vaulting actions.

CHAPTER 6

Learning Experiences for Statics

This chapter offers 11 learning experiences in the skill theme of statics. We have developed learning experiences for the three categories of statics, which include the characteristics, principles, and types of balance.

The following chart provides a quick outline of the focus and suggested grade range for each learning experience. At the end of the chapter you will find additional suggestions to stimulate the development of further gymnastics experiences for children.

Mini-Index

Focus	Name	Suggested grade range
Characteristics of balance: stillness, control, tightness	Patches and Points	Pre-K-2
Principles of balance: base of support, center of gravity	Push and Pull	1-2
Types of balance: symmetrical and asymmetrical	Same, Different	1-2
Types of balance: inverted	Shoulder Stand	2-3
Types of balance: perform a balance on the floor, then perform the same balance on a piece of equipment	Copycat	2-3
Types of balance: dimensions (small, big, wide, narrow)	Dimensions	3-4
Types of balance: balancing with weight completely or partially on equipment	Statues	3-4
Types of balance: inverted	Bottoms Up	3-4
Types of balance: developing a partner sequence using equipment	Twins	5
Types of balance: various types in relation to equipment	See What I Can Do	5
Principles and types of balance: countertension and counterbalance, relationship to partner	Lean on Me	5

PATCHES AND POINTS

Objectives

As a result of participating in this learning experience, children will improve their ability to

- balance on a variety of large and small body parts, using characteristics of good form (standard 1);
- name several classic gymnastics balances and invent solutions to balance problems (standard 2); and
- develop a simple balance sequence: balance, weight transfer, balance (standard 1).

Suggested Grade Range

Primary (Pre-K to 2)

Organization

A large, open space is needed, with mats arranged in scatter formation. Children should spread out in personal space using the mats.

Equipment Needed

You will need one mat for every two children.

Description

"Today we will begin with an easy jog. Pick your knees up. Move quietly, on light feet. When I say freeze, make a wide shape. Freeze! Go again. When I say freeze, make a narrow shape. Freeze. [Repeat several times, using a variety of shapes.] Now travel, using your feet very, very quickly and then very, very slowly. When you come to a mat, jump across it with two feet. Try long jumps. Good—now short, quick jumps. Now skip while you travel between the mats. Lift your knees high and push your toes into the floor. Stop. This time, when you come to a mat, lower yourself slowly into a long, tight, narrow shape like a pencil. [Demonstrate, lying down with your arms over your head.] Roll across the mat. Get up and skip on to the next mat. Ready? Go. [Repeat several times.] Now that we're warmed up, I want you to get with a partner and sit two to a mat so you're facing me. You won't be working with a partner, but you'll be working beside a partner on the same mat. You have to agree to cooperate and perhaps take turns. I'll be watching to see if you make a good choice for your partner. If not, I may have to ask you to change partners so you can work hard at balancing. Let's all sit in our gymnast sit (I). That's right—legs together, toes pointed, body tall, arms at your sides (R). We also call this a long sitting position. Let's quickly do some other positions (E). [Review tuck, front support, back support, shoulder stand, straddle stand, and straddle front support (E).] Now I'll call out the position names, and you move from one position to the next (E). Ready? Front support . . . tuck . . . back support . . . long sit . . . shoulder stand . . . tuck.

"Today we are working on balancing in different positions. Some of the positions have names. Others don't. We'll be using different body parts to balance. Can you name some body parts we've already used? [Feet, hands, seat, shoulders.]

"The smaller body parts we use to balance on—let's call them *points*. Let's call our larger body surfaces *patches*. Can you name some points? [Hands, feet, elbows, knees, head.] Can you name some patches? [Seat, shoulders, tummy, thigh, forearm, shin.] On your mats, let's see if we can balance on some of these patches and points (E). I'll get you started. How about your right forearm and right thigh [free leg up, straddled] (E)? How about your seat and two hands [legs in pike or straddle position] (E)? How about your tummy [back arched, arms out] (E)? Now balance on one knee and the opposite hand, the hand on your other side (E).

"Now I'll give you some choices (E). Figure them out. Balance on one patch and two points (E). On four points (E). Three points (E). Two points (E). One patch and one point (E). Can you make a wide balance [then narrow balance] using patches (E)? Points (E)? Can you make a balance where your head is lower than your hips (E)?

"Now comes the fun part. Let's see how to put two balances together into a sequence (E). A sequence has a beginning and an ending, with action in between. Make sure you hold your beginning balance until you can count to three. The beginning balance is a signal saying, 'Watch me, I'm ready to start.' I want you to show me stillness—that you have control (R). Then move into your second balance. Hold your second balance until you can count to three. It says, 'I am finished.' Choose one balance; move smoothly out of that balance into a new one. [For example, shoulder stand with legs straddled, rolling, rocking down into a V-sit with hands supporting.] You don't have to move much to get into a new balance (R). You can use a rolling, rocking, sliding, or steplike action with the hands or feet to move smoothly into your second balance.

"Let's see you try different balances on patches and points and smoothly link them to your second balance (E). Make up your favorite sequence [balance, transfer, balance] and practice it several times to make it look really good (A). [If appropriate, encourage students to make two sequences. In one sequence, they make the transfer fast: balance, quick action, another balance. In another, they make their transfer very slowly: balance, move slowly out of that balance into the second balance.] Make sure you hold your balances until you count to three to show control, with a good beginning and ending (R). Then find a partner and show him your sequence [after repeated practice].

"Stop. Everyone come here and sit down. Quick. Who can tell me the name of one of the balances we did today? Right, Molly, front support. Yes, Rinji, squat. Good, Billy, V-sit. We also invented some that didn't have names, didn't we? What does it take to balance well? Yes, Kaitlin, your body tight. Good, José, stillness, counting to three for control. You are already becoming good gymnasts."

Ideas for Assessment

- Are the children conscious of good form? Although ability levels vary and children will try easier or harder balances (see figure 6.1), whichever balances children choose, they should do them well. Check for good bases, alignment, support, lines, tight bodies, and control (holding for 3 seconds).

- When appropriate, focus on good transition movements while linking one balance to another. The children should work to remove extra steps, glitches, and unnecessary movements. Often a short step, a twist, a turn, or a movement from one adjacent body part to the next is the best way to get smooth weight transfer. Check the children for good transitions in their sequence work.

Figure 6.1   Basic balance positions.

How Can I Change This?

- Make up a visual symbol for different body parts (hand, foot, large oval for seat, circle for head; see *Balance Puzzles* in the appendix). Make a series of visual charts or posters for different balances. Play a game in which you hold up one chart, then another, getting the children to solve the visual balance puzzles one after another.

- More advanced learners can try longer sequences. For example, they might link three balances with two transitions: balance, move, balance, move, balance.

Ideas for Teaching Fitness

Balancing while maintaining stillness and control develops muscular strength and endurance. For example, a V-sit develops abdominal strength and endurance. A front support position develops muscles of the arm, neck, back, glutes, and legs.

Ideas for Integrated Curriculum

- Name the body parts that children balance on. You can use common terms such as hand, foot, tummy, bottom, and thigh, or you can use more anatomically correct terms such as abdomen, butt, gluteus maximus, and quadriceps.

- Before the lesson, prepare worksheets on which you write out the beginning of a sentence: "In one balance I balanced on my _____, _____, and _____. In another I balanced on my _____." Give the children a list of words they can select from to complete their sentences.

- Have the children draw a picture of their favorite balances. They can use stick figures or regular bodies. Help them to be aware of patches, points, and as much detail as they can include, such as elbows, knees, abdomen, and so forth.
- Have the children draw or write out their sequences using the visual symbols in *Write Your Sequence Using Gymnastics Notation* in the appendix. They can use stick figures to draw their balances or more abstract symbols to signify patches and points. For example, a large circle could be a patch, a small circle could be a point, and a triangle could be a knee. An egg shape could be the abdomen. An arrow with a straight line could signify a slide into a new balance. An arrow with a curved line could signify a rolling action into a new balance. This activity gives children the opportunity to work on their writing skills.
- Have the children name the classic gymnastics balance positions, increasing their movement vocabulary. Show them pictures of Olympic gymnasts.
- Help the children analyze their balances. Which are most stable? Which are least stable? Why? Talk about what makes a good balance.

Ideas for Inclusion

- All children can balance in a static position regardless of their abilities or restrictions. Challenge each child within his or her level of ability. Let children be creative. For example, a child using crutches could do a front or back support position by placing the crutches forward or backward and using the feet as a third base of support. A child in a wheelchair could sit, place a forearm patch on one side of the chair, and extend the free arm or leg (or both) up, out, or to the side.
- In a similar fashion to the sequences in the lesson, children with special needs can develop their own sequences with the use of their wheelchair, crutches, and other assistive devices.

PUSH AND PULL

Objectives

As a result of participating in this learning experience, children will improve their ability to

- vary the number of body parts they use as bases of support for balancing with good form (standard 1);
- identify factors that make some balances more stable than others (standard 2);
- work cooperatively with a partner to determine stable balance positions (standards 2 and 5); and
- develop a simple balance sequence: balance, weight transfer, balance (standard 1).

Suggested Grade Range

Primary (1 to 2)

Organization

A large, open space is needed, with mats arranged in scatter formation. Children should spread out in personal space, using the mats.

Equipment Needed

This learning experience requires one mat for every two children or one carpet square for each child and an index card and pencil for each child.

Description

"Today we will work on choosing good balance positions. We'll start with a warm-up. I want to see everyone skipping around on the floor (I). Stay off the mats. Show me your best skip (R): high knees; light, springy feet; and up on the balls of your feet. I see arms swinging, too. Good! Change speeds—try slow; now faster (E). OK, change directions—forward, sideways, backward (E). Skip while you turn or spin around (E). Stop. Watch me. This time skip, and as you get close to a mat, jump and land on two feet. Lower your body to the mat and roll. Finish your roll by coming to your feet (E). OK? [Signal start.] Keep going—skip, jump, land, roll. Stop.

"Now that we are warmed up, find a partner you know you can work with and sit down beside a mat. Today we are going to learn why some balances are stronger or more stable than others. You and your partner will take turns balancing and helping. When it's your turn to balance, do the best you can. When you're the helper, you will help by questioning and by gently pushing your partner from one way to another. I'll show you what I mean as we get started. Now, decide who will balance first. The balancer should choose two body parts to balance on (I). I see several of you have chosen two feet. That's a good way to begin. Let's watch here. Ashley is standing with two feet together. What if I were to face her and gently push her from the shoulder [demonstrate]? Yes, she would fall over. OK, what if you stand with your feet wide apart (R)? [Have a student demonstrate.] If I push gently from the side, you are strong; you don't fall over. But, if I push you from the front or back, it's easy to lose your balance. So, how could we make a standing balance the most stable, so you won't fall over (R)? See if you and your partner can figure out a way. One partner can gently push. I'll give you a hint. You may need to make your body or feet look different than what we just did. Try this now, and make sure both you and your partner get a chance. [Stop.] Talk to your partner about how to change the balances to become as stable as possible.

"I saw some of you get a good balance by bending to get lower, moving your feet apart into a stride or straddle position, and making a wide base [demonstrate]. These ideas help set strong balances. But gymnasts rarely stay standing still, except when they're done with a routine. So, let's try some balances on two other body parts besides the feet (E). How about a hand and a foot? Your seat and hand? Show me another balance you think of. Of all these, which do you think is the most stable? Show this one to your partner now, and talk with your partner about why you think it's the most stable. Then watch their balance and listen while they tell you why they think it's a very strong balance. [After some time] What answers did you discuss?

"Yes, Li, keeping your body low. OK, Kelly, a wide base and staggered feet or body parts can all help make your balance strong and stable (R). Now, let's try the same types of balances but use two [three, four, or more] bases of support for the balances (E). Take turns with your partner. See which way is most stable and strongest by having your partner gently push you when you have made a balance and are ready (R). Which balances are most stable? Why? Remember, choose good gymnastics balances. I want to see good balances—think of what every part of your body is doing. [During practice] Remember, the more bases of support you have, the more stable your balance is (R). When your body is low and your base is wide, you have better balance (R). I want to see good, strong muscles (R). Tighten your muscles—no wobbly, loose bodies (R). Keep your eyes looking at one place to help you hold your balance while you count to three (R). OK, stop.

"Sometimes gymnasts use a balance to take them into their next move. They may stretch, bend, or lean in one direction or another until they feel their body topple or fall. Then they step, twist, turn, or roll to regain their balance. A good gymnast is always in control. Let's all try this. Choose a balance. Hold it. Now lean or topple. Lose your balance, but move into a new balance (E). Go ahead and try different ways to balance (E). Choose one you like and practice it several times (A). Balance, transfer, balance. Then watch your partner. Tell them why they made good choices from what you know now about good balance positions.

"OK. Everyone in. I'm going to give everyone an index card and a pencil. Before you leave class today I want you to write down one or more ideas that help you balance well (see chapter 4, figure 4.9, on page 75). Leave your cards and pencils in the box at the door as you line up to leave."

Ideas for Assessment

- Children may be tempted to see who is the strongest and push each other out of balance. The purpose of the helper is to push *gently,* offer resistance, yet allow the performer to succeed at the balance. The goal is for the children to discover good principles of balance. Develop a worksheet with pictures of children balanced in different positions—some stable and some unstable. Have the students circle the ones that are stable. Have them write on a sheet of paper what the cues are for good balance principles—wide base of support, low center of gravity, center over base, good lines, stiff body, control (3 seconds), eye focus.

- As a closure to class, show the children a balance pose by demonstrating it yourself; have them tell you or write down why they think your position is or is not a good balance.

- Children should be challenging themselves as gymnasts. Standing, kneeling, or lying down flat may be stable positions, but these are not aesthetic, challenging balances that gymnasts would choose. Keep children focused on high-quality work (see figure 6.2). Check to see if children are challenging themselves within their ability level. In instances where they are not, challenge them to balance in a more difficult balance. Offer them some suggestions.

Figure 6.2   Children's balances should incorporate principles of quality movement.

How Can I Change This?

- Add a range of levels. Choose balances on one to four bases at a high, medium, or low level.
- Add the factor of extensions—wide and narrow, different bases.
- Add different body shapes, using various numbers of bases.

Ideas for Integrated Curriculum

- Bring in objects such as a pencil, a pyramid, a tall vase, and a wide bowl. Talk about the stability of these objects. Is a pencil more stable when standing on end or when lying on its side? Why? Which is more stable, a tall vase or wide bowl? Why?
- Examine the positions that various athletes assume when preparing to begin their sports: a runner; a linebacker, an offensive lineman, and a defensive lineman in football; an infielder in baseball; a swimmer. Which positions are the most stable? Why? Why do you suppose athletes use these readiness positions?

Ideas for Inclusion

- Children who use crutches can create balance positions similar to the ones in the *description section*. The crutches function as an extension of the arms and legs. By reaching out to the side, front, or back, children can lengthen or widen the base of support and become more stable.
- Children in wheelchairs can be shown sport chairs. Racing chairs tend to be long and narrow to produce forward speed similar to that of a sprinter coming out of starting blocks in track. They are stable front to back but less stable side to side. Chairs for games such as tennis or basketball are wide, giving sideways stability, and allow for stopping, starting, and quick changes of direction. Many chairs also have camber in the wheelbase, which offers stability in addition to making it easier for the hands and arms to manipulate the wheels.

SAME, DIFFERENT

Objectives

As a result of participating in this learning experience, children will improve their ability to

- balance in a variety of selected symmetrical and asymmetrical shapes (standard 1) and
- develop a simple sequence that includes a balance, a travel, and balance (standard 1).

Suggested Grade Range

Primary (1 to 2)

Organization

A large, open space is needed. Children should spread out, using mats.

Equipment Needed

Have one mat for every two children if possible; otherwise, carpet squares or a large parachute can be used for balances.

Description

"Today's lesson is about using our bodies symmetrically and asymmetrically. Those are big words. Do you know what *symmetry* means? It means that both sides of your body look alike or are doing the same thing. See if you can move by making your body work symmetrically (I). Yes, jumping from two feet to two feet is symmetrical. Try short, quick jumps; now do long, powerful jumps (E). How about going from feet-together to feet-apart jumps (E)? Can you think of other ways to move symmetrically (E)? Good, Zachary, bunny hops! Two feet, two hands forward and backward. I see some children doing forward and backward rolls. Great! Now, what about moving *asymmetrically* (E)? This means the two sides are different. Yes, a hop is asymmetrical (E). One foot is on the floor and the other is up. Running is alternating feet; skipping is, too (E). Try lots of other ways (E). Go fast and slow. Try moving forward, backward, sideways. Move with straight and curved pathways, too.

"Now that we're warmed up, let's sit on the mat in a gymnast sit (I). Arms are at our sides. Are we symmetrical or asymmetrical? Yes, symmetrical. Now put your arms out to the sides parallel to the floor (E). Are they still symmetrical [same]? Try a V-sit (E). Is this symmetrical or asymmetrical? Yes, a V-sit is still symmetrical. How could we change this (E)? Yes, Latasha, you could bend or stretch one arm or leg in a different position to make your body asymmetrical. Now do the same experiment from a front support, back support, and bridge position (E). Start symmetrical. Move one or two arms or legs to make your body asymmetrical (E). I'll come around and watch as you change your shapes.

"Try other balance shapes with different bases (E). Let me see you start symmetrical and change to asymmetrical (E). You can also start asymmetrical and change to symmetrical (E). Show me how you would do this. I want to see a definite asymmetrical shape that moves smoothly into a symmetrical shape. Nice job, Bill! You too, Marta.

"Now let's put this into a sequence (A). Choose a symmetrical balance. Hold it still. Add a traveling action, steplike or rolling. Finish in an asymmetrical balance. Try it several ways. Then choose your favorite combination. Practice now until it is your best work.

"Finally, let's do just the opposite sequence (A). Start in an asymmetrical balance and change into a symmetrical balance by using a good weight-transfer or steplike action. As you work on the sequence, think about how you use your time (E). Can you change the balance quickly? Slowly? Which do you like best? Whatever you choose, practice it several times. Show your sequence to a partner.

"Stop. Everyone gather here. Sit down. Who can tell me what the word *symmetrical* means? Yes, same on both sides. What were some examples of symmetrical balances? Yes, a V-sit could be one. What does the word *asymmetrical* mean? Yes, it looks different on the two sides. What were some examples of asymmetrical balances? Yes, balancing on one leg. Good work today! Line up at the door by using a symmetrical traveling action."

Ideas for Assessment

- Stillness is essential in balancing. Check to see if the children can hold their balances for three seconds to show control.

Figure 6.3　Sample symmetrical and asymmetrical balances.

- Sample symmetrical and asymmetrical balances are shown in figure 6.3. Call out "same" (symmetrical) or "different" (asymmetrical) and have the children balance accordingly. Check to see if their balances are appropriate. Create a worksheet with symmetrical and asymmetrical balances. Have the children circle the symmetrical balances. Have them put a cross (X) on the ones that are asymmetrical.

- Are the changes in balances and from balances to traveling (using single steplike or weight-transfer actions) logical and smooth? Are the children avoiding extra steps, glitches, and indecision? Their movements should be intentional and purposeful.

How Can I Change This?

- Keep the sequence the same (balance, travel, balance), but add a second focus to each balance. For example, balance 1 starts symmetrical, but through the change of an arm or leg position, it becomes asymmetrical. Balance 2 starts asymmetrical and changes to symmetrical.

- Lengthen the sequence. Use three balances and two travels: balance, travel, balance, travel, balance. Ask for two symmetrical balances and one asymmetrical, or vice versa. One traveling action could be symmetrical and one asymmetrical. Traveling actions may be chosen from steplike movements on the feet, movement on the hands and feet, rocks, rolls, and sliding.

Ideas for Teaching Fitness

Balancing in symmetrical and asymmetrical positions with good form and stillness requires the development of strong muscles in all parts of the body. Holding balances for lengths of time also helps to develop muscle endurance.

Ideas for Integrated Curriculum

- Teach an awareness of geometric design. Create lines with the arms, legs, and trunk that are parallel or perpendicular to the floor. Bend the arms, legs, or hips at right, acute, and obtuse angles. Make curved body shapes—smooth and round.

- Relate the symmetrical and asymmetrical body shapes that the children make to the concepts they are learning in mathematics.
- Compare the concepts of same and different to synonyms and antonyms in language arts.
- Show pictures of gymnasts, bridges, buildings, machines, and pieces of art. Ask the children to pick out lines, angles, and designs from the pictures that illustrate symmetrical and asymmetrical designs.
- Have the children name or write out the names of the muscle groups they are using to help them hold the muscles still when balancing in symmetrical and asymmetrical positions.

Ideas for Inclusion

- Children of all ability levels can move and balance in symmetrical and asymmetrical ways. They can lie on the floor, sit in a chair, and travel a chosen distance across the floor by using their arms or legs symmetrically or asymmetrically. They can also lie or sit on a scooter board or another piece of equipment and move about symmetrically or asymmetrically.
- While balancing on the floor or a piece of equipment, children can make symmetrical or asymmetrical shapes from sitting, lying, or standing positions. The idea is to challenge each child to work within his or her ability level.

SHOULDER STAND

Objectives

As a result of participating in this learning experience, children will improve their ability to

- demonstrate a successful shoulder stand, establishing a stable base with good alignment of the hips and legs over the base (standards 1 and 2);
- select a variety of ways to move smoothly into and out of the shoulder stand (standard 1); and
- develop a movement sequence involving steplike traveling actions onto and off a box or bench, a shoulder stand, and a resolving action that allows repetition of the sequence (standard 1).

Suggested Grade Range

Primary (2 to 3)

Organization

A large, open space is needed with the children spread out with mats. This lesson also is manageable on a gym floor or outdoor grassy area using carpet squares or a large parachute. Arrange mats in scatter formation with good spacing between them, and place a box or bench beside each mat.

Equipment Needed

You will need one mat and a bench or box for every two children.

Description

"Today we will start with stretching and balancing. Later we'll make a sequence by moving into and out of a balance. Now, everyone get into a gymnast sit position (I). Bend forward and reach for your toes. Reach and hold while you count to 15 (R). Open back up and use the movement to rock back onto your shoulders (E). Hold yourself up by pushing your arms down against the floor (R). You can also bend your arms at the elbow and place your hands on your hips (R). Tighten your seat; squeeze those buns together (R)! Tighten your tummy and legs, too (R). Point your toes (R). That's good, Jamie. Your hips should be over your shoulders and your legs straight up. OK, rock back down (E).

"Now, let's create a sequence (E). Watch as I demonstrate. You'll sit long, reach for your toes, rock back to a shoulder stand, rock out of your shoulder stand to a straddle seat, reach smoothly to your left and right legs, rock back to a shoulder stand, come back down to a long sit, and push up to a back support. I'll talk you through it once, then you'll try it on your own. Ready? [Go through sequence.] Start over.

"Now let's experiment with what to do with our legs in a shoulder stand (E). Get back up into a shoulder stand. Try these as I talk you through it. Straddle your legs and make scissor movements slowly. Feel the stretch in your lower back and the back of your legs. Let your feet come slowly down behind your head. Bend one leg, but keep the other leg straight. Write some letters of the alphabet with one leg. Try it now with two legs. Stop. Rock out of your shoulder stand to a sitting position (E). OK, take a rest!

"Good stretching! Now we're ready to learn more ways to come out of our shoulder stand balances (E). Get back into your shoulder stand. Hold your balance tight. Begin rocking back toward your feet. OK, whip your legs under you (R). Bend your knees so the feet come close to your seat (R). First try to be long and tall, then short and small. Can you stand up—rise to your feet—without using your hands on the floor (R)? That's one way to resolve the shoulder stand: return to two feet. Practice it several times.

"Now get back into a shoulder stand. Watch me. You're going to twist and turn at the hips as you rock out (R). You'll turn partway to one side and come up on both your knees (E). Think long and tall, then short and small. No hands on the floor (R)! That's right—bodies tall, hips over your knees, and shoulders over your hips (R).

"Now, get back into a shoulder stand. Next you'll bend one leg under and come out of the shoulder stand to one knee and your other foot (E). Can you come out of a shoulder stand to a one-foot rise to a stand (E)? [Also have them try using a backward shoulder roll to come to a knee and a foot or to two knees (E).] Try each way several times. Pick your favorite two or three ways and really get good at them (E).

"OK. Now we're ready to make a sequence (A). Start by running, hopping, or skipping around the floor. When you come to a mat, jump high, land softly, lower your body, rock back into a shoulder stand, and resolve the shoulder stand as you choose. Then return to traveling on your feet to another mat. Go ahead and repeat this several times (E). [Signal stop.] OK, let's add the box or bench now (E). Travel on the floor using good running steps and jump up onto the bench or box. Do three quick, bouncy jumps on both feet and then one big, explosive jump off the bench. Land softly on your feet. Lower yourself to the floor by squatting or sitting. Then rock back into a shoulder stand. Resolve it. Move off and start over. [Demonstrate.] Try this now. I'm going to look for smooth sequences. [Pinpoint several students, if desired.] Keep the sequence the same this time, but when you're in a shoulder stand, slowly and smoothly move your legs into three different shapes (E). Resolve, or come out of, your shoulder stand ready to begin the sequence again and again. Practice this with your different leg positions. I'll come around and help you out with some hints. [Allow sufficient practice.]

"Stop. Everyone come in. Have a seat. Who can tell me three different ways to come out of, or resolve, a shoulder stand? Yes, Tonya, two knees; good, Ashley, a knee and a foot; right, William, a backward shoulder roll to a knee and a foot. Very good, you remembered. There are other ways, too. What are some words that help us keep good form? Yes, long and tall, short and small. You really learned a lot today. Resolving balances, such as a shoulder stand, in the ways you did today helps make smooth transitions as you move from one position or balance to another. That's all for today."

Ideas for Assessment

- Good momentum and timing are keys to successful resolutions of the shoulder stand. For rocking out of the shoulder stand, the children should keep the body long to establish momentum and speed. Then they should make it short to establish a quick rotation for coming upright to a resolution of their choosing (figure 6.4). Check each child's rocking action for long and tall, then short and small.

Figure 6.4   Sample resolutions of the shoulder stand.

- The children should learn not to use their hands to assist in pushing up out of a rocking action. Use a checklist to see who can resolve their shoulder stand into a new position (two knees, a knee and a foot, coming up to a one- or two-foot stand).
- As children perform the shoulder stand, look for good alignment, with the toes pointed, the legs straight or bent in aesthetic positions, and varying leg positions. Gymnasts should always strive for good lines, shape, and form. Check to see which children are striving for good aesthetic shapes while in the shoulder stand position.

How Can I Change This?

- Perform shoulder stands on a box, bench, or other piece of equipment.
- Work at one mat and a bench or box. Create a sequence that includes a traveling action to the bench, a balance completely or partially on the bench, a roll off the bench into a shoulder stand, and a resolution out of the shoulder stand into a balance of choice.
- Synchronize one of the lesson's sequences with a partner. The children mirror or match leg positions inverted in a shoulder stand.

Ideas for Teaching Fitness

- Balancing in a shoulder stand requires strong arms and shoulders. In addition, the gluteal and abdominal muscles must be strong to hold a vertical position.
- While upside down in the shoulder stand, children can put the legs into straddle, scissors, butterfly, and other positions. Each of these positions requires flexibility.

Ideas for Integrated Curriculum

- For a stable base in a shoulder stand, the weight should be on the shoulders and upper arms to the elbow. No weight should be on the neck or head. The shoulders and arms are strong and provide a sturdy base for support.
- Good vertical alignment over the base provides stability. Hips, knees, and feet should be vertical over the elbow and shoulder base.
- To resolve the shoulder stand, use rotary motion around a horizontal axis. To establish speed and momentum, stay long. To rotate quickly around the axis, tuck and get small.
- Teach the children the difference between upright and inverted balances. An inverted balance is one in which the head is lower than the hips. Compare upright and inverted balances with upright and inverted geometric shapes when using the concepts of flips or translations in mathematics.

COPYCAT

Objectives

As a result of participating in this learning experience, children will improve their ability to

- choose and perform a balance on the floor and then perform the same balance on a piece of equipment (standard 1);
- name several classic gymnastics balances as well as invent new solutions to balance problems (standard 2);
- develop a simple balance sequence—balance off equipment, weight transfer, balance on equipment (standard 1); and
- assist a partner or small group by sharing observations about skill performance during practice (standard 5).

Suggested Grade Range

Primary (2 to 3)

Organization

A large, open space is needed. For each piece of large equipment such as a box, bench, beam, bar, or horse, a small piece such as a hoop, hurdle (wand supported by two milk crates), or rope should be placed nearby (6 to 10 feet away).

Equipment Needed

Both large and small equipment are needed for this lesson. Boxes, benches, beams, bars, horses, tables, chairs, and the like should be coupled with ropes, hoops, hurdles, and so forth. Use mats, carpet squares, or a combination of the two for protection under and beside the large equipment.

Description

"Did you ever notice how strong and flexible gymnasts are? Today we'll work on our strength and flexibility as we warm up, and then we'll concentrate on our balances off and on equipment. Let's begin with jumps on two feet (I)—powerful, explosive jumps. Get into a slight crouch and swing your arms back (R). Then explode! Spring up. Use your legs (R). Reach for the sky with your arms [demonstrate] (R). Go. Stop. Now, while still jumping, take short, quick, resilient jumps (E). Use springy feet (R). Bounce, bounce, bounce. [Demonstrate.] Go. Stop. Combine the two types of jumps (E). Quick, resilient. Explosive, powerful. Bounce, bounce, bounce, big rebound jump. [Demonstrate.] Go. [Repeat several times. Signal stop.]

"While still spread out on the floor, everyone stretch, topple, lunge [refer to the *Clock Face* learning experience on page 110 in chapter 5] (I). Remember, this sequence of stretch, topple, lunge is designed to get your arms over your body straight like a pencil, with arms over your head (R). Then, tip or topple forward. As you lose your balance, take a step and bend forward at the waist (lunge), placing your extended arms down just in front of your lead foot. Take your weight on your hands and kick your extended trail leg up into the air. Come back to your feet softly [demonstrate]. As you take weight on your hands, hold your handstand as long as you can (A). Count to three. Shoulders over hands (R). Hips and legs over hands (R). Tight bodies (R). [Children may work with a partner by taking turns and spotting for each other.] Go. Stop. Next, continue taking weight on your hands [step, topple, lunge] as you move into, out of, onto, off, over, and along the small and large equipment placed on the floor (E). I want to see bunny hops, cartwheels, and temporary handstands. [Signal go and stop.] You're working hard today! We sure are getting stronger leg and arm muscles.

"Now we're going to work to make our bodies more flexible. Spread out on the floor and get into a long sitting position (I). Bend forward and touch your toes. Hold for 10 to 15 seconds [count]. Remember, this is a pike position. While remaining in a sitting position, straddle your legs and bend to touch your right toes, then your left toes (E). Bend your legs at your knees and place your feet together. Clasp your hands together and place your elbows on your knees. Push down and hold for 10 to 15 seconds [butterfly] (E). Rock up into a shoulder stand (E). Tight bottoms. Long, strong legs straight in the air (R). Straddle your legs and twist right and left (E). Rock back down out of your shoulder stand into a long lying position (E). Push up into a back bend (E). Use strong arms and legs! Feel your tummy stretch. Repeat the whole sequence three times [demonstrate] (E). Long sit, touch toes. Straddle, touch right, touch left. Shoulder stand, twist right, twist left. Back bend. [Signal go and stop.]

"While you're resting, sit up straight and listen. Today we're going to do balances on the floor and then try some of those same balances on a piece of equipment (I). Let me show you some we already know by name. V-sit. Front support. Rear support. Tip-up. Long sit. Straddle stand. [Demonstrate.] Let's try each of these balances on the floor first (E). Go. Stop. Now, let's do these same balances using the small equipment (E). Do each of the balances while placing your body over, in, out, and along the small equipment. Go. Stop. Next comes the real challenge. Try each of these same balances on the large equipment (E). You may have to adapt some of the positions on different pieces of equipment. For example, front supports on the floor and bench are the same. But a front support on the beam or bars may be a vertical position. [Demonstrate.] Try a balance on the floor, then the same balance on the large equipment. Go. Stop. Repeat the process on a different piece of large equipment (E). [Signal go and stop.] [Refer to figure 6.5.]

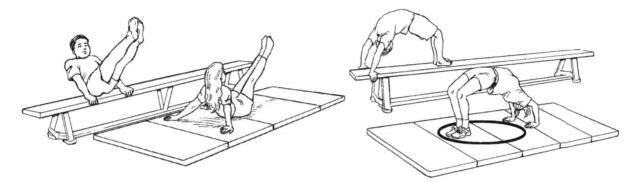

Figure 6.5 Perform a balance on the floor and then the same balance on the equipment.

"Now, let's try some new ways to balance (E). How about a forearm and foot? [Demonstrate.] What about two hands and a foot? [Demonstrate.] You can try balancing on other body parts as well. Think about the shape of your body as you balance. Stretched. Curled, twisted shapes. Wide and narrow shapes. High-, medium-, and low-level shapes. Belly-facing-up-and-down shapes. Let's see what you can do. Remember—try each balance on the floor by being over, on, in, out, or along a piece of small equipment. I want to see good, defined shapes (R). Good, strong bases. Hold each balance for three seconds. Then try the same balance on a piece of large equipment near you. This is how you are being a *copycat* today. You may have to adapt your balance on the large equipment. Where will you hold on? Make sure your base is stable. No shaking or being unsteady. [Signal go and stop.] Move to a new piece of small and large equipment. First try several new balances on the small equipment. Then try the same balances on the large equipment. [Signal go and stop.]

"You've had a chance now to practice several balances on the floor, using small and large equipment. As our last activity, I want you to choose your three favorite balances (E). It's your job to do the balance on the floor first using the small equipment, then use a traveling or rotation action to get to the large equipment placed next to the small equipment. [Demonstrate.] Balance floor, travel, balance equipment. Then, move to a new place and try your second balance on the floor by the small equipment, travel or rotate to the large equipment, and balance in the same way on the large equipment. Repeat the process for the third balance—new piece of small and large equipment. Go. Ashley, I like the way you balanced on your tummy while arching your back inside the hoop, used a pencil roll to move toward the box, and balanced on the box in the same position. Good work, Jeremy. Way to balance on two forearms and one knee (belly facing the floor) over the hurdle. Then, you did an egg roll to arrive at the bench and moved very smoothly into the same balance on the bench. Super job! [Allow for continued practice.] Stop. Remember that I'm looking for good gymnasts (R). I want to see good steplike travels, good rolls, good cartwheels. I want to see good transitions into and out of your balances at the small equipment and large equipment. No hesitation. No extra, unneeded movements. Go. Get back to practicing. [Signal stop.]

"Finally, I want you to choose one balance that you like the best or that you think is the most original, not like anyone else's (A). Practice that balance sequence at one place. For example, I could do a back bend on the floor over the rope, lower my body into a long stretched position on my back, do a sideways pencil roll to the bench, get up and lie down on the bench, and press up to a back bend on the bench [demonstrate]. Balance small equipment, travel, same balance large equipment. Do it several times until you make it your best work. Memorize your sequence so you can do it the same way over and over. Remember—you're no longer moving from place to place; you're staying at one piece of small and large equipment. [Signal go and stop.] Now, when I say go, I want you to get into groups of three. Your group of three should be made up of people who are at different pieces of equipment. For example, one group may include one person from a bench, one person from a beam, and one person from a chair. Go. Sit down in your group of three. Your very last task is to go around and show each other your sequence. When it's your turn to watch, find something nice to say about what you like in the performer's routine. Go. Show time! Stop. Excellent work today. You sure are a bunch of copycats! Please line up at the door."

Ideas for Assessment

- The children must commit to high-quality balances. You should see good, strong bases and nice lines and body shapes. Develop a checklist for high-quality balances. Check the children for a strong base, good lines, and whether they hold their balances steady (three seconds).
- Are the children performing a given balance on the floor, then using the small equipment, then the large apparatus?
- Smooth, logical transitions into and out of balances are important—especially on large equipment. Look for logical weight-transfer actions that are well thought out and under control. Check each child for smooth transitions between balances.
- Traveling actions must be gymnastics-like. Do not allow children to race around or have any speed contests. Expect high-quality rolls, cartwheels, skipping, and so forth. Check the children for the quality of their traveling actions—light, controlled, with good mechanics.
- Children should give thought to traveling in different directions and pathways and at different speeds and intensities to show variety. For example, if one travel is a skip forward, the next might be a cartwheel sideways. If one is a strong, powerful, controlled jump, the next might be a soft, light sliding action. Check the children's sequences for changes in direction, pathway, speed, and other factors.

How Can I Change This?

- Reverse the sequence. Balance on the large equipment first, then perform a weight-transfer action to the floor and finish with a copycat balance (i.e., the same balance) in relation to the small equipment.
- Perform the sequence with a focus on the concept of time. Move into or out of the balances quickly or slowly. Or make the traveling or rotation actions quick or slow. Convey sharp contrasts in the element of time. For example, balance on the floor in relation to the small equipment, transfer weight slowly toward the large equipment, then copycat balance on the large equipment. Or balance on the large equipment, move quickly off the equipment, then copycat balance on the floor in relation to the small equipment.

Ideas for Teaching Fitness

Balancing in and holding different positions on the floor and then on the equipment require strength and flexibility.

Ideas for Integrated Curriculum

- Bring in a book about an artist such as Monet, Cassatt, or Van Gogh and show how an artist might sketch or paint the same subject in several ways—changing colors, textures, size, or other elements. In much the same way, a gymnast can do the same balance on the floor and then on the equipment. The medium has changed.

- In mathematics children learn to do slides and translations, turns and rotations, and flips and reflections. In art children explore the same concepts through tessellations. Tessellations are the re-creations of patterns such as prints and mosaics. Repeated patterns may be accomplished through translation, rotation, or reflection. When children perform a balance on the floor and then repeat the balance on a piece of equipment, they are essentially doing a translation.

- Listen to a piece of music with a given thematic pattern—such as ABA, ABAC. Simple folk-dance music with two or three parts such as "Lott Is Todd," "Crested Hen," or "Blackberry Quadrille" or a piece of classical music such as "Circus Music" or "Romanye" from the RCA Adventures in Music series are good examples. Each time the composer changes themes (from A to B) or returns to a theme (back to A), notice that though one or more elements may have changed, the basic notes (melody) are still there. As in the preceding example, the artists may perform the same balance under different conditions.

- Have the children name the balances they can do. Let them invent names for new balances they create. They can write out or draw their own sequences.

- Watch routines of Olympic gymnasts. Show examples where a given balance or move is done in a floor exercise and then again in an apparatus routine.

- Compare a student's given balance on the floor and then on a piece of equipment to a slide or reflection in mathematics.

Ideas for Inclusion

Although balance positions may be modified for children with special needs, all children, regardless of ability, can create a given balance on the floor, in a chair, or in other ways and then modify it while using a piece of equipment.

DIMENSIONS

Objectives

As a result of participating in this learning experience, children will improve their ability to

- balance while using different dimensions of the body—small, big, wide, narrow (standard 1);

- develop and perform a gymnastics sequence using a variety of dimensional body shapes (standard 1);

- describe their gymnastics sequence using two or more variables of dimension simultaneously (standard 2); and
- communicate with other students in a manner that describes what they saw and liked about their sequences (standard 6).

Suggested Grade Range

Intermediate (3 to 4)

Organization

A large, open space is needed. Children should spread out with one or two at each mat. This lesson is also manageable on a gym floor or outdoor grassy area using carpet squares or a large parachute. Arrange mats in scatter formation with good spacing between them. If you want to teach this learning experience about dimensional shapes using equipment, provide one box or bench per mat.

Equipment Needed

This learning experience requires one mat for every two children. Otherwise, carpet squares or a large parachute can be used for the dimensional balances and development of the sequence work.

Description

"Hello, everyone. Today we will begin our warm-up by doing some stretching and strengthening exercises. They will all be related to making our bodies big and small, wide and narrow. Those are dimensions of our bodies in space. Let's start by sitting in a V-sit position. Keep your legs straight and straddle them out wide. Lean back on your hands as you spread your arms out wide as well. Hold your tummy tight while you hold this position for 15 seconds. This exercise is strengthening your abdominals. Next, roll over onto your belly and assume a push-up position. Your hands should be below your shoulders with arms straight and your legs close together. Keep your body stiff like a tabletop. This is an example of the body being in a narrow dimension. Hold this position for 15 seconds (or do 10 push-ups). This exercise strengthens your triceps muscles. Now, go into a child's pose (yoga) position. You are on your knees and shins all tucked up nice and small with your chin near your knees. Your arms are resting on the floor, extended back toward your feet. Feel the nice stretch in your lower back. Next, move to a standing straddle with your arms and legs spread out wide. This is a very big body dimension. From this position, touch your right hand to your left foot by bending over at the waist. Feel the stretch in your hamstring muscles (back of leg) and up through the side of your torso. Come back up into the straddle position. Then, touch your left hand to your right foot by bending over at the waist. Do this exercise 10 times. [Add several more exercises of your choice that emphasize big and small, wide and narrow body dimensions. During each exercise, point out what muscle groups are being strengthened or stretched]. Stop. Everyone come in and sit down in front of me.

"As you may guess from our warm-up exercises, the emphasis on today's lesson is performing balances using different dimensions with our bodies. (I) We will focus on making our bodies big, small, wide, and narrow. Who can tell me what the word *big* means? Yes, Ishan, big means to make your body take up as much space as possible. What about small? Good, Ila, small means to make your body take up as little space as possible. How about wide? You've got it, Karaivi. Wide means to spread out in a sideways direction. And who can tell me about narrow? Good, Max. Being narrow means to pull in to the center and be as skinny as possible. When I say go, we will get up and find a personal space on a mat. [If need be, you can share a mat with a partner and take turns if necessary.] First, we'll try some different big shapes. (E) So when you get to your space, make a big shape of your choice. Try to hold your shapes steady for at least three seconds. I want to see good balance positions, not wobbly ones (R). Go. Good, Johnny, I see you are in a big star position balancing on your hands and feet with your belly facing up toward the ceiling. Celia is balancing on her two hands and one foot with her belly facing the floor. Her other foot is placed up in the air with her leg straight. Way to go! Now try some more big balance shapes. Try them at different levels (E). Can you make a big shape at a low level? A medium level? A high level? Can you make a big shape that is symmetrical (E)? Asymmetrical? Now, we'll try some small balances (E). Try your first one. Good, Nashant, I like how you are balanced on your back all tucked up with your arms around your shins. That's it, Sachin, you are on your shins with your knees bent and your torso is bent backward. Now try some more small balance shapes. Try them at different levels (E). Make a small shape that is symmetrical. Now asymmetrical (E). Next, let's try some wide body shapes (E). Excellent, Naomi. I like how you are balanced on your foot and hand, all spread out in a star shape. Way to go, Esther! I like how you're balanced on two feet and one hand with your belly facing up and your free hand spread wide as well. Stop. I want to make sure that we keep correct principles of balancing in mind at all times. Shoulders over hands, hands or feet planted firmly, tight bodies, eyes focused on a spot (R). Hold your balances for at least three seconds. I do not want to see wobbly and unsure positions. Try several more wide balances at different levels (or symmetrical or asymmetrical) (E). Now let's do narrow shapes (E). Try your first one. I like how Molly is in a pencil shape balanced completely on her side. Good job, Ricky. You are surely narrow in that back support position. Try several more narrow balances: low, medium, high, symmetrical, asymmetrical (E). Stop. Everyone come in and sit down in front of me.

"What I want us to do next is begin to put our dimensional balances together into sequence work. We'll start simply with one balance and transition smoothly into a second balance. Let me give you an example. [Demonstrate.] I could start on a knee and a foot. My leg with the support foot is spread out wide. My torso is erect (straight up, vertical). My arms are spread out wide. So we can think of this balance as wide at a medium level. From here I could choose to perform a forward rolling action into a shoulder stand. As I perform the roll under control, I can stop the rolling action and balance on my shoulders with my elbows on the floor and my hands on my hips. Now my torso and legs are straight (vertical) with my toes pointed. My new balance position is narrow at a high level. Can anyone think of a way I could smoothly move out of my first balance to the same or different ending balance? Yes, Frank, I could have rolled sideways or backward. Or, I could have dropped using my hands to a front support position and moved into a push-up balance (long and narrow at a low level). When I say go, I want you to go back to your work spaces and create your own mini-sequence (E). Choose a first balance. It might be big, small, wide, or narrow. Then, figure out a smooth transition move into a second balance. Your transition move could be a step, rock, roll, or sliding action. Think. What is logical? How can I get from here to there without any extra, unnecessary movements? Your second balance can be of the same type as the first (big to big, wide to wide) or it can be different (small to big, wide to narrow). You choose. Who can tell me what we are going to do back in our work spaces? Inga? That's right, Inga. We are going to create one balance (dimensional), make a transition move, and perform a second balance. Everyone clear? Go. [While the children are working, move from one person to another and give them feedback on their work.] Stop. Stay where you are. Listen. Once you have one sequence down and have done it several times to get out all the kinks and unnecessary movement and feel like your balances are as good as you can make them, try a second, completely different sequence (E). Think small to big, big to small, wide to narrow, narrow to wide, wide to wide but change levels, narrow to narrow but change levels. Go. [Go around and help students, provide feedback, make sure children are staying on task.] Stop. Come in and gather in front of me. You are making good progress in putting together a simple sequence (shape, transition, shape). I see some excellent dimensional shapes (big, small, wide, and narrow). I see some smooth transitions from one shape to another.

"What I want you to do now is put together a more complex sequence (A). It will involve choosing four shapes and linking them with three transition moves. You get to choose the shapes in your sequence, but they must show contrast (see figure 6.6).

Start: low, long, narrow, stretched shape on side

Roll onto tummy, then onto back

Tuck knees to chest

Roll over into small, tucked shape to knees

Roll sideways into a shoulder stand: high, narrow

Rock out of shoulder stand to wide leg straddle: one arm support—big, extended shape—medium level

Finish: drop down to V-sit—wide arms, narrow legs, medium level

Figure 6.6   Make up a sequence of big, small, wide, and narrow shapes.

For example, you might choose small at a low level, big at a low level, wide at a medium level, and narrow at a high level. [Demonstrate.] What else might you choose? Yes, Sarah, wide, wide, narrow, narrow. Yes, Jason, big, big, small, small. Yes, Susan, big, small, wide, narrow. The tricky thing will be to choose smooth transition moves from one balance to another. You may choose from steplike actions, sliding, rocking, and rolling. You need to think logically. How can I get from this position to my next position smoothly without any extra steps, gestures, awkward moves, or unnecessary movement? See what you can do. Go back to your spaces and begin work. Go. [Go around to as many students as possible and watch their work. Make comments and suggestions. Provide feedback on what they are doing well and what they could improve on. After a period of practice, give the students a signal that they have one to three more minutes to polish and finalize their sequences.] Stop. What I want you to do now is select a partner who has not seen your work. Sit down next to them at a mat. Take turns showing them your sequence and observing theirs. Talk to each other and tell them what you liked about their work and maybe give them an idea that you have on how their sequence might have been improved. [During this time as the teacher you should move about the class and observe both the active gymnasts and those observing. Give them feedback on their performances, but feedback is probably more important to the observers who are learning to provide support and advice to their peers.] Good work today. You are learning how to be good gymnasts! Good-bye for now.

Ideas for Assessment

- Have the children draw a picture of each of their balances. They can use stick figures or draw two-dimensional figures. If a mannequin is available, have them manipulate the mannequin to show their balance positions showing three dimensions.

- Have an observing partner verbally describe each of the dimensional balances in the active partner's sequence. Or, have the observing partner write a description of one or two of the active partner's dimensional balances.

- Have the observing partner tell the active partner what they liked about the transitions from one-dimensional balance to another or describe how they think the transitions from one-dimensional balance to another could be improved.

How Can I Change This?

- Add complexity to the sequence: two wide and two narrow balances with smooth transitions, three small and three big balances with smooth transitions.

- Within a sequence, change two dimensional factors at one time. For example, use a smooth transition to move from a low-level, wide balance to a medium-level, narrow balance.

- Add a piece of equipment such as a box or bench. Wide and narrow balances can be completely or partially on the equipment.

- Perform a wide-to-narrow balance sequence with a partner. Balances may mirror or match the partner.

Ideas for Teaching Fitness

- As part of the warm-up or cool-down phase of the lesson, perform muscle strengthening balances. Hold positions for 10 to 15 seconds (front support, back support, V-sit). Talk about what muscles are stabilizing the body and what muscles are being strengthened. Emphasize good form while holding positions.

- Increase muscle endurance by repeating several balances three to five times each.
- Perform stretches to increase flexibility during warm-up or cool-down. Move the arms, legs, and torso from positions of contraction to extension. Hold poses for 10 to 15 seconds each.

Ideas for Integrated Curriculum

- In an effort to develop language arts skills, have the children verbally describe each of their balance shapes in their sequence using dimensional terms. Or, have the students describe their balance shapes in writing using dimensional terms.
- Compare body shape dimensions with mathematical size and shape dimensions. Combine two or more factors simultaneously. For example, a big, wide, high-level balance; a small, narrow, low-level balance; a large triangle with open space; a small rectangle with filled-in space.

Ideas for Inclusion

This learning experience is about creating different dimensions with the body. All children with special needs can profit from passive and active experiences in stretching the body wide and pulling in to make it narrow. They can also make big and small dimensions. Whether on the floor, in a chair, or on crutches, children can develop strength and flexibility by making balance shapes that show the dimensions of big, small, wide, and narrow. They can also make transition moves from one dimension to another by themselves or with assistance.

STATUES

Objectives

As a result of participating in this learning experience, children will improve their ability to

- demonstrate a variety of ways to balance while body weight is completely or partially on the equipment (standard 1),
- develop a simple sequence of moving into and out of a balance on the equipment (standard 1), and
- work cooperatively with a partner by assisting with balances and suggesting ways to improve the sequence (standard 5).

Suggested Grade Range

Intermediate (3 to 4)

Organization

A large, open space is needed. Children should spread out with two or three at each box, bench, horse, table, chair, or other large piece of equipment.

Equipment Needed

Though standard gymnastics equipment is nice to have, you can substitute or supplement it with boxes, benches, tables, chairs, and the like. Outdoor playground equipment is also useful.

Description

"We're going to work on balancing on equipment today, but before we do, let's warm up. Get into a long sitting position (I). Twist your torso to one side and put both hands on the floor. Rotate and press up into a push-up position (E). Angry cat [curve and press your back up] (E). Happy cat [curve and press your belly toward the floor] (E). Return to a long sitting position. Twist your torso to the opposite side and repeat (E). [Demonstrate.]

"Get up and run about (E). Let me see good, controlled runs (R). When you get to a mat, use a roll of your choice to get into a long sitting position (E). Repeat that sequence on the next mat. Return to your feet and run off. Repeat this sequence several times as you move from mat to mat.

"This time, run, hop, and jump about (E). When you get to a piece of equipment, jump onto, off, or along it in different ways (E). Move away to another piece of equipment and repeat. [Signal stop.]

"Everyone get a partner and move to one piece of equipment (I). Sit down. We're going to work on balancing today (I). We'll start on the floor [mat]. Choose several ways to balance. Think of using several body parts to balance on (E). Think about being wide, narrow; high, low; symmetrical, asymmetrical. Challenge yourself to be a good gymnast. Anyone can lie on the floor or kneel on all fours. But how would a gymnast make a balance (R)? [Good lines, definitive angles, extensions, and eye focus.] Help your partner with his balances by making suggestions on how he could be even better. Choose three of your favorite balances (E). Hold each one for three seconds before moving into the next. [Signal stop.]

"Now we're going to take our balances to the equipment (E). We can use our bodies to balance partially or completely on the equipment. [Demonstrate.] These are some examples. Two parts on, two parts off. One part on, two parts off. Complete weight on the equipment in a V-sit position. Complete weight on the equipment with two hands and one knee supporting your weight. [Refer to figure 6.7.] Now it's your turn. Take turns with your partner. When you're not doing a balance, be helpful to your partner by encouraging her or making suggestions. Go.

"I see that most of you are trying body parts you would normally think of to support your body weight on and off the equipment. Maybe try some different body parts (E). What about using your shoulders, upper arms, lower arms, thighs, shins, or tummy?

Figure 6.7   Using good form, balance partially or completely on the equipment.

See what you can do. Work hard. Make your balances gymnastics-like (R). Hold your balances for three seconds. Show good lines and extensions. Choose a point of focus with your eyes. Go. Great work, Sara. I like how you're balancing with your forearm on the equipment and your feet in a scissor position on the floor. Your side is toward the ceiling. Nice, Virginia. I like how you're balancing with your calf muscles [gastrocnemius] on the equipment and your elbows and forearms on the floor. Your belly is facing the ceiling. Mike, your bottom is sagging. Tighten up those tummy and gluteal muscles. That's much better. [Signal stop.]

"To finish this lesson, I want you to pick your favorite way to balance on the equipment. Your body may be partially or completely supported on the equipment. Your task is to find a way to smoothly move into or out of that balance (A). You have two choices (R). Start away from the equipment. Use a roll, slide, wheeling action, or other weight-transfer movement to arrive in just the right place (no extra steps or adjustments) to smoothly go into your balance. [Demonstrate.] Or start in your balance position on the equipment and use a roll, slide, wheeling action, or other weight-transfer action to move off the equipment. [Demonstrate.] Take turns with your partner. Be helpful by spotting or giving suggestions when needed. Go. [Signal stop.]

"When I say go, I want everyone to find a new partner. Your job is to take turns. First, one partner will perform the sequence while the other watches (A). Then you'll change roles. When it's your turn to watch, your job is to look for the weight-transfer action, the smooth transition, and the balance. Notice whether the balance is completely or partially on the equipment. Notice what body shape the person is in while balancing. Use the rating scale as you observe your partner's sequence. [See figure 4.6 on page 73. Use the sample rating scale as a guide and make up one of your own appropriate for this sequence using the equipment. The rating scale should emphasize the important parts of this sequence: weight-transfer action, smooth transition, the balance completely or partially on the equipment, and the body shape. Also, create the same type of three-point rating scale for the children to use.] When the sequence is finished, tell your partner what you saw, what you liked best, and one way you think she might be able to improve the sequence.

"Next, you'll have a short time to work on improving your sequence. Then, get a new partner and go through the performance and observation experience again. Take a turn to perform your improved sequence while your partner watches critically and gives you feedback about what you observed, what they liked, and how you might improve. Stop. Gather in close in front of me and sit down.

"You worked very hard today on some sequence work using balances on equipment. You also found some excellent ways to move smoothly into and out of those balances. I especially liked the way you worked with your new partners at the end of the lesson to use the checklist to review each other's sequences. Working cooperatively with a partner is a good way to check each other to make sure you've included all of the elements of the routine and to encourage each other to do your best work. That's it for now. Good-bye."

Ideas for Assessment

• Children have already done balance work on the floor. Their transfer to balancing on equipment should produce the same-quality work. Children should exhibit placing the center of gravity over the base. They should have strong bases (whole hand on the floor, elbows locked, shoulders over wrists, hips over knees, and so on). They should show good extensions—toes and fingers pointed (see figure 6.7). Develop a worksheet to determine whether each child understands the application of good principles of balance on the equipment. (See the assessment ideas for good balance positions on the floor from the *Push and Pull* learning experience in this chapter and adapt them to balance positions on the equipment.)

- Smooth transitions are critical. Children should experiment proximity to equipment, angles of approach and exit, choice of weight-transfer action, and other elements until they fit. Movement into or out of a balance should be natural, smooth, and flowing, with no extra steps or glitches. Make up a worksheet to assess whether each child exhibits each of these characteristics.

How Can I Change This?

- Add a second balance at the beginning or end of the preceding sequence: balance off the equipment, weight transfer to arrive, balance on the equipment. Or balance on the equipment, weight transfer off the equipment, balance off the equipment.
- Add both a beginning and an ending balance: balance off the equipment, move to arrive, balance on the equipment, move away from the equipment, balance off the equipment.
- Synchronize a balance sequence with a partner: mirrored balance off the equipment, simultaneous or copied move to arrive, mirrored balance on the equipment, simultaneous or copied move away from the equipment, mirrored balance away from the equipment.

Ideas for Teaching Fitness

As in balancing on the floor, balancing either partially or completely on a piece of equipment will develop muscular strength, endurance, and flexibility. For example, doing a back bend on a bench with either both hands and feet on the bench or hands on the floor and feet on the bench will help develop strong arm and leg muscles. Holding the position for longer periods (10 to 30 seconds) will develop muscular endurance. Arching the back with the belly toward the ceiling will develop torso flexibility.

Ideas for Integrated Curriculum

- Bring in pictures of gymnasts, dancers, architecture (e.g., bridges, buildings), and art sculptures (e.g., Alexander Calder) that emphasize taking weight and distribution of weight. Encourage children to create body designs similar to the pictures they see. Have children write about why some buildings, bridges, and balances are more stable than others.
- Compare balances on equipment to statues on a pedestal (e.g., Rodin's *Thinker*, Degas' *Little Dancer*). What move did the statue make to get into that position? How would he or she choose to exit that position?

Ideas for Inclusion

Most students can adapt balances such as a front or back support either partially or completely on the equipment. For example, while in the push-up position, children can balance on the floor with their knees rather than their feet to make the balance easier. Other children can use the wheelchair or crutches as their piece of equipment for balancing. The key is that all children can be successful in balancing on equipment by adapting the task to their level of ability.

BOTTOMS UP

Objectives

As a result of participating in this learning experience, children will improve their ability to

- demonstrate a variety of inverted balance positions (where the head is lower than the hips) with a stable base (standard 1);
- design and perform a short sequence that includes an inverted balance (standards 1 and 2);
- identify by name some traditional inverted balances, such as the tip-up, tripod, headstand, forearm stand, and back bend (standard 2); and
- create their own inverted balances (standard 2).

Suggested Grade Range

Intermediate (3 to 4)

Organization

A large, open space is needed. Children should spread out in a scattered formation, with one or two children to a mat or carpet square.

Equipment Needed

You will need one mat or carpet square for every one or two students.

Description

"We're going to work on balancing upside down today, but before we do, we need to warm up. Let's start with some sideways movement (I). Slide right or left. Make good slides, up on the balls of your feet (R). Quick feet. Stay off the mats. Move in straight pathways, not curved pathways (R). Now keep going sideways but cross your feet (E). This is called the *grapevine step:* The right foot goes in front of the left and then behind it. [Demonstrate.]

"Next, move sideways any way you choose with your feet (E). When you get to a mat, jump onto it, land, and roll (E). Then get up and move off, again in a sideways direction. Ready? Give it a try! Stop. This time, do the same sequence: sideways, jump, land, and roll, but end the roll in a long stretch position (E). From there, go into a shoulder stand and stretch your legs in different ways [demonstrate] (E). Resolve the shoulder stand by coming to your feet, and move off sideways (E). Then you're going to begin the sequence again. So it goes sideways, jump, land, roll, shoulder stand, stretch, resolve. Try this now. [Signal stop.]

"A shoulder stand is one way that you already know to balance upside down. Today you will learn about balancing upside down in other ways. One way to be upside down is to have your head lower than your hips. See if you can find a way to balance so your head is lower than your hips (I). Yes. I see Bill doing a back bend. I see two hands and a foot on the floor with the other foot high in the air. Good, Jessie! I see lots of creative ways to balance upside down.

"Now, for the next 10 minutes I want you to try four traditional inverted balances (E). They are called a *tip-up, tripod, headstand,* and *forearm stand.* First, I'll show them to you and give you good practice cues. Then you can practice each inverted balance at your mat [or carpet square]. A partner may help spot for you if you think you need some help. Try only those balances you feel comfortable with and ready for.

- Tip-up—squat with hands shoulder-width apart, elbows out, arms strong, knees on the elbows, and rock forward.
- Tripod—begin in same position as the tip-up. Place the forehead (hairline) on the floor. Make a triangle and keep knees on the elbows and the body tight; stay tucked.
- Headstand—same as the tripod. Your body is tight. Press the legs up and use a straight up-and-down alignment with your hips over the base and the feet and knees over your hips.
- Forearm stand—your forearms (elbows to your hands) are on the floor, shoulder-width apart. Keep your body tight and press up into a vertical alignment.

"OK. Everyone practice. [During this time, go around to each student and provide feedback and keep students focused on their tasks. Refine their work to the specifics of each task. For example, use the cues to improve the quality of the skill they are working on: Tip-up has strong arms, knees on elbows, lean forward; tripod has hairline of forehead on floor, triangle, stay tucked. Provide spotting where necessary.] Stop.

"Now, in addition to trying these balances, see if you can invent some new balances of your own (E). The only rules are that you must have a good base and that your hips must be higher than your head. [Signal stop.] You sure are working hard!

"Everyone has tried several ways to balance upside down. We call that an *inverted* position. As gymnasts, you need to learn to get into and out of inverted balances smoothly. Everyone, think of an inverted balance you like and how you can practice getting into that balance smoothly (R). Will you roll into it? Step into it? Think of the balance as unfolding little by little. Maybe count in order—one, two, three, four—to help you get it flowing. You need to get out of the balance just as smoothly as you got into it. Choose your balance and practice it now. [During practice] Always stay under control. You may want to step out lightly in just the same way that you got into the balance. Maybe you want to tuck and go into a roll. Try several inverted balances and work on getting into and out of each of them smoothly (E). [Signal stop.]

"For the last part of the lesson you'll be making up a sequence (A). You should do two balances of your choice. One or both of the balances can be an inverted position. Connect your two balances with whatever weight transfer you want. Balance, transfer, balance. Experiment and then choose the sequence you like best. Practice it several times so you can show it to a partner. Go! When you finish showing your work to a partner, gather in here.

"What was the main part of the lesson about today? Yes, inverted, also known as upside-down, balances. How did we define an inverted position? Right, the head lower than the hips. Using a steplike traveling action in an inverted position, move to line up at the door. OK, stand up. Walk back to your classroom."

Ideas for Assessment

- Just as in their upright balances, children should use correct alignment in their inverted balances (see figure 6.8). Check to see if their elbows and shoulders are over their wrists, their knees and hips are over their feet, their hips are over their head, and so forth.

Figure 6.8 Inverted balances.

- In the tripod and headstand positions, some children will align head and hands in a straight line. Point out the stability of a triangle. Check that the head is out in front of the hands, creating a triangle with the forehead as the apex.

- Children should keep tight bodies to maintain control (see figure 6.9). If they let go from an inverted position, they will flop or crash to the floor. Check to see that their muscles are firm and flexed.

- Children should be able to hold their balances for three seconds to show adequate control. Periodically count to three to check if children can hold a balance.

- As in all sequence work, smooth transitions from one balance to another are required for high-quality work. Check to see if each child's transitions are logical and smooth, with no extra moves or unnecessary actions.

Figure 6.9 Children must have full control of their bodies in inverted balances.

How Can I Change This?

- Combine an inverted balance with the warm-up sequence. Travel sideways to the mat, jump, land, assume an inverted balance, and resolve the balance by moving back to the feet. Repeat.
- Increase complexity by adding a balance. Try three balances, including at least two inverted positions. Use two methods of weight transfer to connect the three balances.
- Perform an inverted balance sequence with a partner. Partners mirror or match movements. Perform side by side, face to face.

Ideas for Teaching Fitness

When performing inverted balances, children often support a portion of the body weight with the arms and sometimes with the head. Holding the body in a firm, strong position under control requires the development of muscular strength in the arms and neck as well as other body parts.

Ideas for Integrated Curriculum

- Sometimes balances that can be done one way can be mirrored or rotated into other positions on the floor. For example, a child may stand upright and curve the body into a C. A child could then make the same C on the floor in an inverted position (two hands and two feet on the floor with the belly facing up or down). A child could also lie on the floor on the side in a C position. When assuming the same body shape in different poses, a child is learning about reflections and rotations as in mathematics. Ask the children what other body shapes can be performed using reflections and rotations.
- A triangle forms a strong, sturdy base. Have the children look at pictures of bridges and buildings to see how triangles are often used in engineering and architecture to form strong, artistic designs.

TWINS

Objectives

As a result of participating in this learning experience, children will improve their ability to

- develop a sequence that includes individual balances both on and off equipment, with a focus on partner relationships (standard 6); and
- work cooperatively and productively with a partner to develop a balance sequence using equipment (standard 5).

Suggested Grade Range

Intermediate (5)

Organization

A large, open space is needed. Spread out benches, boxes, or both to permit a safe working space for each set of partners. Place mats beside benches and boxes.

Equipment Needed

You will need one bench or box and a mat for every two students. Milk crates, folded mats, tables, and carpet squares can substitute for or supplement commercial gymnastics equipment. Each child will need an index card and a pencil. Music and a CD or cassette player are also needed for this lesson.

Description

"Today you're going to choose a partner and pretend you're twins. The objective is to look alike. When I say go, find a partner and spread out. Go. Thanks! You sure did that quickly! Now, I'm going to play some music [slow, flowing], and we'll start by stretching using partner mirror movement on the spot [right where you are] (I). Remember that mirroring your partner means that if you look in a mirror, you and your partner look the same. If one partner has the left hand in the air, the other partner will have the right hand in the air. [Demonstrate.] One person will lead; the other will follow. Perform movements that take you into long sitting positions, straddles, toe touches, standing with a lean right and left, twist. Begin. You choose how to continue to stretch. Try to get so good that I can't tell who is leading and who is following (R)! Try some balances you know (E). Front support, back support. Straddle stand. Back bend. Move your arms and legs to create symmetry and asymmetry (E). Stay with the music, moving slowly and smoothly (R). Link your mirroring movements. Trade roles with your partner and continue (E). Stop. Now, I want you to begin to move about the gym on the floor with your partner (E). [If you want to continue background music, make it faster.] You don't have to mirror each other, but I do want you to lead and follow (R). I want to see good steplike actions on the floor (R). Perhaps you could perform cartwheels on the floor or rolls on the mats (E). Use other weight-transfer and rotation actions as well (E). When you get to a box or a bench, jump or hop on, off, over, and along (E). Create a shape in the air as you spring off (E). Keep it going. Move to all of the spaces in the gym. Remember to vary your directions, pathways, levels, speed, and so forth. [Demonstrate.] Go. Stop. Trade roles with your partner (E). If you want, move side by side with your partner and do the same actions (E). [Signal go and stop.]

"OK. We're all warmed up. Now, as partners you're going to select one piece of equipment—a box or a bench. You're going to work as individuals and as twins to create a sequence (I). The idea is to look like and move the same as your partner (R). Your sequence must include the following elements:

- Use two or more identical (mirrored) balances on the floor.

- Use one or more identical (mirrored) balances on the bench or box.

- Use traveling or rotation actions, or a combination of the two, to create smooth transitions as you move toward and away from the equipment and link each of the balances. Timing is important. You must strive to be the same.

"Mickey, what are we going to do when I say go? That's right—we're going to create a sequence. Start in a partner balance on the floor, using a mirror image. Move to the piece of equipment—partners move together in the same way. Create a partner balance on the equipment that uses a mirror shape. Move off the piece of equipment—partners move together in the same way. Create a partner balance on the floor that uses a mirror image.

"Today is about being identical twins. Remember, it's important to work cooperatively and productively with your partner. Choose balances that you both can do (R). If one person chooses a balance the other can't do, the sequence won't work. Sharing ideas and cooperating with your partner are what I'm looking for. Begin your work by starting on the floor off the equipment. Choose a shape you can mirror with your partner. It must be gymnastics-like and still. Go. Stop. Try several more balances you can mirror with your partner. Go. [Allow ample practice.] Stop. Let's watch Terry and Lori. See their balance—they're like identical twins. Their balance is very still, and the balance is very gymnastics-like. They have good straight and curved lines. They have a good steady base and good support. From all the balances you've tried so far, choose one—the one you like best or the one that's the most challenging. Go back to work. Make your balance the best it can be. [Signal stop.]

"Next, from your chosen balance you must find a way that you can move identically or simultaneously to arrive at the equipment (E). Your movement may be steplike using feet only; steplike using hands and feet; or a weight-transfer action such as a roll, rock, or slide. The movement must also be logical so as to exclude unneeded actions (R). If you're at a low level, perhaps a roll or a sliding action would be most appropriate. If you're inverted (shoulder stand), perhaps a rocking action will help you arrive. If you're balancing at a high level on your feet, perhaps several jumps or hops while changing direction or pathway would be most appropriate. [Demonstrate.] Go. See what works best for you. Stop. Let's watch Missy and Shirley. They are starting in a balance on two hands and one foreleg. The second leg is stretched out behind them. Good mirroring. They've chosen a roll to help them arrive at the equipment. They've figured out just how far away from the equipment they need to be so that one roll enables them to arrive at the equipment simultaneously and precisely. They're identical and well timed. No extra steps. Go back and do your best work. [Signal go and stop.] I see some excellent work developing!

"Your next job is to choose a balance you can perform on the equipment (E). Experiment. Remember, I'm looking for good balances (R). Stillness—hold balances for three seconds. Twins—be a mirror of your partner's balance. [Signal go and stop.] Now pick your best or favorite balance (E). Start from the beginning. Balance off the equipment. Move to arrive. Balance on the equipment. Twins all the way! I'm looking for good balances, stillness, good timing, no extra steps. Try it several times. Work out the glitches. [Signal go and stop.]

"The next step is to move off and away from the equipment and finish in a final twins balance on the floor (E). From your balance on the equipment, how can you best, most logically move off the equipment (R)? For example, if you're balancing at a low level, perhaps you can slide or roll off. If you're balancing at a higher level on your feet, perhaps you can jump or hop off the equipment. [Demonstrate.] Work with your partner. Make your movement off the equipment different from your movement to arrive. Make your ending balance different from your beginning balance. Maybe change your shape, level, or base. Go to work. [Signal stop.]

"Finally, let's put the whole sequence together (A). Balance, move to arrive, balance on the equipment, move to depart, balance. I'll be looking for good balances and good transition moves. Most important, I want to see twins moving simultaneously, looking alike (R). Go to work. Polish your sequence. [Practice.] Stop. OK. Your classroom teacher has arrived. Let's give him [her] our best performance and show how good we are at becoming gymnasts. And let's show how well we can cooperate. Do your sequence three times so your teacher can see all of your work. Go. Stop. Thanks. I saw excellent shapes, lines, and stillness; different levels; upright and inverted positions; and different bases while you were balancing. I saw good transitions and linking actions. Most of all, I saw twins working hard at timing their actions to move simultaneously and look alike. Give yourselves a hand! [Lead applause.] Before you leave I'm going to give you an index card and a pencil. On a scale of 1 to 10, rate yourself on how hard and well you worked with your partner today. In one word [phrase, sentence], describe yourself as a gymnast. For example, I might rate myself an 8 and say, "I felt like my upside-down balance made me feel strong yet somewhat dizzy." Or "I liked working with Jerry today. He suggested several ways we could balance as twins." When you're finished writing, put your cards in the box at the door and line up. Thanks."

Ideas for Assessment

- Children need to cooperate well together. Both should have input and make decisions. Be aware of one partner who is dominating. Have the children rate themselves on their level of cooperation on a point scale from 1 (low) to 10 (high). Have them write out why they placed themselves at that level. Read the responses and see if you agree.

- Children need to work at their ability level. Be aware of mismatches. If one partner is of high ability and the other is of much lower ability, they might frustrate each other. Check to see if each of the partnerships is working, and intervene when necessary.

- Children need to select balances and traveling actions from their previous work. The key is to focus on what is gymnastics-like. What would a gymnast do? You are not looking for children to be running around out of control. Nor are you looking for cheerleader poses or ready positions for sports actions (figure 6.10). Develop a worksheet on which the students write out or diagram their sequences from start to finish. Use a still or video camera to record their performances. Have the students check the images later for quality. As a teacher, work with the students to make suggestions on how they might improve their performances. Allow the students to have follow-up time to get better.

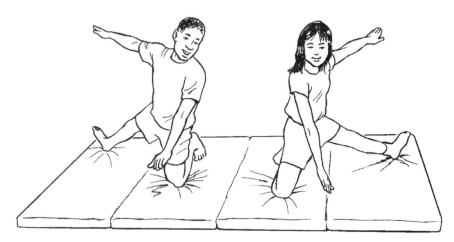

Figure 6.10   Make a twin shape with your partner.

- Timing is the key to this learning experience. Partners must synchronize their movements. A silent count, a wink of the eye, a nod of the head, or a click of the tongue may be a signal for a smooth transition from a held balance to movement. How well are the students synchronized? Rate them on the extent to which their mirrors and their transition moves are logical and smooth.

How Can I Change This?

- Use matching rather than mirroring movements to create the sequence.
- Focus on one or more of the BSER process variables during their sequence (refer to table 3.8 on page 57).
- Choose a piece of music and choreograph the sequence to it.

Ideas for Integrated Curriculum

- The process of creating a sequence in gymnastics is much like that of rehearsals in band, choreography in dance, and drawing up plays in games. It is also the same as writing in English. To create well-written sentences or paragraphs, you need to experiment with words and make some changes until you get it right. As a result, sequencing is much the same as developing story plots in language arts.
- Working together is part of any successful enterprise. Each person contributes to the success of the whole.

Ideas for Inclusion

Special-needs students can and should be a part of experiences that require partner cooperation and sequence building. In a given class, partnerships may vary from two or more special-needs students working together to a typical student working in cooperation with someone with a special need (see Elizabeth's Story in chapter 1, page 19). By working together, children can begin to appreciate the benefits of cooperation and sharing (standard 2) as well as accepting the skills and abilities of others (standard 4). Children can also learn to seek out, participate with, and show respect for people of similar and different skill levels (standard 6).

SEE WHAT I CAN DO

Objectives

As a result of participating in this learning experience, children will improve their ability to

- select and perform various balances on multiple pieces of equipment (standard 1),
- develop a sequence that involves balancing on two pieces of equipment with a smooth transition between the pieces (standard 1), and
- work cooperatively and productively with others in sharing equipment (standard 5).

Figure 6.11 Equipment should be paired together.

Suggested Grade Range

Intermediate (5)

Organization

A large, open space is needed. Place equipment together in pairs: a box and a bench, a bench and bars, a horse and a box, and so forth (figure 6.11). Equipment may be arranged parallel to each other, at right angles, and at a variety of other angles.

Equipment Needed

This learning experience requires a variety of large apparatus—boxes, benches, bars, horses, hanging ropes, beams, or tables.

Divide children into groups of two to four so that there is one station of equipment for each group of children. Place mats beside and under equipment.

Description

"Today we are going to do balances on pieces of equipment and link our actions between the equipment. During this lesson it will be important to cooperate while sharing equipment.

"Before we do that, start by spreading out in the room for a warm-up. From a long sitting position, stretch and touch your toes (I). Straddle your legs; lean right and touch your toes (E). Lean left and touch your toes. Twist around right and left to stretch your torso (E). Do a back bend (E). OK, stand up and do some other stretches (E).

"Begin running about—in and out, but don't touch the equipment (E). Good running steps, quick feet, high knees (R). Now, when you get to a piece of equipment, travel over or along it, using your hands and feet (E). Move to open spaces and free equipment. I don't want to see long lines and anyone waiting a long time. Practice several ways of using your hands and feet on the equipment—maybe bunny hops, walking, or cartwheels (E). [Signal stop.]

"This time, as you are on the equipment, stop and make a balance of your choice (E). The balance may be completely or just partially on the equipment. It may be upright or inverted. It may be symmetrical or asymmetrical. It may be a stretch, curl, or twist. As you come out of your balance, transfer your weight to the floor (E). You might use a jump or a roll. See what you can dream up. [Go and stop.] Now we have the beginning of a sequence (E). Run on the floor. Arrive at a piece of equipment. Travel on the equipment using hands and feet. Balance on the equipment. Move away. Start over. Try this again; make sure you visit all of the equipment as you travel about the gym. Use different balances at each of the pieces of equipment (E). Keep it going. [Signal stop.]

"Have you noticed that the equipment is arranged in pairs today? You might find a bench and a box, bars and a bench, or a beam and a box close to each other. Some are parallel to each other, others are perpendicular. You are to select one pair of apparatus and develop a sequence there (I). The only rules are that there should be no more than four children at any one pair and that you work cooperatively with the others at whatever place you choose. When it's not your turn, you should be watching and helping others by giving suggestions, thinking of choices for your sequence, or practicing your sequence on the floor. Your sequence has to have these elements:

- At least one balance on each piece of equipment
- A traveling or rotation action to create a smooth transition between pieces of equipment
- A variety of body shapes and levels: inverted and upright, symmetrical and asymmetrical positions

"Experiment with some possible choices for five minutes. Select your best or favorite balances (E). Make the linking actions between balances smooth (R). For example, you could choose rolling, stepping, or wheeling actions to help you travel and transfer weight between pieces of equipment. You should not need extra steps to arrive at a piece of equipment (R). Feel free to move the equipment closer together or farther away or add an extra action to fill in the voids (R). The key is to make the flow natural— nothing extra, no glitches or hiccups (R). Practice until you get good at it. Then show your sequence to someone on the opposite side of the gym (A). [Signal go and stop.]

"After you've taken turns being a performer and an observer, talk to each other. Tell each other what you liked about the sequence. Give at least one suggestion on how the sequence could be improved. Go back and practice. Do the sequence again for each other. [When finished, ask the following questions.] Did the sequence get better this time? How? [More polish, fewer glitches, better lines, better body stillness, eye focus.]

"Thanks for working so hard together today. I really like seeing you cooperate and help each other improve your work. It's exciting to see you become such good gymnasts and so responsible in your work habits. See you soon."

Ideas for Assessment

- Check students for controlled, high-quality balances. Balances on the equipment and the floor must be held for one to three seconds. Whichever balances the children choose should have good lines.
- Variety is important in the selection of balances—one high, one low; one symmetrical, one asymmetrical; one upright, one inverted. The children should make good choices. Does each child's sequence show differences in the selection of balances?
- Transitions, or linking actions, should be smooth and flow into and out of balance positions, with no extra steps or wasted movements. As children move toward, away from, or between pieces of equipment, are the movements smooth and logical? Check each child's sequence for smooth transitions.

How Can I Change This?

- Add complexity to the sequence by moving from the first piece of equipment to the second and back to the first, using three balances and two transition moves.
- Combine the balances on the two pieces of equipment with balances on the floor: balance on floor, transition, balance on equipment, transition, balance on floor, transition, balance on equipment, transition, balance on floor.
- Add a third piece of equipment. Balance on the three pieces of equipment with two transitions.
- Choreograph the sequence to a piece of music.

Ideas for Teaching Fitness

As children build more complicated and longer sequences using different pieces of apparatus, they will become stronger, have more muscular endurance, and maintain or increase their flexibility through practice.

Ideas for Integrated Curriculum

- During your gymnastics unit, show some routines of Olympic gymnasts performing floor exercises and on apparatus. Include gymnasts from various countries. (You can find lots of interesting routines on YouTube.) Also have the children research the topic of Olympic gymnastics through books or magazines or over the internet. In coordination with the classroom teacher, have them do investigative reports and write stories comparing and contrasting results of different countries, special interests about the athletes, similarities and differences among routines, and so on.
- Have the children write about themselves as gymnasts—their likes and dislikes. What do they find challenging? Do they see themselves improving? How does gymnastics help them become more fit?
- Have a discussion about what makes something interesting, whether in art, dance, or science. For both performers and spectators, the answers usually involve competence and variety. The better that people become at something, the more chal-

lenged and engrossed they feel and the more likely they are to continue. Variety creates new challenges. A spectator appreciates differences and contrasts. Gymnasts seek variety in their balances and sequences to please themselves and spectators.

Ideas for Inclusion

Children of all ability levels should be able to develop a sequence using apparatus. Help special-needs students know what they can do and what limits they have. Then, encourage the children to change the type or height of equipment, distance between pieces of equipment, type of balances, type of weight-transfer movements, and so on to develop a sequence that meets their level of challenge. In some instances accommodations should be made to assist children in performing a balance through active or passive support or to change the type of weight-transfer actions to incorporate the use of crutches, braces, or chairs.

LEAN ON ME

Objectives

As a result of participating in this learning experience, children will improve their ability to

- select and demonstrate three or more partner balances in good form, including good countertension and counterbalance (standard 1);
- link partner balances with traveling and rotation skills to develop a sequence (standards 1 and 2); and
- wisely select a partner (based on ability level, body size, and weight) with whom they can work productively (standard 5).

Suggested Grade Range

Intermediate (5)

Organization

A large, open space is needed. Children should spread out in scatter formation, with a set of partners at each mat or padded area.

Equipment Needed

Mats or carpet squares (or both) are needed for this activity. Provide one mat or carpet square for every two children and 5 to 10 photocopies of figure 6.12 on page 164.

Description

"Today you will work with a partner to create balance shapes. In fact, you'll do the whole lesson with a partner. Choose someone you know you can work with productively—not necessarily your best friend. You should consider size, weight, and strength. Stand next to your partner now. Good. Let's start by playing follow the leader (I). The leader may choose to hop, skip, jump, cartwheel, or whatever. When you get to a mat, you may choose to roll (E). Don't go too fast; you want your partner to stay with you (R). Consider changes of direction, pathway, speed, method of travel, method of rotation, and level (E). After a few minutes, trade roles with your partner (E).

Figure 6.12   Sample partner balances.

"Now go with your partner to a mat and sit down next to it. We'll work for a bit on strength and flexibility. First, stand facing your partner. One person extends the arms straight out in front. Press your palms up, while your partner creates resistance by pushing down (E). Now press your arms out while your partner provides resistance by pushing in (E). Next press your arms in, while your partner provides resistance by pushing out (E). Take turns with your partner.

"Stand with your back to your partner, arms raised to the side and back. Have your partner gently and safely pull your hands closer together, arms parallel to the floor (E). Finally, stand back to back with your partner and hook elbows. One of you rocks forward and lifts the other onto your back (E). Feel your tummy and legs stretch?

"I'm going to show you a few pictures of partners balancing. In any partner balance the partners must use good principles of countertension and counterbalance to be successful. If one partner leans one way, the other partner must lean in the opposite direction to create a balance. Look at these pictures carefully and decide, together with your partner, on three balances that you would like to try (I). Go to your mat and try them. Feel free to come back and look at the pictures. You can also invent some partner balances of your own (E). Be safe, but see what you can do. Work until you can do three different balances. Be sure to choose balances that both you and your partner can do. [Refer to the balances in figure 6.12.]

"A partnership requires both people to work together. If one particular partner balance doesn't work, change it so you can do it or try a different one (R). Notice that some balances take the partial weight of your partner. Others take your partner's complete weight. Select ones that you can do best. [Signal go and stop.]

"Now that you can do three different balances, let's think about how to get into and out of those balances smoothly (E). How do you get from here to there? For example, as the base, one partner could roll into a back-lying position from a forward, backward, or sideways direction. The second partner then could use a roll, cartwheel, or stepping action to arrive at the head, feet, or side of the support person. Once there, without hesitation move smoothly into the partner balance. Go back and try each of your balances. Work hard at smooth transitions into and then out of your balances (R). Move to arrive, hold, move out. [Signal stop.]

"Finally, we'll build a sequence (E). Choose two of your three balances. Start your sequence with an individual balance away from your partner. Use some form of weight transfer to arrive. Go into your partner balance. Move away to a second individual balance. Move together to your second partner balance. Finish and hold. Your individual balances may mirror, match, and contrast shapes or levels. [Self-balance, move, partner balance, move, self-balance, move, partner balance.] Go to work. Do your best! If you need some help, come and ask. [Signal stop.]

"OK, several minutes have passed. I can see that you're working very hard. Wherever you are in developing your sequence, show it to a second pair and allow them to comment. Then watch their sequence and comment on it. Be constructive and helpful in your comments. What do you like? What suggestions for additions or improvements do you have (R)? Go back and practice your sequence. Work hard for several more minutes to polish your routine. I want to see stillness in the balances, good timing, and smooth transitions in your traveling or weight-transfer actions.

"Stop. Everyone come in. You will now receive a gymnastics routine score sheet. [See *Gymnastics Routine: Partner Balances With Mat* on page 244 in the appendix.] I'm going to ask you to judge one new set of partners, whose routine you haven't seen, using the rating scale I give you (A). Watch the routine twice. Rate it on quality for each of the elements on the scale. You'll be looking for five elements worth 2 points each, or a total of 10 points. When you see errors, deduct a half point. At the bottom of the score sheet be sure to write something you liked about the sequence. When you're finished, put your rating sheets in the box on my desk over in the corner of the gym. Thanks for your hard work."

Ideas for Assessment

• Children need to use good alignment and strong bases of support to take each other's weight (figure 6.12). Good body mechanics are a must: knees over the feet, hips over the knees, and shoulders over the hands. The top person should place the weight in positions of strength, not in the middle of a sagging back. Check each set of partners for good alignment and strong bases of support.

- Children may need suggestions on creating smooth transitions into and out of a balance. In general, the base person needs to arrive just ahead of the top person, to settle and be ready to assume the partner's weight. The top person must initiate an action to move away. Rolls, twists, turns, and stepping actions often create the best transitions. Check each set of partner routines for smooth transitions—no extra steps, glitches, or hiccups. Are the transitions logical and intentional—out of one balance and into the next without extra or unnecessary movements?

- Some partners will go right to work. Other children will be more hesitant or begin by talking. Your job is to keep everyone task oriented and productive. Give suggestions; pull back and observe. Make sure everyone makes enough practice attempts. Are the students working productively? Are they staying on task?

How Can I Change This?

- Simplify the sequence. Use one partner balance with a self-balance before and after it.

- Add more complexity by using three partner balances, with appropriate transitions into and out of each balance.

- Focus on partner relationships. For example, all traveling actions and rotations could have a face-to-face or side-by-side orientation. One partner could move above and the other below.

- Focus on timing. Perform one of the weight-transfer or rotation actions quickly and a second slowly, in a sustained fashion, to create contrast.

Ideas for Teaching Fitness

When partners work together in counterbalance and countertension positions, each partner must be strong. Supporting or lifting the weight of another person helps children develop muscular strength. In addition, many of the partner balance positions help children to develop or maintain flexibility.

Ideas for Integrated Curriculum

- Emphasize principles of good balance used in science, such as the base of support and center of gravity. These principles are the keys to the success of partner balances. In general, when using the arms for support, the arms should be straight—elbows locked with shoulders over wrists. When in a kneeling position, legs should be bent at right angles to the torso, with the hips over the knees. Body weight for the supported person should be placed over the points of strength of the base person.

- Bring in pictures that emphasize balance. Old cantilever structures, flying buttress structures, buildings by Frank Lloyd Wright and other architects, and the work of Alexander Calder and other artists are examples. Use these pictures to show how people in various occupations use principles of balance as a basis for their work.

Ideas for Inclusion

As emphasized in the *Twins* learning experience in this chapter (page 156), working with a partner often provides opportunities for students of varying abilities to work together. This learning experience served as the main focus for the partner balance sequence with Elizabeth described in chapter 1. Children of all abilities can succeed in this learning experience. At times, balance positions may need to be modified to accommodate individual children's abilities to perform counterbalance and countertension balances. As a rule, let the children and your knowledge of them dictate what they are willing to try. At times provide extra support or spotting as needed.

ADDITIONAL IDEAS FOR LEARNING EXPERIENCES

PRINCIPLES OF BALANCE

Triangle

Use a sheet of paper or an index card. While it is straight and unbent, try to stand it up on edge. You can't do it. Now bend the sheet or card in half, creating an apex. Now balance the paper or card on edge with the apex facing a direction—up, down, left, right. In the same way, show the children that they cannot do a tripod or head-stand when the head and arms are in a straight line. They must place the head out in front and the hands back 6 to 12 inches (about 15-30 cm), creating an isosceles triangle.

To Move or Not to Move

- Use a round piece of fruit, such as an apple or an orange, or a ball. Show the children that as long as the object is round, it will roll easily. Now, cut the piece of fruit in half or take some air out of the ball. When the fruit or ball has a flat surface, it has a wide base of support with a lower center of gravity. Use this as an example to help children understand that when they create balance positions, their supporting surface must be flat on the floor and they must create a wide, stable base with a low center of gravity.
- Use a bowling pin, bat or racket, batting tee, tricycle, bicycle, unicycle, wagon, and other children's toys as an experiment in balance. Which toys are the most stable? Why? Have the children try different types of balance and predict which toys will be the most stable in the various positions. Why?

Simple Machines

Use a rod or dowel that is 3 to 4 feet long (1-1.2 m). At one end place a 1-pound weight (about 0.5 kg). At the other end place a 2-pound weight (about 1 kg). Where would you have to locate the fulcrum to get the dowel to balance horizontally? Why? As children perform various counterbalance or countertension balances, how far do they have to lean in or out to account for differences in weight or leverage with a partner?

TYPES OF BALANCE

Shape Up

- Focus on body shape as an emphasis on learning experience. Have the children create shapes that are straight, bent, curled, and twisted. Have them make the shapes on the floor and on equipment. Make the shapes from supported and suspended positions. Start in one shape and then change into another shape.
- Join two balances together—one stretch and one curl. Work out a favorite move that allows you to create a smooth transition from one to the other.
- As children work in pairs, one partner makes a stretched shape and the other copies it; then one makes a curled shape and the other copies it. The partners trade roles and repeat.

Even, Uneven

- Create symmetrical shapes on the floor (even). Create asymmetrical shapes on the floor (uneven). Move from one symmetrical shape to another. Move from one asymmetrical shape to another.

- Find different ways to balance on, under, and along a piece of apparatus in symmetrical ways. Find various ways to balance on, under, and along a piece of equipment in asymmetrical ways. Balance in a symmetrical way, use a symmetrical weight transfer, and balance in a different symmetrical way. Do the same with asymmetry.

Bridges

- Create a bridge shape with your front facing the floor. Create a bridge shape with your back facing the floor. Create a bridge shape with your side facing the floor. Do several variations of each. While in a bridge shape, keep your hands and feet still and walk around in a circle. Find ways to move quickly and slowly from one bridge shape into another. Travel from a high bridge shape into a low bridge shape by turning or rolling.

- Make a bridge shape on or against a piece of apparatus. Make a high bridge shape on the apparatus. Come down onto the floor and turn or roll into a low bridge shape.

- As children work in pairs, one partner creates a bridge shape. The second partner tries different ways to travel under or over the bridge—jumping, leaping, rolling, crawling, and so forth.

Contact

Have the children create balances using a variety of bases of support. Balance with one, two, three, and four body parts touching the floor. Have them use different body parts to support their weight. Can they balance on their bellies, forearms, elbows, knees, thighs, side?

How Low Can You Go?

Children can also perform balances at different levels. Have them create balances at high, medium, and low levels. Ask them to create balances at various levels on the floor and then on equipment. Have them create balances with a particular body part at a high, medium, or low level—feet at the highest level, seat at a medium level, tummy at the highest level, and the like. Instruct them to create a balance at one level and then smoothly move into a balance at a different level.

Up, Down

Create a learning experience that encourages children to experiment with a variety of upright and inverted balance positions. Define each work. Upright means head above the hips. Inverted means head below the hips. Rather than the more traditional upright balances such as a front support, V-sit, or scale or the more traditional inverted balances such as a tip-up or headstand, have the children experiment with alternative positions. Try upright and inverted balance positions with a variety of bases of support, different levels, different body shapes, as well as other elements. Toward the end of the learning experience, they should select their favorite or most original upright and inverted balances and put them into a sequence: upright balance, transition, inverted balance; or inverted balance, transition, upright balance.

Changing Times

Develop a lesson with a focus on moving from one balance into another quickly, then in a sustained fashion. Change from one balance to another quickly, then in a sustained fashion on the floor, then on equipment.

Forces of Nature

Change from one balance to another softly or lightly. Then change balances in a very powerful way using a lot of force. Combine changing balances using various amounts of force with time variations. Move from one balance to another quickly and lightly. Then change balance positions slowly in a sustained manner with a lot of force.

Go With the Flow

Move from one balance position to another in a free-flowing manner. Then move from one balance to another in a bound, tense manner.

Relatively Speaking

- Have the children develop balance positions with a focus on the relationship of one body part to another—seat above head, knees above head, elbows below belly, forearms below knees, and so on.
- Develop balance positions with relation to a piece of equipment—face the equipment, back to the equipment, side to the equipment. Create a balance position over the equipment and under the equipment. Create a balance position from a support position on the equipment and from a hanging or suspended position on the equipment. Balance partially on the equipment and completely on the equipment. Perform one balance on the equipment and one balance off the equipment. Use a smooth transition.
- Develop balance positions with relation to a partner. Balance in a position on, over, or under a partner. Create balances that have partners facing, back to back, and side by side. Create balances that mirror or match those of a partner. Develop balance positions with a partner on equipment.

Larger Than, Smaller Than

Children learn the concept of *size gradations* in mathematics. In gymnastics children can make a shape and then make another shape that is larger than, smaller than, or equal to the size of the first shape. They can also make a shape and then make a second shape that is higher than or lower than the first shape.

Roll the Dice

Make up several die (singular form of the word *dice*) by taping together six pieces of heavy paper (e.g., manila folders) into a cube. On one of the die, write the numbers 1 to 6 to indicate the number of bases of support. On another, write levels (high, medium, and low) two times each. On another, write the type of shape (straight, curled, twisted) two times each. You can develop additional die to indicate extensions and patches and points. Roll each of the die to determine the type of balance the children should create. For example, one roll could yield balancing on three body parts at a medium level in a twisted shape. By rolling the die two different times, you could develop a sequence. The first roll dictates the first shape; then students use a smooth transition to get into the second shape.

Tessellations

In art, the concept of *tessellations* can be used in creating patterns like mosaics. A *translated pattern* is one that is repeated by sliding it up or down, right or left, or diagonally. In the same way, children can create a shape, then perform a traveling or weight-transfer action in a chosen direction and perform that shape a second time. A *reflected shape* is like one in a mirror. Children can create one shape and then perform a mirror image of it. A *rotation* is a shape that is turned 90 or 180 degrees. Children can make a shape that is right-side up and then do the same shape upside down (e.g., stand up with arms extended, then do a handstand; or V-sit with arms and legs extended into the air, then support the body with the arms and feet with the seat in the air). Or they can create a shape and then perform it again by lying down and doing the shape on the side.

Mirror, Mirror on the Wall

- Working with a partner, children create balance positions that are mirrors of each other. Mirroring can be done face to face or side by side. Then, the children use the same balance positions with one person changing shape to create matching balance positions. Perform a sequence that starts in a mirroring balance. Use a smooth weight transfer into a matching balance.
- Partners create mirroring and matching balances on equipment. Create a sequence in which partners start in a matching balance, use a transition move, and finish in a mirroring balance.

Teeter-Totter

Have partners experiment with countertension and counterbalance positions with their weight completely or partially supported on a piece of equipment. Choose a favorite partner balance in a countertension or counterbalance position. Then create a sequence where partners start with an individual balance on the floor. After holding the balance, partners use a traveling or weight-transfer movement to arrive at or on the equipment. The sequence finishes with the partner balance. Do the same type of sequence, starting with the partner balance on the equipment. After holding the balance to show control, the partners use a transition movement into individual balances on the floor.

CHAPTER 7

Learning Experiences for Rotation

This chapter offers 11 learning experiences in the skill theme of rotation. We have developed learning experiences for the three categories of rotation: characteristics of rotation; principles of rotation; and movement around the vertical, horizontal, and transverse axes.

The following chart provides a quick outline of the focus and suggested grade range for each learning experience. At the end of the chapter you will find additional suggestions to stimulate the development of further gymnastics experiences for children.

Mini-Index

Focus	Name	Suggested grade range
Characteristics of rotation: rocking, rolling	Balls, Eggs, and Pencils	Pre-K-2
Characteristics of rotation: rocking, rolling in backward direction	You've Got It All Backward	1-2
Principles of rotation: radius of rotation	Sit-Spins	2-3
Movement around axes: rolling in a forward direction	Roll, Roll, Roll Your Body	3-4
Movement around axes: turns	Taking a Spin	3-4
Movement around axes: cartwheels	The String Challenge	3-4
Movement around axes: using equipment	A Roll by Any Other Name . . .	3-4
Movement around axes: using rotation for transitional moves in sequences	Let's Make a Connection	4-5
Movement around axes: around equipment	Hip Circles	4-5
Movement around axes: rotation sequences with a partner	Partner Task Cards	4-5
Movement around axes: developing more advanced rotation skills by transferring weight from feet to hands to feet	Feet, Hands, Feet	4-5

BALLS, EGGS, AND PENCILS

Objectives

As a result of participating in this learning experience, children will improve their ability to

- demonstrate control in simple rocking and rolling actions (standard 1);
- select, from a variety of choices, ways to move into and out of a roll (standards 1 and 2); and
- put a simple sequence together involving a travel, a roll, and a balance (standard 1).

Suggested Grade Range

Primary (Pre-K to 2)

Organization

A large, open space is needed. Children should be in scatter formation with one or two to each mat or carpet square.

Equipment Needed

This learning experience requires one mat or carpet square for every student, or at least one for every two students.

Description

"Good morning! Today we will learn how to make our bodies roll as a way of turning around. But first, let's warm up. Our lesson is about turning, so let's start by jogging, being careful to avoid the mats and carpet squares (I). As you jog, turn your body in a spinning fashion around a vertical axis, like a beater on a mixer, but not too fast (R). Stay under control. Be careful not to bump into others. Go easy, round and round. Can you hop on one foot and turn around (E)? What about using two feet to jump and turn around (E)?

"We don't want to do that too long or we'll get dizzy. Everyone find a mat or carpet square and sit down beside it. We'll start our rolls as part of our warm-up and stretching. Everyone get in the long sitting, or gymnast sit, position (I). Reach one hand way across your body. Keep your legs, seat, and tummy tight as you roll over and return to a long sitting position (R). You just rolled, or transferred weight, from your seat to your side, to the front, to the other side, and back to your seat. We'll call that a seated roll. Easy!

"Try it again, rolling back in the other direction (E). Good! This time, roll halfway over into a push-up position (E). We call this a front support position. Arch your back up like an angry cat (E). Now let your back sag and stick out your tummy like a happy cat (E). Nice! Roll the rest of the way and come back to your long sit (E).

"From a sitting position, tuck up into a ball; bring your knees and chin to your chest. Rock back and forth, from your back to your shoulders, and then to your feet (I). Rocking is like rolling—you transfer your weight from one body part to the next. It's kind of like a rocking chair. Try rocking back and forth. Think about how you're transferring your weight. Stay tucked in tight, like a ball, to help you (R). Now lie down and open up into a long stretch, just like a pencil. Keep your legs, seat, and tummy tight and see if you can rock to one side and then the other (E). Rock from side to side. Keep it up. Yes! That's good. That's pretty easy, right? OK, stop.

"We are ready to roll now. A roll helps you turn over from one body part to the next. Adults call that weight transfer from one body part to the next. The secret to good rolling is to make yourself round in the direction you are moving. When I say go, try rolling like a pencil (I). I want to see tight bodies. Choose one direction and roll from your back to your side, to your front, and to your side. Go. [During practice] Can you roll over and over three times (A)? What about going the other direction to your other side (E)? Stay in your personal space! Stop.

"This will be fun—you'll get to feel like a pretzel. Watch what I do [or have a student demonstrate], and then you'll get to do it. First get into a kneeling position on your hands and knees (E). Pick up one hand and lead it through your body tunnel and out the hole between your other arm and leg. Lower your shoulder and begin rolling: shoulder, back, hips, feet, kneel. You want to keep your head off the floor. Try it now. [During practice] Stay tucked, like for a fall. Make it smooth—I don't want to hear your body hitting the floor (R). Now use the other hand to lead the other way, with the other arm through the tunnel (E). Try both ways by yourself a few more times. [Signal stop.] OK. Let's tuck up into an egg shape and roll sideways (E). Good, Karen and Joey, from your shins, side, back, side, shins. Roll the other way [direction] too (E). Try these in your own space a few times. [Stop.]

"This next one is a little harder (E). I'll have Jeremy and Shonda show you first. Squat down, hands on the floor just in front of you. Tuck your body—knees and chin close to your chest. OK, now raise your seat, look under your legs, and let yourself roll! Try to keep your head off the floor. Are you ready to try it? Remember, tuck, behind up, roll! Try it in your space now. [During practice] Stay tucked. Your weight goes from feet to hands, to shoulders, to back, to hips, to your feet (R). Nice tuck, Johnny. Nice job keeping your head off the floor, Cindy. Try a few more rolls. Stop.

"We now know several ways to roll. Who remembers one way? Yes, Sheryl, seated. Good, we also have [pencil, shoulder, sideways like an egg, and forward like a ball]. What I want you to do now is think about how to get into and out of these rolls (E). For example, can you go into a roll from standing? Sure. Let's get ready to try this. Lower your body into a squat, and then roll. Try this a few times. Nice tuck, Arisa! Stop. This time, choose a balance on three or four body parts and see if you can roll out of that balance (E). I'm going to come around and watch. Try different balances and go into different rolls—not just forward (E). Stop.

"You can end your roll in different ways (E). Let's see if you can figure some of these ways out. [If you see students do these, pinpoint them to other students. If not, suggest that students try each way.] Straddle seat. Two knees with your body straight. V-sit. Straddle on two feet. Kneel on one leg with the other out in a straddle position. Now, practice several different ways of finishing each different type of roll—your choice (E). Stop.

"Let's finish by putting a short sequence together (A). You'll travel on the floor using good running, hopping, jumping, or skipping. When you come to a mat, lower your body, roll, get back up, and move a different way to the next mat. Try a different roll at each mat you come to. So it's travel, roll, and travel again. Go! Stop.

"Everyone come here quickly. Sit down. Who can tell me how to make your body roll really well? Yes, you must be round and stay tight, or tucked. When you rock or roll, where does your weight go? Right, from one body part to the next and to the next. What directions can we rock or roll? Good, Rinji—forward, backward, and sideways. What were the names we gave to the rolls today? Yes, Tonja, seated, pencil, shoulder, egg, and forward rolls. Good remembering! What shapes were our bodies in when we did all of these rolls? Yes, Felipe, long stretched [egg, ball, curled]. You sure learned a lot today. See you next time."

Ideas for Assessment

- In pencil- or log-rolling actions, children tend to initiate the action with the upper torso so the legs trail. They should contract abdominal, gluteal, and leg muscles so that the body rotates as one unit (see figure 7.1). Check to see if each child is keeping the body tight and rolling with the body as a single unit.

Figure 7.1   When doing a sideways pencil or log roll, roll as a tight, single unit.

- In forward-rolling actions and the shoulder roll, children tend to open up, or become "unglued." This is a reflex action. They can grasp the shins to stay tucked: chin and knees to the chest (figure 7.2). Check to see whether the children are staying tucked.

Figure 7.2   When rolling forward, stay tucked in a ball.

- To finish a roll in a different position or body shape (e.g., straddle position or wide shape), control must be established. It helps to perform the roll more slowly and to keep the muscles tight rather than flop and let go (see figure 7.3). Are the children performing their rolls under control in a manner that allows them to create a smooth transition into a shape or their next action?

Figure 7.3   A roll can be finished in various positions, including a straddle position or V-sit.

- Momentum is a key to any rocking or rolling action. The initial push or falling action should generate enough momentum for the body to make a complete roll without extra, unwanted movement. For example, in a forward roll the body should be round and tucked, and weight should return to two feet. No extra hand movements on the floor should be necessary for regaining balance at the end.

How Can I Change This?

- Have children work on individual sequences at their own mats. Travel to the mat, lower the body to the mat, roll, and resolve into a balance.
- Combine turning and spinning traveling actions with rolls on the mat. Approach with a spin, turn, or whirl. Then jump, land, crouch, and roll.
- Change the sequence. Roll out of one balance into a new balance. Balance, roll, balance.

Ideas for Teaching Fitness

- Performing rolling actions requires children to have strong muscles so they can move under control.
- Performing a variety of rolling actions and resolving them into balance positions require children to maintain or increase flexibility.

Ideas for Integrated Curriculum

- Bring several objects to class, such as a pencil, an egg, a ball, an orange, a cube, a rectangular solid, and a cone. Talk about the properties of things that roll smoothly: They are round, transfer weight from one place to the next easily, and move around an axis. Why do some things not roll smoothly? Because they are flat and have edges or corners.

- Rolling in different directions and in different body shapes helps children develop body and spatial awareness as well as develop their movement and language vocabulary.

Ideas for Inclusion

- Rolls can be modified to allow all children to succeed. Some can do seated rolls while others are doing shoulder or forward rolls. Some nonambulatory children will be able to roll on the floor. Others can do spinning or turning actions in a chair.
- Children can modify their rolls by using specially designed equipment such as donuts, inclined planes, and large balls.
- Children who have slowly developing neurological systems may exhibit lingering reflexive actions. These children may profit from active or passive manipulation or spotting. The key is to overcome their tendencies to use the tonic labyrinthine and symmetrical tonic neck reflexes. Sometimes shifting weight from side to side or forward and back may be the best they can do. They need to overcome their reflexive actions to move on and be able to perform voluntary movement—in this instance, rocking and rolling.

YOU'VE GOT IT ALL BACKWARD

Objectives

As a result of participating in this learning experience, children will improve their ability to

- demonstrate control in rocking and rolling actions in a backward direction (standard 1);
- select, from a variety of choices, ways to move into and out of rolling in a backward direction (standards 1 and 6); and
- put a simple sequence together involving a travel, a roll in a backward direction, and a balance (standard 1).

Suggested Grade Range

Primary (1 to 2)

Organization

A large, open space is needed. Children should be in scatter formation with one or two to each mat or carpet square.

Equipment Needed

You will need one mat or carpet square for every one or two students as well as blue and red poker chips and a box to put them in.

Description

"Today is backward day. Everything we do is going to be backward. We'll start by running backward (I). Good running! Stay on the balls of your feet (R). Use quick feet (R). Be careful to watch where you're going (R). Move to open spaces (R). Who can jump backward (E)? Try short, quick jumps (E). Now try longer jumps (E). What about hopping backward (E)? When one foot gets tired, use the other (E). Can you skip or gallop backward (E)? Try that! Stop.

"Move to a mat or carpet square. Watch me show you what to do next. You'll squat down into a ball shape, with your knees and chin to your chest. Stay up on the balls of your feet. Also stay tucked, but put your arms up and point your thumbs to your ears. From there, you'll rock back to your heels, then to your seat, your back, your shoulders, your hands on the floor. Stay tucked up as you do it [demonstrate] (I). Ready to do it on your own? Try it a few times. Each time, start all over from a squat. [Signal go and stop.] This time, when you go back, I want you to stay tucked up (R). See how Audrey is doing it? From there, push with your hands and rock back in the other direction: shoulders, backs, hips, feet (E). OK? Do this several times on your own. [During practice] Stay tightly tucked. Stop.

"You're doing great. Now we're going to try to roll all the way over backward (E). We're going to try it several ways, from easy to hard. You choose the way that you think is best for you. [Have a student demonstrate the choices you present. Perhaps introduce three; invite students to try additional choices you may present later.]

- [Entry level] (E) We all have this big thing on top of our shoulders called a head. It gets in the way of rolling backward. We're going to get in our backward-rocking squat. Tilt your head to one side and put your ear on your shoulder. You have now made a big open space to roll over on the other side: tilt left, roll right. Ready? Crouch, feet, hips, back, shoulders, over to the feet.

- [Backward roll on an inclined plane] (E) [To create an inclined plane, use a folded mat as a base to raise one end of two benches placed side by side. Place a mat on top of the benches (see figure 7.4).]

- [Backward roll on a level surface] (E) Squat, tuck, rock back, push with hands, back to feet.

- [Backward roll from a stand] (E) Stand, squat, rock, push, feet.

- [Backward roll into a straddle stand] (E) Stand, squat, roll, straddle your legs.

- [Backward roll from a pike position] (E) Stand, pike, hands, rock back, push, extend, pike, stand.

- [Backward roll from a stand into an extension] (E) Stand, squat, rock, push, extend (handstand position), snap down to feet.

Figure 7.4 Sample variations of the backward roll.

[All children in the class should practice at least one type of backward roll that is appropriate for them.]

"Now that everyone can roll backward at least one way, we will work at selecting ways to move into and out of your rolls (E). It's like asking the question 'What's next?' or 'Where do I go from here?' One choice is to use traveling actions on your feet. For example, you could run, jump, land, squat, roll, return to your feet, and move on. Another choice is to create a balance, roll backward, which is a weight transfer, out of that balance into a new balance or onto a knee and a foot, onto two knees, or onto two feet, and then move into another traveling action. For example, you could go from a shoulder stand, roll over backward to a knee and a foot, push up into a cartwheel, and travel off on your feet.

"So let's summarize what kind of sequence you can create using a backward roll. You can

- travel, roll backward, travel (E);

- travel, roll backward, balance (E); or

- balance, roll backward, balance (E).

"While you work at your own mat or carpet square, I want you to try one or two of these ideas. Practice each one three or four times. Then choose the one sequence you like best and work at it a few more times to get the bugs out (E). Go! [During practice] I want to see stillness in the balances, good lines, and good shapes (R). I want to see smooth backward-rolling actions (R). And remember, work on smooth transitions into and out of balances and rolling actions (R). OK, stop. Now that most of you have your sequence memorized and in good shape, find a partner to show it to (A). Partners, tell the performer what you liked about the sequence. Maybe make one suggestion on how to change or improve it the next time. Then show them yours.

"Stop. Come in. Who can tell me what we worked hard on in today's lesson? Right, rolling backward. What were some ways we tried rolling backward? Good, you remembered. Inclined plane, from a stand, into a straddle stand. I'm going to show you a backward roll. As you leave, if you think I do it well—with good form and in all the right ways—put a blue poker chip in the box at the door. If you think my form could be improved, put a red poker chip in the box." [See page 76 in chapter 4 for the poker chip survey.] [Perform the roll.]

Ideas for Assessment

- Rolling backward is difficult for young children until they learn to inhibit their postural reflex to open up. It is critical to help them learn to stay tucked, with knees to the chest and feet close to the seat. Check for each of these factors in both rocking and rolling.

- Proper positioning of the arms and hands is critical: arms bent, elbows up, hands flat on the floor, thumbs in close to the ears (figure 7.4). Check to see whether the children place their hands in the proper position near the head. Each factor is critical to the success of getting enough lift to clear the head in a successful backward roll.

- Sufficient arm strength is critical to rolling in a backward direction. Before this lesson, make sure you have the children take weight on the hands in a variety of ways to build arm strength. Check to see whether each student can momentarily take weight on the hands.

How Can I Change This?

- Add a bench or box. Use the backward-rolling action to move toward or away from the equipment in the creation of a sequence.
- Work with a partner. Create a short partner sequence using a backward roll: travel side by side, jump, land, roll, symmetrical and matched balance.

Ideas for Teaching Fitness

- Rocking and rolling backward generally require strong abdominal muscles to stay tucked. Also, the arm muscles, especially the triceps, must be strong. As you warm up and throughout the lesson, build strength experiences with the children.
- Rocking and rolling backward require good neck, torso, and hip flexibility. During the warm-up, make sure the children stretch the whole body but especially the neck, torso, and hips.

Ideas for Integrated Curriculum

- Doing anything backward is unnatural. We do not have eyes in the backs of our heads; we cannot see where we are going. Rolling backward, sitting down in a chair, walking backward along a line, and walking backward on a balance beam will develop tactile-kinesthetic perception. Tactile-kinesthetic perception is one of Howard Gardner's multiple intelligences.
- Children can write their sequences on a journal page by using symbols or sentences for their actions to develop language and writing skills.

Ideas for Inclusion

Children who have slowly developing neurological systems may exhibit lingering reflexive actions. These children may profit from active or passive manipulation or spotting. The key is to overcome their tendencies to use the tonic labyrinthine and symmetrical tonic neck reflexes. Sometimes shifting their weight from side to side or forward and back may be the best they can do. They need to overcome their reflexive actions to move on and be able to perform voluntary movement—in this instance, rocking and rolling backward.

SIT-SPINS

Objectives

As a result of participating in this learning experience, children will improve their ability to

- spin around several times, under control, from a sitting position (standard 1);
- combine actions of spinning with balances, traveling, and weight transfer into simple sequences on the floor and on boxes or benches (standard 1); and
- describe how lengthening and shortening the radius of rotation affect the rate of spin (standard 2).

Suggested Grade Range

Primary (2 to 3)

Organization

A large, open space is needed. Arrange boxes, benches, and mats or carpet squares in scatter formation to permit free movement. One mat should be beside each piece of equipment.

Equipment Needed

You will need one mat or carpet square for each child, or at least one for every two children, as well as one box or bench for every two children.

Description

"We are going to have fun today learning how to make our bodies spin and rotate like a top! Let's begin first with light, soft running (I). Run at someone, and as you get close, avoid them (R). Approach big, fade, and move away. Relax—don't be stiff (R). This time do a double high five with people you meet (E). You'll run, approach, jump, land, and then move away. [After several tries] Stop.

"Now, let's take that same idea of run, approach, jump, and land to open spaces (E). This time you'll be working by yourself. Each time you run, you will hurdle or spring jump into the air and rotate a quarter or half turn to face a new wall when you land. Use your head, feet, and arms to help you spin, like this. [Demonstrate.] Notice how I moved my head and arms in the direction I was spinning (R)? As you land, spread your arms and legs to help you balance (R). Bend and land under control (R). Ready? Go. [During practice] As you get better, you can go faster in your approach. As you take off, hurdle into the flight (one foot to two feet) like a diver or a vaulter (R). If you're really good, you might try rotating three-quarters or a full turn (E). Control is important. Stick your landings before moving on. Run, hurdle, jump, turn, land [squash], move on. [Signal stop.]

"Let's sit on the floor in a long sitting position. Get on the floor, rather than on a mat, right now because we need a slippery surface to do the next skill. Watch what I do first; then you'll try it. Tighten your tummy and your legs and get into a V-sit position. Swivel both legs to one side and place both hands on the floor on the other side. Push hard with the arms and swivel your legs back to the other side. Do this several times so you build momentum [push, swivel, push, swivel, push, swivel] (I). Try this on your own. [Signal go and stop.] As you do it this time, push hard, then tuck your knees to your chest and grab your arms around your shins (R). Try this and see what happens. Yes, you spin round and round fast! If you shorten your body, you spin faster. Next time, at the end of your spin, lengthen your body back to the V-sit (R). Lengthening your body helps slow the spin. Try this several times. [During practice] Get control by spinning on your seat. We don't want any wipeouts by spinning off onto backs or shoulders. Move your body parts symmetrically to help keep control (R). OK, stop.

"Let's see if we can put these sit-spins into a sequence on the floor (E). You'll run, hurdle, jump, and land, just as before. Then lower, V-sit, sit-spin, then resolve your sit-spin with a roll into a balance of your choice. Can you remember all that? Practice it several times so your sequence gets good. Go. [During practice] Work for quality. [After repeated practice, signal stop.]

"Next, let's try doing sit-spins on the equipment (E). First, find a space on a box or bench. [Allow time.] When you do your spins on the equipment, I want to see perfect control on your sit-spins. Go. [During practice] Good. I see nice, tight bodies. You look like gymnasts with good control. Try to spin faster once you feel comfortable on the equipment. Tuck your body during the spin to go faster (R). Try spinning in both directions (E). Stop. This time, use your hands and arms to control and finish your spin and end with your whole body lengthwise on the bench [or box], with your back or shoulders supported on the bench (E). [Signal go and stop.]

"Next, do a sit-spin and freeze in a shape of your choice (E). Think, *Where can I go from here?* as you continue on the equipment or exit the bench or box onto the floor. Use different types of weight transfer such as rolls or a stepping action. Explore. Stop. I want to show you some of the ways your classmates have solved this challenge. [Point out several students.] Some of your classmates linked their sit-spins with shoulder balances or a roll or a rocking action on the equipment. Some children ended their sit-spins in different positions, such as a V-sit, straight legs, or one leg straight and one leg bent on the bench. When the sit-spin ends with straight legs, you should take it into a full-body roll onto the mat or a stepping action onto the feet. Try some of these ways and others that you can think of. Go. [During practice] You've got the idea. Work hard! I want to see controlled movements—no flops! [Signal stop.]

"You've done a great job with sit-spins both on the floor and on equipment. I want you to have a chance to create a movement sequence to demonstrate your talents (E). Your sequence should begin with a sit-spin on the equipment, move out of the sit-spin and off the equipment in any way you choose, then include a roll and a balance. Work for good quality. You are going to perform the sequences for your classroom teacher when he [she] comes in to meet you. I want you to show him [her] your best work. [Signal go and stop.]

[To the classroom teacher] "Welcome to the end of our class. Today we have worked very hard at developing a new skill called a sit-spin. Everyone has developed a sequence. First, half the class will perform their sequences (A). Then the other half will do the same. We want you to notice all of the sit-spin actions and watch the variety of ways the children move out of the sit-spins into a roll and balance. [Performances.] Thank you for being our audience. The class is really working hard in gymnastics."

Ideas for Assessment

Children must show control in their rotation movements. The use of the arms, legs, head, and other body parts is important in initiating and stopping rotation (see figure 7.5). Emphasize good control, including an aesthetic, focused, controlled sense of spin. Are the children using their arms and legs in appropriate ways with good timing to spin fast, then slow to perform this task under control? Spinning feels good and is fun for youngsters. What you don't want is crash and burn by rotating onto the back and shoulders out of control, with students sprawled out across the floor.

Figure 7.5   Do a controlled push and tuck to initiate a spin.

- Children must control their sit-spins on the bench to avoid losing their balance and falling off the equipment (see figure 7.6). Observe whether the children can begin and end their spins in a controlled manner. Are they falling off? Be sure that mats are placed under the equipment. Children can help serve as spotters to provide safety.

- Transitions (linking actions) are important in the sequence work. As children come to a stop from the sit-spin, their

Figure 7.6   Sit-spins can be performed on equipment.

bodies should move quite naturally into a rocking, rolling (weight-transfer), or balancing action. Are the children exhibiting good, controlled linking actions? No holes, gaps, long breaks, or breakdowns should be evident.

How Can I Change This?

- Simplify the sequence if necessary: start in a V-sit, sit-spin, transfer weight to a balance of the student's choice on the floor.
- Have students move into a sit-spin on the equipment and incorporate that into the sequence: mount, balance, sit-spin, balance, dismount.

Ideas for Teaching Fitness

Sitting in a V-sit or performing sit-spins requires the development of abdominal strength. As a lead-up to this learning experience, work with children to develop their abdominal muscles. Exercises such as bent-knee sit-ups and crunches are helpful. If children tire quickly and their abdominal muscles begin to quiver, move on to another activity and return to more sit-spin work at another time.

Ideas for Integrated Curriculum

- Make sure children understand the principle of lengthening and shortening the radius of rotation. A shortened radius (body tuck) will cause a faster spin; a longer radius will make the spin slower and more controlled. Illustrate the use of this principle in other gymnastics skills (handsprings, somersaults) and in such sports as diving, figure skating, dancing, and roller skating.
- Relate the rotary action to that of a spinning top or a bicycle wheel. What else do you know that is affected by shortening or lengthening the radius of rotation (e.g., swings on a playground, pendulum on a grandfather clock)?
- Spinning around an axis helps children to develop the vestibular mechanism. This in turn helps them with spatial awareness. To spin around effectively, children need to learn to focus on a spot to help keep them from getting dizzy.
- Have the children write about how they can open up and close in to make their bodies spin slower or faster.
- Have the children write about how they feel when they are spinning around. Ask them to identify other experiences that stimulate the vestibular mechanism, such as amusement park rides, spinning on a swing, spinning on a scooter board, diving, and ice skating.

ROLL, ROLL, ROLL YOUR BODY

Objectives

As a result of participating in this learning experience, children will improve their ability to

- demonstrate a variety of exits from a forward roll (standard 1);
- perform a forward roll from a stand, a forward roll in a pike position, and a forward roll in a straddle position (standard 1); and
- develop a creative movement sequence that involves a combination of five rolls, with at least one of those rolls performed fast and a different roll performed slowly (standards 1 and 2).

Suggested Grade Range

Intermediate (3 to 4)

Organization

A large, open space is needed, with mats scattered around the room.

Equipment Needed

This learning experience requires one mat or carpet square and one piece of chalk (optional) for each student. You will also need an index card and a pencil for each student.

Description

"We will continue working with the concept of rotation today. To begin, find your own space on the floor. OK. Do some cartwheels in a circle [demonstrate] (I). You can either draw a big circle with chalk on the floor or imagine a big circle in your mind. [Signal go and stop.] Can you do cartwheels in a circle like a clock and then in the other direction [counterclockwise (E)? Make the cartwheels continuous (R). Try not to take any time between your cartwheels as you complete the circle. Try it again. Now, jog around the gym, and when you come to a mat, do a forward roll. Then get up and perform a cartwheel (E). You can do more than one forward roll on the mat if the mat is long enough. Go! [During practice] Land on two feet after your roll (R). Stay tucked throughout the roll (R). That's it! Freeze!

"Let's review some of the rolls we already know. From earlier lessons we know how to do seated rolls, forward rolls, pencil rolls, backward rolls, and shoulder rolls. Today we'll experiment with how these rolls can be resolved or finished (I). For example, when you start a regular forward roll, you can finish it in a long sitting position, on two knees, on a knee and a foot, on one foot, or coming to a stand on two feet (E). [Demonstrate one or a few of these options; see Shoulder Stand on page 137 in chapter 6.] You may have to twist or turn your body some as you rotate to finish in these positions (R). Try several rolls and finish them in different ways (E). Go! [During practice] Pencil roll to V-sit (E). Backward shoulder roll to a knee and a foot (E). That's it; keep trying new ways. Good work! Stop.

"Everyone come and sit in front of this mat on the floor. I'm going to show you how to do a roll from a standing position [demonstrate] (E). Stand tall. Take a walking step and begin to bend or lean forward. Lead with the opposite arm. As you lower your body, take weight on your forearm, then your upper arm, shoulder, and back. The idea is to use this as a safety roll if you think you are going to stumble and fall. Arm, shoulder, back, roll. Stay tucked throughout the roll and come up on your feet (R).

"Sometimes you see volleyball players or martial arts performers roll like this. Any questions? Why don't you go to your space and try it? Try it many times. [During practice] Stay tucked in the roll. That's it. Try not to use your hands. Come up to a knee and a foot or return to a standing position on two feet. Stop.

"Sit down where you are and watch me. Next, we're going to learn how to do a roll in a pike position [demonstrate] (E). Start standing. Pike, hands, roll, puuuush, pike, stand. Place your hands on the mat and take your weight onto your upper back. Keep your head tucked. Your head and neck should never touch the mat. Go. [During practice] Instead of tucking your body as you have done in all the other rolls, keep your legs straight and your hips bent in a pike position. You can land in a long sitting position or try to come up to two feet (E). Coming up to two feet is a challenging task. Try it. [It may be best to teach only the skillful students this roll.] Stop.

"Finally, our last roll is a straddle roll [demonstrate] (E). Start in an erect standing position. Place your hands on the mat out in front of your body. Push with your legs. Tuck your head. Take your body weight on your upper back. Keep your legs straight and next sweep them wide to a straddle position. Puuuush your body up so you end up standing in a straddle position. Think stretch, hands, roll, straddle, puuuush! Try it. You have to roll quickly and really push your body up with your hands (R). If that's too difficult for you, end sitting on the mat in a straddle position (E). [Signal go and stop.]

"Your sequence for today involves a combination of five rolls of your choice (E). Who can tell me one of the rolls we have learned in this unit? Yes, Latasha, the shoulder roll [safety roll, backward roll]. OK, Mark, forward straddle roll [pencil roll, backward shoulder roll]. We have learned many ways to roll. In your sequence the rolls must link smoothly together (R). Be sure I can tell when the sequence begins and when it ends. Be creative. One of the five rolls must be done fast and one must be done very slowly (E). Work hard on them. Show me how well you have learned to roll. Go!

"Stop. I want everyone to see the variety of roll sequences you have developed. Count off into three groups: 1, 2, 3 . . . . OK. I want all the 1s to show us their sequence while the 2s and 3s watch (A). Now it's the 2s' turn. Now it's the 3s' turn. To finish I'm going to give you this index card and a pencil. On the card write down the names of three different rolls that you can do. Also write down three quick ideas that you think are important to help you roll well or smoothly. When you're finished, put your card in the box and line up. Thanks."

Ideas for Assessment

- Students may have difficulty with one or more of the rolls. Prepare a checklist with the class roster in a vertical column on the left and each of the types of rolls listed in a row at the top. Check to see which rolls each child can perform. Be prepared to simplify the tasks that children are having problems with. For example, allow the legs to bend in the straddle roll. Remember, we want each child to be successful and to feel challenged at his or her own level.

- Check to make sure that each child is rolling safely. Be sure students take their body weight on the upper part of the back and never on the head or neck.

- For doing a safety roll, the secret is achieving rounded body surfaces, transferring weight from one body part to the next, and giving with or lowering the body as it gradually moves from an upright to a rolling position on the floor (see figure 7.7). Watch for children using each of these characteristics in their rolls: rounded surface, transfer of weight to adjacent body parts, giving or absorbing body weight, transition to a finishing position.

Figure 7.7 Forward safety roll.

Figure 7.8   Forward straddle roll.

- Be sure students push hard and extend upward with their arms on the pike and straddle rolls (see figure 7.8). To be successful, they must push with the hands.

How Can I Change This?

- With more advanced children, you could teach these skills in an earlier lesson on rolling.
- After each new roll the students learn, have them link it to different actions, such as a balance, before you teach the next roll.
- Add a piece of equipment. Use the rolls to approach or move away from the equipment. Allow less-advanced children or children with less ability to finish their roll in a straddle or pike long sitting position or a straddle or pike V-sit position. You could also allow them to bend their legs and press up into a standing position to finish the roll.

Ideas for Teaching Fitness

Rolling from a variety of positions and resolving rolls in a variety of ways develop strong muscles and flexibility.

Ideas for Integrated Curriculum

Discuss the importance of rolling in various sports. In volleyball, baseball, football, and basketball, for example, athletes use rolls for safety and to return to their feet quickly during play. Have the students write in their journals about experiences they have had or could have where they could use a roll to be safe and not get hurt.

Ideas for Inclusion

- Some children with delayed neurological development can benefit from working on rolling over—prone to supine or supine to prone—in a coordinated fashion.
- Children with lingering reflexive actions can lie on a big ball and, with some assistance, roll toward the front, back, or side and work on inhibiting their parachuting reflex.
- Children can spin around on a scooter board from lying and sitting positions to stimulate their vestibular mechanisms. They can also spin around in a swing or cargo net device.
- Children who can perform a basic roll such as a seated roll or pencil roll can work at beginning and ending their rolls in different body poses or shapes.

TAKING A SPIN

Objectives

As a result of participating in this learning experience, children will improve their ability to

- execute quarter, half, and full turns around the vertical axis during the flight phase of a jump (standard 1);
- land under control after rotating during the flight phase of a jump (standard 1); and
- understand the roles of the head, arms, and legs in initiating rotation around an axis and in controlling the landing (standard 2).

Suggested Grade Range

Intermediate (3 to 4)

Organization

A large, open space is needed for this activity, with mats, benches, and boxes spread out a safe distance apart from each other. Place mats beside benches and boxes.

Equipment Needed

This learning experience requires one mat and a bench or box for each student, in addition to one hula hoop or carpet square for each student.

Description

"Today we will be jumping with turns in the air, like ice skaters or dancers (I)! Let's start with good jumps. Everyone use your feet in different ways to jump on the floor now. That's it: from two feet to two feet, from one foot to two feet, from two feet to one foot. Jump several quick jumps in a row, like hopscotch. Jump as high as you can (E). Let your jumps take you somewhere in the room (E). Travel forward, backward, sideways (E). Go straight, zigzag, in a curved line (E). [Signal stop.] Good.

"Now, each of you get a hoop [or carpet square] and take it to a personal space in scatter formation. Spread out and use the space wisely. Stand inside your hoop and face one wall. You'll try to jump and turn a quarter of the way around so you end up facing the next wall (E). Watch me. [Demonstrate.] As you do it, think about what you can do with your body to help you turn. Try it several times. [Signal start and stop.] OK. Who can tell me what body parts help to turn you (R)? Yes, Billy, your arms move, or rotate, in the direction of the turn. Yes, Shelley, your head, too. Did you notice that your legs push in the opposite direction [action, reaction] to help you rotate? Let's see you use your arms, head, and legs [demonstrate] to get better turns now. Still quarter turns; think turn and land. Start and finish inside the hoop or on the carpet square.

[After several tries] "Your turns are getting much better, but even with such good turns I still see some of you crashing to the floor on your landings. What can we do to land better (R)? Yes, spread the feet apart, bend at the knees, keep the back straight, head up, and arms spread. Good. Now think spread, bend, and head up. Let's work at better landings now. Go. Yes, that's it, great!

[Move on to half and full turns with children who can handle the greater difficulty (E). Emphasize an increased use of the arms, legs, and head to initiate turns and control landings, as well as increased height to allow time to turn.]

"Now we will use turns to jump off the equipment (E). Place your hoop on the mat about one foot away from a bench or box. What you'll do is step up onto the bench [or box], jump down with a quarter turn, and land in the hoop [demonstrate]. Think jump, turn, land, hold. Ready? Go ahead and try it. [After time for several tries, signal stop.] Remember to land the same way you did when you were turning on the floor. Spread, bend, and head up (R)! Count for three seconds to show control after you land (R). Try this now, thinking of landings. Stop. Now travel to all the different benches and boxes and jump, turn, land, and hold at each one (E). [For those children who are doing well, allow half and full turns.] Stop.

"Go back to the piece of equipment where you started. Let's put the turns in the air into a sequence (E). Watch as I demonstrate. You'll start away from your bench or box, use your choice of steplike actions to approach the bench, jump up onto it with a one-foot takeoff, and do a two-foot landing. Then jump off, turn, and land. Go into a roll or wheeling action of your choice and finish in a balance. The sequence is travel, jump, jump, turn, land, choice, balance. Work hard so you can show me your best. Go!

"Stop. I've seen some great sequences. You really have learned to make turns in the air during flight. Who can tell me what body parts help to get your turn going? Yes, the arms, head, and legs. How do you stop your turn when you land? Good—spread and bend. Very good; see you next time."

Ideas for Assessment

- Children tend to jump out and land far from their starting points. The purpose of jumping with a vertical turn is to jump up to allow time for rotation and still get a controlled landing. Check each student for a controlled landing—feet spread, arms out, back straight, head up, knees bent.

- Develop a checklist to help watch for the following cues. Head turn: The head turns in the direction of a rotation. Wrap: A gymnast turning right wraps the left arm around the body. Push: Use the feet to push at takeoff, which will initiate the turning action from the floor (see figure 7.9). Throw: Throw arms in the direction of the turn.

Figure 7.9   Jump and turn, landing softly.

How Can I Change This?

- Up to this point turns have been from a jump-forward orientation. You can also jump sideways or backward to initiate the turn. Start on the floor and, once control is established, do jumps off the equipment.

- Try jumping with turns onto equipment. Start with quarter turns. As children gain confidence, allow them to do half turns.

Ideas for Teaching Fitness

- Strong, powerful legs are needed for exploding upward or outward into the air. To help develop their leg strength, children can jump over dowels raised at various heights. At heights such as 6 inches (15 cm), children can perform consecutive jumps back and forth. At increased height, such as 12 to 18 inches (about 30-45 cm), children can perform singular jumps over the bar. To further develop leg strength, children can jump up onto raised surfaces such as folded mats, benches, or boxes.

- Jumping rope with quarter, half, and full turns is also good practice for developing leg strength.

Ideas for Integrated Curriculum

- Compare turns to the points of a compass: 90 degrees equals a quarter turn, 180 degrees equals a half turn, 360 degrees equals a full turn.

- Refer to points of orientation as north, south, east, and west.

- Relate jumping and turning to simple scientific principles. Newton's third law of motion—action and reaction—comes into play as the feet push down and away and the jump goes up and around. Wrap the arms to decrease the radius of rotation and turn fast. Spread the arms to slow down and stop, keeping the turn under control.

Ideas for Inclusion

- Depending on children's methods of locomotion, they can practice quarter, half, and full turns. In a wheelchair they can use their arms to help them turn. On crutches they can use two crutches and one leg. Nonambulatory children can lie on their bellies or backs and turn the stated rotations.

- Children in wheelchairs can also learn to jump their chairs by using an upward thrust of their shoulders and torso if they have the strength and ability to do so.

THE STRING CHALLENGE

Objectives

As a result of participating in this learning experience, children will improve their ability to

- transfer weight from the feet to the hands and onto the floor, bench, or box and then back to the feet as they rotate around the transverse axis (standard 1);

- develop strength in the arms and shoulder girdle (standard 4); and

- develop flexibility in different joints by using stretching exercises (standard 4).

Suggested Grade Range

Intermediate (3 to 4)

Organization

A large, open space is needed, with boxes or benches (or both) scattered around it. Place mats beside each box or bench.

Equipment Needed

This learning experience requires one piece of chalk, one piece of string (6-8 feet long, or 1.8-2.4 m), tape, one box or bench, and one mat for each student. You will also need one photocopy of figure 7.10.

Description

"Today, let's begin by using steplike actions from one mat to the next. When you come to a mat, take your weight on your hands and feet as you travel across it (I). Do bunny hops along a bench or side to side, or even vault over the bench by putting your hands down and kicking both your legs to one side (flank vault) (E). Remember to keep your arms straight and your body tight (R). [Signal start and stop.]

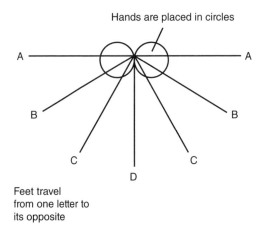

Figure 7.10 Diagram of a cartwheel performed over the string.

"While we're still warming up, think of different ways to stretch your body (E). Stretching is important to developing and maintaining flexibility in the joints. Try different stretches now to make sure you stretch the muscles in your arms, shoulders, back, tummy, and legs (E). Good. I see some back bends; Johnny is straddling his legs while sitting and bending forward; I see others, too. Think of four different stretches. Go over them several times and do each one well. [After some time] Team up with a partner now and teach your partner the four stretches—without talking (E). Then perform your partner's sequence of four stretches. Together choose the four best stretches from the eight stretches and put them into a sequence that you can do together.

"Now we're ready for the main part of our lesson, which is to take weight on the hands (I). As we take weight on our hands, we develop strength in the arms and shoulders. Gymnasts, and all other people, too, need strong upper-body muscles. Earlier you learned to take weight on both your hands at the same time. Today we're going to take weight on the hands one at a time. When I say go, everyone get a partner. You and your partner should get one piece of chalk and find a mat to sit down next to. You'll then draw this picture on your mat. [Show students figure 7.10.] Go!

"I see you're all ready, so we'll start by taking turns with your partner. You start on the letter B and stretch, topple, or fall forward, then lunge (R). If you're on the left B, place your left hand in the circle; then place your right hand on the other circle and come down on the right B, with one leg following the other. You land softly first on the leg you did not step with (R). Watch as Jeremy demonstrates. You want to think *stretch, topple, lunge, hand, hand, foot, foot*. Go ahead and try it; you get four turns, then switch with your partner. The purpose of this is to develop upper-body strength and the wheeling action of a cartwheel. The stretch, topple, lunge is a movement that helps make this a smooth sequence. Keep your legs and arms straight as you wheel around. Keep tight bodies; land softly and in control (R). Go. [During practice] Try to do this from both sides of your body (E). Sometimes your right hand goes down first and sometimes your left hand goes down first. Stop.

"We are going to add a piece of string to make this a more challenging task (E). One partner, get a piece of string and tape and wait for my directions. [When all are ready] Tape one end of the string down on the floor at the point where all the lines meet. One of you will hold the other end of the string up in the air for your partner. The string should be long enough so that whoever holds it can stand far enough away from the performer to avoid being kicked. The string can be held at various levels, depending on where your partner wants it. The higher the string, the more difficult the cartwheel is. If you're moving first, you place one hand on each side of the string, one at a time, and wheel your legs over it. Watch as I try it. I'm glad my string was low! Good quality is important—think of our stretch, topple, lunge, hand, hand, foot, foot. Go ahead and start, beginning and ending on the letter C. [Give other alternatives as necessary (E), using teaching by invitation or intratask variation.]

- Start on C, take weight on hands, return to the opposite C.
- Start on B, return to D.
- Start on B, return to the opposite C.
- Start on B, return to the opposite B.
- Start on B, return to the opposite A.
- Start on A, return to the opposite A.
- Tie or tape a piece of string to the top of a bench or box (E). One student holds up the string, and the other cartwheels from a position on the floor. The hands are placed on the bench or on each side of the string. The feet land on the floor or the opposite side of the string.

[Signal stop.] "As you get better and feel more confident, have your partner raise the level of the string to increase the level of challenge (E). Make sure you try cartwheels over the string from both the left and right sides of your body (E). [More advanced students can learn advanced Olympic gymnastics skills of rotation through transverse and horizontal axes, such as front and back walkovers, roundoffs, and front and back handsprings. These are beyond the scope of this learning experience. They are presented in the Feet, Hands, Feet learning experience on pages 205-210. Also, consult such references as Hacker et al. (1993) and Cooper and Trnka (1989).]

"Let's end our lesson with a movement sequence (A). Let's take weight on the hands, using a wheeling action. Perform a roll of your choice, then finish in a balance [wheel, roll, balance]. Practice this over and over until you are ready to perform it. Go! [During practice] Make sure you have good linking actions (R). One action should lead right into the next without stops or extra movements. Your sequence should flow together. Work hard. Are you ready to perform your sequence? Stop.

"Girls stand, boys sit. Girls, you will go first. Show us your sequence. OK, boys, now it's your turn. Thanks! Everyone sit down. You're really learning a lot about cartwheels and rotation. Who can tell me what it takes to do a good cartwheel? Yes, Li, hand, hand, foot, foot. Straight arms and legs like spokes in a wheel. As I watched your sequence work, I saw many good efforts at smooth linking actions. I saw very few extra movements, stops, stutters, or glitches. Thanks for your hard work."

Ideas for Assessment

- Students must strive to keep their arms and legs straight while performing wheeling actions. Check to see whether their bodies are tight, with elbows locked and shoulders over the hands. Are students landing on the foot opposite the one they stepped with?
- How high can the string be raised and still allow for a good cartwheeling action over it?

How Can I Change This?

- Do a sequence of wheeling action, roll, and balance on the floor with equipment or with partners.
- Add a balance at the beginning: balance, wheeling action, roll, balance.

Ideas for Teaching Fitness

- Taking weight on the hands requires strength in the arms and shoulder girdle. Children can begin by doing bunny hops. They can also kick up into a handstand position with the help of a partner and hold the position for an increasing number of seconds—5, 10, and 15.
- Push-ups and upside-down push-ups from a handstand position can help the strong get even stronger.
- Performing a cartwheel requires good flexibility. Have the children perform several stretching exercises where they extend and reach up high and wide. Have them straddle their legs while standing and bend their hips to the front, back, and side while reaching with the arms.

Ideas for Integrated Curriculum

A cartwheel should be like a wheel turning on a bicycle. Hands and feet are the tires. Arms and legs are like spokes in the wheel. For the wheel to work well, the spokes need to be straight, tight, and stretched.

Ideas for Inclusion

Special-needs children who can take weight on their hands in an inverted position should do so. Other children who cannot support their weight while upside down can develop arm strength by trying to take their weight in a front support or back support position on the floor or in a more upright position from a piece of equipment such as a balance beam. They can straddle their legs to make their movement more like a cartwheeling action.

A ROLL BY ANY OTHER NAME . . .

Objectives

As a result of participating in this learning experience, children will improve their ability to

- demonstrate control in rolling actions used to move onto, along, or off equipment (standard 1); and
- develop an action sequence that includes the use of a roll onto, along, or off equipment (standards 1 and 2).

Suggested Grade Range

Intermediate (3 to 4)

Organization

A large, open space is needed. Children should be in scatter formation, with one or two to each piece of equipment.

Equipment Needed

At least one box, bench, low beam, or table is needed for every two students. Folded mats, 4 to 6 inches (10-15 cm) high, can substitute. Place mats and carpet squares beneath or beside the equipment.

Description

"You already are very good at rolling in different ways and in different directions. Today we'll use rolls to move onto, along, or off the equipment. It will be challenging for you! First, let's warm up by jogging on the floor in open spaces (I). Light, up on the balls of your feet with springy, quick feet. Change your speed—faster and slower. Change directions. Jog. As you come close to a mat, transfer smoothly into jumps. As you get to the mat, go into a roll and return to your feet. Keep moving to another mat. Jog, jump, jump, jump, land, roll. Good! Stop.

"We'll start today by rolling off our equipment (I). Everyone move to a piece of equipment you'd like to begin at and sit down beside it. First we'll get on our equipment in a squat or kneeling position. Watch as I do it first [or have a student demonstrate]. From this position, place your hands down on the floor (R). Stay tucked, chin and knees to the chest (R). Rock forward a little and transfer your weight to your hands and arms (R). Make your arms strong. Your bottom goes up; roll over to your feet (R). Think you can try it? Go ahead, everyone try it a few times. Stop.

"What about rolling off sideways from a pencil position (E)? Place one arm and leg down on the floor and roll (R). See if you can lie on your back or be in a shoulder stand and roll off backward (E). Use your hands to control your body position by holding on to the equipment (R). Go ahead and practice rolling off.

[Signal stop.] "Well, I see we can roll off! Now let's try rolling onto the equipment (E). Stand facing your piece of equipment, just like Danny and Meghan here. Put your hands on the equipment. Tuck your chin to your chest (R). Begin to lower your body and take your weight on your hands and arms (R). Jump, bottom up, tuck, and roll. Your weight should go from the feet to the hands, to the shoulders, back, hips, and feet. Stay tucked. [Demonstrate.] Everyone try this. If you need to change to a different piece of equipment, you may—but ask the person who is there already. Good. Practice this several times. Stop.

"Next, you'll turn around with your back to the equipment (E). Sit on the equipment and rock back. Feel for the equipment with both hands beside your head (R). Stay tucked and push with your hands (R). Roll over to your feet. [Demonstrate.] This is a hard skill. Not everyone might want to do it. Some of you might want to do it with a spotter. See if you can find a way to roll onto the equipment in a sideways direction (E). [After a few minutes] Stop.

"For you to be able to roll along a piece of equipment, it must be fairly long (E). We can use the tables, benches, and folded mats for that. [Surfaces should be wide and low to build confidence. Only accomplished children will want to use a standard-width balance beam.] Remember to try to do your rolls just as if you are on the floor. I will be looking for these points to make sure you are doing the skill correctly (R):

- Forward roll—tuck chin to the chest; bottom up; transfer weight to the hands, shoulders, back, hips, and feet.

- Backward roll—tuck; weight goes from the feet to the hips, back, shoulders; push with the hands and back to feet.

- Sideways roll—tight body; roll like a pencil or log.

"Try not to get nervous just because you're on an elevated surface. If you can do your roll on the floor on a line, with practice you will develop the precision and control on the equipment. We've started on low, wide surfaces on purpose for your safety. You can also ask for someone to help spot for you. [Mats can be stacked on both sides of a low bench or beam to reduce falling.] Practice each skill several times. Stop.

"Now let's put these rolls into a sequence (A). You may choose the type of sequence you want.

- Start with steplike travel to equipment, then a roll of your choice onto the equipment, and finish in a balance on the equipment.
- Start in a balance of your choice on the equipment, roll off the equipment, and finish in a balance of your choice.
- Start in a balance on the equipment, go to a roll of your choice along the equipment, and finish in a balance of your choice on the equipment.

"Stop. Wow! I'm impressed, seeing the great variety as you perform your rolls onto, off, and along the equipment. Let's show off your work. Everyone whose sequence involves a roll onto the equipment will perform their routine first. Everyone else watch. Great ideas! Nice transitions! Now, everyone whose sequence involves a roll along the equipment, perform your routines. Yes, those were good rolls, and you maintained control. Finally, everyone whose sequence involves a roll off the equipment, perform your routines. I'm just as impressed with your work. Good weight transfers in your rolls off the equipment. They were smooth; I didn't see clunking or crashing. Thanks for your hard work."

Ideas for Assessment

- Children should execute these rolls on and off equipment as if they were on the floor (figures 7.11 and 7.12). Check each child for good form and smooth weight transfer.

Figure 7.11   Rolling off the equipment.

Figure 7.12   Rolling onto the equipment.

- Some children may be very apprehensive about trying one or more of these rolls. Don't force the issue. Find their comfort level; simplify a given roll by stacking extra mats. Provide spotting for those who want it. Allow children to choose a roll they are comfortable with. First master the roll on a line on the floor. Are the children performing at their level of ability?

- When sequence work starts, look for smooth transitions into and out of rolls and onto and off the equipment, without extra steps, indecision, or glitches. Children should maintain good control.

How Can I Change This?

- Make the sequence more complex by combining rolls. For example, use steplike travel to equipment, roll onto equipment, balance on equipment, roll off equipment, finish in a balance.

- Make up a partner rolling sequence in which partners mirror or match each other. For example, use a cartwheel to arrive, jump onto equipment, lower into a balance of choice, roll off equipment, and finish in a balance of choice.

Ideas for Teaching Fitness

Performing rolling actions onto, along, and off equipment requires good strength and flexibility. To develop overall body strength, have the students tense selected muscle groups and then relax them in an isometric fashion. Build up to making the whole body tense in a small, crouched position and then relaxed in a long, stretched position. To develop flexibility, have students tuck their bodies up into a small ball—chin to chest, knees to chest—then rock front to back (shoulders to feet) and side to side.

Ideas for Inclusion

Instead of rolling onto and off equipment, have children roll down an inclined plane forward, backward, and sideways. Gravity will help them complete their rolls. Good form is still essential.

LET'S MAKE A CONNECTION

Objectives

As a result of participating in this learning experience, children will improve their ability to

- balance in a variety of upright and inverted positions, move smoothly into a roll, and end in a balance (standard 1);

- move smoothly from one balance to another in a variety of ways (standard 1);

- explain that a combination of maintaining a round body shape and momentum can help a person to roll and return to feet (standard 2);

- detect, analyze, and correct errors in personal movement patterns (standard 2);

- accept responsibility for selecting movement choices that are suitable and safe for each person's ability (standard 5); and

- design unique gymnastics sequences (standard 6).

Suggested Grade Range

Intermediate (4 to 5)

Organization

Mats are scattered throughout the learning environment.

Equipment Needed

One mat per student or per two students is needed. One flip camera per four students is optional.

Description

"If you were told you could get a new bicycle or skateboard, you would probably select what you thought was the best or coolest of all the choices. What would you look for to help you make this decision? OK, some of you said what looks the best and others mentioned what would help you to ride the best. Today we are going to pretend that Olympic judges are here to view your best performance. From previous work in our gymnastics lessons, you have a lot of balances, rolls, and steplike actions that you can now perform. Today you will select a variety of these actions that you do best and put them together in a unique gymnastics sequence. We are going to learn how to make connections between parts of sequences to help them look the very best we can. Our focus words today are *transition* and *flow*."

"We will warm up by traveling in general space (I). You may choose how you will travel. I expect to see a variety of locomotor skills, pathways, levels, and speed. Some of you may choose to vary the force of your travel. However, when I hit the drum one time, you must change at least one of your travel choices and continue your travel without stopping (E). Your change must be so smooth that the judges hardly notice when you made the transition. [After two or three turns, stop and refine if it appears they are not planning the next move.] As you are traveling, you should be planning your next move and the way to transition into it (R)."

"Now, have a seat on a mat and we will work on performing balances and using body rotations to make smooth transitions out of these balances. Start by performing an inverted balance of your choice. You will need to hold the balance showing good tight muscles, extensions, and stability for five seconds (I).

"Go into and out of the same balance, slowly returning your feet to the place you started. Repeat the same balance, but this time as you come out of your balance, carefully twist at your hips, turning your body so that your feet come down in a different place (E). Continue to practice this same transition or try twisting another direction, but slow the speed of your move by tightening your muscles, showing that you are in control of your body both into and out of your balance (R). Repeat the same inverted balance, but this time use the twist to transition into a new balance (E). Plan your base of support for your second balance. Do not forget to maintain control of your movements. Reduce tension only in the muscles that are required to aid you in twisting, turning, or changing into the shape needed for the new balance (R). Continue to practice until this combination of inverted balance, transition, balance looks like a polished performance (A).

"Next we are going to try a different way to use twisting movements to lead to new balances. Start by balancing on two feet and one hand with your trunk facing the floor. Hold your head up and extend the free arm (E). From this balance, stretch the free body part slowly toward the ceiling and then away from the rest of your body. Twist your trunk and follow the free arm until you end in another balance where your base of support changes and you are now facing the ceiling (e.g., bridge, V-sit) (E). Using the same two balances you just performed, we will try using a roll as the transitional move. Assume the first balance, hold it for five seconds, and then tuck your free arm under your body using a forward shoulder roll to transition into the second balance (E). Remember to control both your muscle tension and the speed of your movement to make a smooth transition (R). On your own, come up with two other balances and a way you can use a different roll to transition between the two (E).

"Finally, create a sequence that includes three of your favorite balances, one of which must be inverted. They may be balances we used today or another day. Use a combination of twisting, turning, and rolling to make smooth transitions from one balance to the next. Do not forget to maintain control of your movements. Reduce tension only in the muscles that aid you in twisting, turning, rolling, or changing into the shape needed for the new balance. Your sequence should be a beginning balance, twisting or turning transitional move, second balance, rolling transitional move, ending balance. Practice the sequence so that it will meet the high expectations of our Olympic judges (A). [Allow half of the class to perform their sequence while the other half pretends to be the judges. They should look for controlled, smooth transitions. Then change roles.]

"Now we are going to practice a transitional move called touch and pop that can be used between other rotational moves or between balances. First, we will practice a forward roll from a standing position and return to a standing position (I). Remember that you must maintain a round body shape and increase your rolling speed to have enough momentum to allow you to return to a standing position. [Practice a few minutes.] You are looking good, but remember to keep that chin on your chest to help with the round shape and push extra hard with your hands to increase your rolling speed (R). Great, now we can add a touch and pop (E). After the roll, as your feet touch the mat, without stopping, you will want to pop off of the balls of your feet, jump into the air extending your arms toward the ceiling, and then land on both feet keeping your arms above your head momentarily in a good gymnastics ending pose. [Practice.] Good use of tight muscles on the pop-up! I noticed you remembered to bend your knees for a good landing. Repeat the forward roll, touch, and pop to your feet, and this time during the pop, execute a quarter turn before you land. Follow the landing with a cartwheel or another roll. Be sure to stay balanced as you pop and land up so you can go right into your next action. Go! Now, add a final touch and pop after the last move, ending in the gymnastics ending pose (E). Here's how this sequence should be:

- From a standing position execute a forward roll.
- Do a touch and pop with a quarter turn.
- Go right into a cartwheel or another roll.
- Follow that with a touch and pop.
- Freeze in a gymnastics ending pose.

"There should be no stops until the end; just touch and go. Great work! I challenge you to try any combination of rolls or steplike actions and jump turns (quarter, half, three-quarter, or full) (A). Be safe and stay within your ability. Maintain control of your muscle tension, speed, and balance to be successful. Be sure to end each sequence you create with a touch, pop, and freeze.

"For your final project today you will create a gymnastics routine that combines both sequences with great transitional moves and flow. You want to *wow* the judges. Start with your first balance sequence and then add one of the sequences that you just practiced. The difficult part will be finding that transitional move that will connect the last balance of your first sequence with the first roll of your second sequence (A). If you need help, I will be glad to assist you with ideas for this part. Practice it at least three times and then your assessment team of four will videotape each other using a flip camera (A). Be sure to use the same-number camera that your group always uses. Tomorrow you will watch your video and you and your peers will determine what you need to do to improve the transition and flow of your routine. Great work today! I know this judge is impressed!" [If video equipment is not available, use a live peer assessment.]

Ideas for Assessment

- Develop a checklist so that peers can assess the critical transition moves.
- Observe for students controlling both muscle tension and the speed of their movement to make smooth transitions.
- Ask students to share their plan sequence and to explain why a particular movement or balance was best.

How Can I Change This?

- Provide specific sequences as opposed to having students create their own.
- Provide an option of a forward roll or a forward shoulder roll.
- Use live peer assessment as opposed to videotaped assessment.

Ideas for Teaching Fitness

- Discuss the need for flexibility in using the stretch and twist moves. Provide students with ideas to increase their flexibility.
- Twisting, turning, and rolling require strong abdominal muscles. Suggest that students do curl-ups at night for at least one minute.

Ideas for Inclusion

- Students with intellectual disabilities may need specific sequences drawn or demonstrated for them.
- Some autistic children may struggle with staying focused during extended practice time. Try providing other options for these students.
- Obese children may not be able to hold weight in some inverted balances or maintain a curled shape during rolls. Options should be provided to allow for success.

HIP CIRCLES

Objectives

As a result of participating in this learning experience, children will improve their ability to

- demonstrate controlled front and back hip circles on a large piece of equipment (standard 1),
- understand the principle of rotation around a piece of equipment (standard 2), and
- perform a movement sequence that includes at least one front or back hip circle (standard 1).

Suggested Grade Range

Intermediate (4 to 5)

Organization

A large, open space is needed. Set up equipment at an appropriate height so that students can safely spin around it. A bar set too high might prevent success for the less-skilled children. Set bars or beams at chest height for standing positions; children should be able to just reach the bar or beam from a long sitting position under the equipment. Spread mats under and around the equipment. Spread the stations around the gym.

Equipment Needed

A variety of large apparatus must be available for you to conduct this learning experience, including balance beams, parallel bars, and horizontal bars. If you have only one or two pieces of equipment, use them as stations and have the children rotate to the equipment. Ideally, you want enough large pieces of equipment to fit four to six students safely at each apparatus. For safety, an adequate number of mats should surround the equipment. If you have sufficient mats, extend them out away from the equipment so that students can develop sequences moving toward or away from the equipment. One drum is necessary, and outdoor playground pieces, such as chin-up bars, are also useful.

Description

"Today, we will use the idea of rotation in a new way with equipment. We are going to rotate around a beam or bar. This activity takes some strength in the abdomen, upper body, and arms, which we have been building up progressively during the year. Let's get started. To begin, jog around the room in any way you choose (I). Whenever I beat the drum, change the speed of the jog (E). Stay off the mats. Freeze! Get with a partner. Think of three stretches for your arms, trunk, and legs (E). Teach your partner the three stretches. You should do six different stretches altogether. Find a new partner and do the same.

"OK. When I say go, find a piece of equipment and stand in front of it, facing me. No more than six of you for each piece of equipment. Go! Support your weight on the equipment in a front support position (I); it looks like this. [Demonstrate.] Take turns with a partner if the space is crowded. Your body and arms must be tight and straight (R). Your hips rest on the equipment (R). Keep your head up (R). Go!

[During practice] "Good. Hold it for five seconds (A). Try to hold it longer (A). Count to yourself; how long can you hold it? Your hands should be shoulder-width apart in a palm-down position, with the fingers away from your body (overgrip) (R). Great, I see strong, tight bodies with good lines. I even see toes pointed. Stop. Now, face the equipment; support your body weight on it and then lift one leg in a straddle position on it (E). Keep your legs straight and your head up (R). Keep your arms straight and tight, your shoulders over your hands (E). Come down to the front support position. Now straddle your other leg on the beam (E). Swing, lean, straddle, and support. Now give your partner a chance.

"What other balances can you create from a front support position (E)? How about swinging both legs to one side and balancing on one hand and your feet [one-hand releases]? How about straddling both legs simultaneously? You and your partner have a few minutes to practice different supports and balances. [Signal stop.]

"Next, we're going to do a form of front and back hip circles (I). We'll start with a front hip circle, which ends in a long sitting position under the equipment. Watch now. [Demonstrate or have a student demonstrate.] Bring yourself into a front support position. Grip the equipment with your fingers pointing toward you, thumbs away (R). Bring your body into a tuck position as you spin around the beam (R). End the rotation by sitting on the floor in a long sitting position. [Demonstrate.] Think support, tuck, spin, sit. Do this with control—no crashes to the mat. Go! [During practice] Keep your body tight. This will give you control. Squeeze your seat and your legs. Stop. If you can do this well, I challenge you to do it with your legs straight, from a pike position. This takes more strength: support, pike, spin, sit. Do it slowly and end up in a long sitting position on the mat under the beam [bar], just as Dawn did. [Demonstrate.] Try it. Good, I see slow, controlled rotations around the beam [bar], with tight seats and legs. Keep your arms bent so your body rotates closely around the beam [bar]; this gives you better control. Once you sit on the mat, add an action away from it, such as a roll, a wave, or a twist back onto the beam [bar] (E). Explore different ways. [Pinpoint a few students for demonstrations.] In a few minutes, I'll have some people show everyone what they've done.

"OK. Next you'll try a type of backward hip circle (E). This is another challenging task. You'll start in a long sitting position under the equipment with hands gripping it in an undergrip, palms facing away from you. Pull up with your arms to get the beam [bar] close to your chest and kick one leg up and over the top of the beam [bar]. Kick hard to get the momentum you need to get over the beam [bar]. Pull and kick. End in a front support position. Neat, huh? Give it a try. [During practice] Keep trying. This takes some strength and timing. You need to keep the equipment close to your hips to be successful (R). Have a controlled flowing action. Spotters can help you by supporting the kicked leg over the beam [bar]. I want everyone to try this several times. Good work!

[More advanced students can learn Olympic gymnastics skills of forward and backward hip circles as well (E). Consult such references as Hacker et al. (1993) and Cooper and Trnka (1989).]

"For today's sequence, start with either a front or a back hip circle; move away from the equipment in a rolling action, taking weight on your hands; end in a balance (A): hip circle, rolling, weight on hands, balance. Remember to make smooth transitions from one action to another. Work for quality. I'm going to come around and watch you. Perform your sequence for a partner, also. Excellent work! That's it for today."

Ideas for Assessment

When children are in a front support position on the equipment, their arms should be straight, with shoulders over the hands. Bodies should be tight, legs straight, and toes pointed (see figure 7.13).

• Students must use proper grips for the hip circles. Thumbs should always be pointing in the direction of the turn. If the students' hands are small, they may have to change their hand position during the rotation to have a safe grasp. Teach this, watching closely; it is important for safety.

• Overweight children may lack the necessary strength for hip circles. Be on the alert for students who might not succeed. Provide them with activities to improve their upper-body strength. (See Ideas for Teaching Fitness later in this activity.)

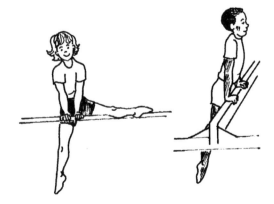

Figure 7.13 Sample balances from a front support.

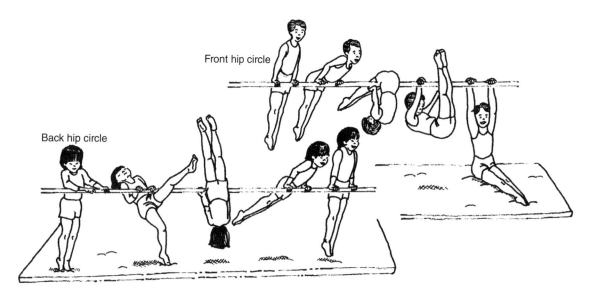

Figure 7.14   Hip circles.

- Make sure all rotation takes place with the body's center of gravity close to the bar or beam (figure 7.14). It is much more efficient mechanically.

How Can I Change This?

- Divide students into small groups. Each group goes to a uniquely designed work station. At each station place a task card that gives some guidelines for developing a creative movement sequence. For example, "Mount, balance, front support, hip circle, long sit, shoulder stand, roll, balance."
- Work with a partner and develop a short sequence that includes a hip circle. They can mirror or match each other's movements.

Ideas for Teaching Fitness

- Holding the body in a front or back support position on a piece of equipment requires good strength in the arms and shoulder girdle. Build toward this strength gradually by putting children in situations in which they support their body weight with their hands—push-up position, coffee grinder, bunny hops, cartwheels, tripod, balance on two arms and one leg in an upright or inverted position, and so on.
- Performing hip circles requires good abdominal strength. Children can do V-sit positions, crunches, and bent-knee sit-ups to build the required amount of strength.
- To be successful at hip circles, a person must also be flexible. Have the children get into a curled-up position on their backs, with knees and chin to chest. Have them rock forward and back from feet to shoulders and return feet to shoulders to feet.

Ideas for Integrated Curriculum

- Teach the students what a good body line is in a front support on the beam. Take a broomstick or ruler and place it against the beam; explain how the child's body should look as straight as the broomstick or ruler.
- In science, children learn about lengthening and shortening the radius of rotation to decrease and increase the speed of rotation. They also learn about center of

gravity and base of support. To perform hip circles with competence, children need to keep the center of gravity near the axis of rotation. Thus they must tuck and keep the knees close to the chest when rotating. They can then lengthen their bodies to slow their rotation and end up in a sitting or hanging position under a beam or bars.

- Rotation around a bar or beam provides an excellent opportunity to talk about centrifugal and centripetal forces.

Ideas for Inclusion

- To develop the readiness skills necessary for doing hip circles around a piece of equipment, work with all children as they attempt to take their body weight completely or partially in a hanging or support position. Work especially on the development of strength in the arms and shoulder girdle.
- Before working at a beam or bar, students can use rocking actions on the floor to initiate the feel of rotation around a horizontal or vertical axis and inhibit their lingering labyrinthine, tonic neck, and extensor thrust reflexes. Rocking from a log or pencil position side to side and from a tuck position forward and back are examples.

PARTNER TASK CARDS

Objectives

As a result of participating in this learning experience, children will improve their ability to

- use a variety of rotation skills in selected movement sequences (standard 1);
- integrate the concepts of meeting, parting, mirroring, and matching into their movement sequences (standard 2); and
- work cooperatively with a partner in designing a movement experience (standard 5).

Suggested Grade Range

Intermediate (4 to 5)

Organization

A large, open space is needed. Four stations should be spread out in the gym:

1. A series of connected mats
2. Mats at the base of several benches
3. A balance beam or horizontal bar with mats under and away from it
4. A second series of connected mats

Equipment Needed

This activity requires mats, benches, and a balance beam or horizontal bar. If you don't have a balance beam or horizontal bar, a second set of benches with mats is acceptable. You should have enough equipment to fit four to six students safely at each apparatus. You will also need task cards to guide the children in the development of their movement sequence (see details for what to include on these task cards in the Description section).

Description

"Today we're going to have a challenging lesson that requires you to cooperate well with a partner and develop movement sequences with a focus on rotation skills. Slide next to a partner. We'll begin our warm-up by moving around the gym—one partner leading and the other following, copying the leader's locomotor patterns. Use jumps, hops, skips, and slides (I). Think about changing your direction or pathway (E). Think about changing your speed (fast to slow or slow to fast) (E). When you come to a mat, the leader will perform a roll of her choice and the follower will copy that roll [demonstrate] (E). Stop. Switch leaders and repeat. [Signal stop.] Now find a mat with your partner and sit down. To continue our warm-up we're going to perform some more rolls that emphasize mirroring and matching and meeting and parting (E). For example, if Johnny and I are partners, we could agree that we will start away from each other in a mirror shape. Out of that shape we could do a forward roll as we come close together. We could then finish in a second shape that is again a mirror image. [Demonstrate.] We could also start in a matching shape that is side by side. We could then lower ourselves to the floor and perform a side-by-side pencil roll and finish in a second matching shape. [Demonstrate.] Your warm-up sequence is to balance, roll, and balance with your partner. You have choices to meet, part, move side by side, and mirror or match. Choose one way to solve the problem, then another way. Begin. [Allow several minutes for practice.] Stop. Come in here to this station.

"That was a good warm-up, but I noticed several things that we need to work on. First, you need to become more synchronized with your partner (R). Begin and end simultaneously with your partner. As a set of partners, you must be an exact mirror or match. Pay attention to the little details (R). Make sure you both are pointing your toes, have your arms bent at exactly the same angle, and have your legs separated the same distance as you balance. I noticed that Susan and Camille were particularly good at this during warm-up. Would you show us your last balance, roll, and balance sequence? See how they were in an exact matching shape to begin? Then they had a signal to indicate when they should start their roll. The speed of their roll was exactly the same. And they finished in another exactly matching shape. Good work, girls.

"Now find a new partner and go to one of the four stations that I have set up. Each station will have four or five sets of partners, so you'll have to take turns performing. We'll be using a variety of the rotation actions we've learned to develop a new sequence that will require you to mirror or match your partner's rotation actions. When you're not using the equipment, you can talk to your partner about balances and rolls that you can use to solve the problem. Who can tell me a type of rotation action we have learned? Yes, cartwheel, sit-spin, hip circle. Right, all the different rolls we've practiced—forward, backward, seated, shoulder, egg. We've used many of these skills with and without equipment. Your job today is to go to a gymnastics station, read the task card, and work with your partner to solve the partner sequence suggested (I). Each station has different equipment and a different task assigned for you. Don't worry about where you start, because you'll get a chance at all of the stations. Partner cooperation will be very important. Now find a new partner and move to your first station. Great, Todd and Rob, you saw that one station had too many people so you moved over to station 3, which had fewer people. Stop and sit down.

[When children get to their stations, they find the following task cards.]

Station 1 (E)

You may start side by side, face to face, or back to back. Perform a roll of your choice with your partner. Remember to mirror or match each other. The roll you choose may allow you to move in the same direction simultaneously, move toward each other, or move apart. Finish your roll in a V-sit. Perform a sit-spin with your partner. Come out of your sit-spin and perform a second roll. The second roll must be in a different direction from the first. Come out of your second roll and finish your sequence with a balance of your choice. Remember to mirror or match your partner's balance (roll, V-sit, sit-spin, roll, balance).

Station 2 (E)

Travel on the bench to meet and then part from your partner. Your traveling actions may include steps, hops, jumps, slides (on feet or on other body parts), or rolls. Either use a wheeling action (cartwheel or round-off) off the equipment or jump off the equipment, land, and perform a wheeling action. Your wheeling action should take you away from the bench. Perform a rolling action of your choice back toward the bench with your partner. Remember to move simultaneously and to mirror or match your partner. Finish your sequence by balancing with your weight completely or partially on the bench in a shape that mirrors or matches that of your partner (see figure 7.15) (travel toward, then away from partner; wheeling action; rolling action; partner balance).

Figure 7.15   Balance on the bench in a shape that mirrors or matches that of your partner.

Station 3 (E)

Start in a front support position on the beam or bar. Mirror or match your partner. Perform a front hip circle and end in a pike seated position on the mat. Select a traveling action that moves you away from the beam or bars (roll, slide on selected body parts, steplike action on the feet). End in a balance shape that mirrors or matches that of your partner. Depending on the way you move away from the equipment, your balance will be at different levels (front support, hip circle, pike position, traveling action, balance).

Station 4 (E)

Begin in a mirror balance with your partner on the mat. Use a roll of your choice to move away from your partner. Balance in a matching shape with your partner. Depending on your balance position, perform a spinning action of your choice (sit-spin; jump with a quarter, half, or full turn; cartwheel). Use a different roll of your choice to move back together. Finish in a different mirroring shape (mirror balance, roll away, matching balance, spinning action, roll together, mirror balance).

"When I say go, I want you to get to work. Remember, I'm looking for good mirroring and matching partner balances. Each part of your sequence should be done skillfully (R). Each balance must show stillness, good lines, and a focus with your eyes (R). I want to see good linking actions as you move into and out of your balances—logical moves, no extra steps, smooth (R). To coordinate your balances with your linking actions, you may want to count or establish a signal, like winking an eye or clucking your tongue, so you both know when to move or hold a balance. I want to see good beginning and ending positions. When we have moved to each of the stations, I'll ask some of you to perform a selected sequence for the class. Go. [Allow students sufficient time to practice at each station. Signal when it is time for everyone to move to a different station until everyone has had an opportunity to work at all four stations.]

"That was a good effort on your part. I like the way you worked responsibly with your partners. I saw you sharing ideas. I saw you trying different solutions to each problem and working out a way you and your partner could perform the sequence. Let's watch Jenny and Kelly do their sequence at station 3. After they finish, I want you to tell me what you saw them do and what you liked about their performance. [Performance and discussion.] Now let's watch Ben and Jameson. [Performance and discussion. Repeat several more times.] Thanks for being such good gymnasts. I'll see you again soon."

Ideas for Assessment

- It is critical that partners time their routines together precisely. Teach the children to count each segment of the sequence quietly to themselves or establish signals so they learn to time each move. Has each set of partners established a signal in an attempt to time their sequence?

- Students may be having a hard time working with a partner. They must be willing to cooperate, and they should be fairly close in ability level to allow for sequences that challenge each person. Check each set of partners for compatibility. Are they cooperating? Do their ability levels complement each other?

- Quality work in the sequence is essential. Be sure that you give them enough practice time to perfect their sequences. Watch for good-quality balances. Expect precise mirroring or matching. Refine for good-quality rotation actions.

How Can I Change This?

- Assign a longer sequence that includes previously learned concepts and skills. Allow several class periods to solve the tasks and practice them so the sequences are of good quality.

- Make up your own tasks that are different from the ones presented in this learning experience.

- Use different equipment. Boxes, horses, tables, chairs, or outdoor equipment such as jungle gyms or horizontal ladders are some examples.

- Make up different tasks for various ability levels. For example, assign highly skilled students tasks that involve walkovers, hip circles, or handsprings. Assign less-skilled students tasks that involve easier movements such as seated rolls, egg rolls, and pencil rolls on and off the equipment.

Ideas for Integrated Curriculum

- Have the students write in their journals about the sequences they performed at each of the stations. What skills did they include? Did they mirror or match their partner? Were they face to face or side by side? Did they meet or part? Which sequence did they like best? Why?

- This lesson provides great potential to work on affective goals (national standards 5, 6, and 7). For example, discuss how to respect your partner's ideas, make decisions with a partner, and compromise. Ask the students to write in their journals about their choice of a partner. How well did they cooperate? Did they each get a chance to have input into their sequences? How did they resolve their differences?

Ideas for Inclusion

This learning experience serves as the basis for the partner sequence work in the story about Elizabeth cited in chapter 1. You know your students best; before assigning this partner task sequence, talk to one or more students who you think might work well with a particular child and ask them whether they would be willing to be his or her partner. Suggest some ways that they can complete their assignment and help the pair during the process if necessary. Provide alternative tasks to allow them to complete the assignment as well.

FEET, HANDS, FEET

Objectives

As a result of participating in this learning experience, children will improve their ability to

- understand the concept that several weight-on-hands tasks overlap as traveling and rotation movements (standard 2);

- develop more advanced skills of taking weight on the hands, such as cartwheels, round-offs, walkovers, and front and back handsprings (standard 1); and

- perform a skillful creative movement sequence that includes at least one of the skills listed in the preceding point (standards 1 and 2).

Suggested Grade Range

Intermediate (4 to 5)

Organization

Scatter mats around a large, open space. Allow enough space between mats so that children can get a good running start to perform their rotary weight-transfer actions on the mats. For several tasks, you will need small stacks of mats, rolled mats, or benches or boxes to design appropriate developmental stages that lead up to the skill.

Equipment Needed

You will need 10 to 15 mats for this activity, with two to three children at each mat. In the warm-up, one jump rope for each child will be placed on the floor to serve as lines on which to move. If you have small mats, attach several together with Velcro.

Description

"We have a challenging lesson today. Previously we've done lessons by taking weight on our hands, such as in bunny hops, vaulting, and handstands. Those activities used weight transfer from feet to hands to feet without a focus on rotation. For example, a bunny hop transfers weight from feet to hands and back to feet without using rotation. [Demonstrate.] Today we're going to take weight on our hands in different ways to focus on rotation. For example, a cartwheel transfers weight from feet to hands and back to feet while rotating around a front-to-back [transverse] axis. [Demonstrate.] We also rotate around an axis when we perform various types of rolls. Today we're going to learn some rotation skills and then end the lesson by creating a sequence that includes a rotation movement.

"You look ready to move! Jog slowly around the gym, and when you come to a mat, transfer your weight from your feet to your hands and back to your feet across the mat (I). Feet, hands, feet, hands, feet. That's it. Good, I see straight arms, flat hands on the floor with fingers spread out, shoulders over wrists (R). Kick your feet up one at a time or both feet together (E). Each time, land softly back on your feet (R). I don't want to hear loud feet or see any crashes to the floor. Terrific! Stop.

"Now find a space on a mat. From a standing position, stretch long with your hands over your head (E). Then lean to the right, and then to the left. Hold each position for 10 to 15 seconds. Do this several times. Now, lie down on the floor. In a long lying position on your back, bend your knees at a 45-degree angle with your feet near your seat. Place your hands near your shoulders with your palms on the floor and fingers pointing toward your feet. Elbows should be pointing up to the ceiling. Stretch your body up and form a bridge [back bend] (E) [demonstrate]. Push your belly up (R)! That's it. When you're tired, lie back down, rest, and try it again.

"Divide into groups of three. You'll take turns to do this next warm-up activity. One person will get into an egg roll position, with his or her back toward the ceiling. The second person will act as a performer. He or she will lie on the back on top of the egg, perpendicular to the egg, with the hands and head on one side of the egg and the feet on the other side of the egg. The third person will act as a spotter. The egg will now rise up onto the hands and knees, pressing the back up high. These actions will place the person who is lying down into a back bend—weight on hands and feet, back arched, belly toward the ceiling (E). Reach for the floor with your arms and rock so that your shoulders are over your hands (R). Look for the floor with your eyes (R). For safety, the spotter can help the performer press up into the back bend. [Demonstrate.] Go. Be sure that every person gets a turn. Try it several times. [For those who lack the flexibility or skill to try this with a partner, pressing up into a back bend from a back-lying position on the floor is a good alternative (E). Those who have more skill might want to go into a back bend from a standing position (E).] Arms up, body stretched. Start bending back while your knees and belly come forward a little. Reach for the floor and look for the floor with your eyes (R). Come down softly on your hands (R). Hold the position and gradually let yourself down to the floor in a lying position. [Spotting is suggested at first. Foam donuts or curved foam mats help in this process if you are fortunate to have them.] Stop. Come in here and gather around this bench [box].

"As I mentioned, today's lesson is about transferring your body weight from your feet to your hands and back to the feet again. We'll do this in the four stations I've set up. As we begin, everyone will try these first three skills. If you are skillful enough, you will try some new skills at the fourth station. As you can see, I've placed some lines on the floor. You've taken weight on your hands before by doing bunny hop, clock face, and the string challenge. Today we're going to try to do a cartwheel in a straight line (I). Start with your body facing the line, feet together on the line. Twist your upper torso a quarter turn and place your lead hand [right or left] on the line. Follow that with your next hand. Then, land one foot at a time. Try to land on the line with your feet (R)—hand, hand, foot, foot. Keep your arms straight—shoulders over wrists (R). Keep your legs straight (R). As you finish, you should be sideways with your feet in a straddle position on the line [demonstrate] (R).

"Let's go over to the second station. The second skill we will all try is a cartwheel over the box [bench], landing on the other side (E). If you want, you can do this at the end of the box [bench] (E). Those of you who feel you can keep your legs straight and get them vertically over your shoulders can try the cartwheel from the middle of the box [bench] [demonstrate] (E). Once again, it's hand, hand, foot, foot. I'll be looking for the same things as when you're doing cartwheels on the line.

"Here at the third station you'll start lying on your back perpendicular to the box [bench] (E). You'll need to have your seat really close to the equipment and place your feet up on the box [bench]. From there you'll press up into a back bend. From the back bend you'll shift your body weight over the shoulders, kick with the lead leg, trail leg following, and come to a standing position facing the equipment. [Demonstrate.] [Spotting is a good idea for this activity.] OK, let's divide into three equal groups. [Allow time to practice, then signal for groups to move to a different station. Make sure everyone gets a chance to work at each station.]

"Nikki, Rashad, Tiffany, and Josh, come to this station. [Ask some higher-skilled students over to the extra station.] I've been watching you, and I think that you're ready to try some even more difficult gymnastics skills. Sequentially we're going to learn five skills. It will take time to work at these skills over several lessons, but I'm confident you can master them. The skills are the round-off, the front and back walkover, and the front and back handspring (see figure 7.16 on page 208).

- *Round-off* (E): Stretch long and high with your hands above your head, just like you do for a cartwheel or handstand. Place your hands like you do for a cartwheel. As the hips and legs come over the top, do a quarter turn at the hips and snap the legs down to the floor together as the hands push hard off the floor (R). There is an instant when the feet and hands are off the floor simultaneously (R). The end position is such that you face the opposite way than you started. [Demonstrate.] Think *hand, hand, twist, snap, push, land.* Your legs come together in the air as you twist and snap. You land with your feet together (R). When you're ready, move away from the mat and take a three-step run up to the mat before you do the round-off (E).

- *Back walkover* (E): Get a partner. You previously did a back walkover off the equipment. This time I want you to do it on the floor. One partner will be the gymnast and the other will be the spotter. When it's your turn, push up into a back bend. As before, rock or shift your weight over your arms and shoulders (R). At the same time, use one leg as a push leg and the other as a kick leg (R). You can also initiate the back walkover from a standing position (E). In this case you start in a stretched position with hands over the head. Again, one leg acts as

Figure 7.16 Challenging ways to perform the weight transfer of feet, hands, feet: *(a)* round-off, *(b)* back walkover, *(c)* front walkover, *(d)* front handspring, and *(e)* back handspring.

a push leg and the other as a kick leg (R). As the kick leg is thrust up, the back arches and hands reach for the floor (R). The head must tilt back as eyes look for the floor (R). Legs are in a scissor position and land one at a time (R). You may also choose to scissor the legs together while in the upside-down (handstand) position and come down with both legs together (E). The spotter can assist by placing one hand in the arch of your back and the other on the kick leg to help you come to an inverted position on the hands and then a standing position on the feet. Think *bend, kick, stand.*

- *Front walkover* (E): Stand in front of a mat with your toes touching the mat. Stretch, topple, and lunge; place your hands on the mat close to your feet on the near side of the mat. Kick one leg up and over your head in a handstand position as you hyperextend (R). The trail leg should follow (R). Continue on over with an arch in your back (R). Land with one foot and then the other, and finish at the end of the mat with your back to the mat [demonstrate] (R). Think *hands, kick leg, arch back, land.* Again, the spotter can support your back during the early practice stages. [As an assist, a raised or folded mat, a bench, or a box can be used as a starting place for the hands (E)]. By placing the hands on a raised surface and rotating to the floor, you have more time to rotate the body before the feet come down to the floor. If you slow down the walkover action to an approach with a kick up into a handstand position and allow both feet to come down simultaneously, you can finish the walkover in a back bend (E).

- *Front handspring* (E): Initiate the front handspring with a running approach to gain momentum (R). As you come to the mat, transfer weight to one foot (hurdle action) and spring into the air (R). The arms are extended overhead in the step-hurdle action (R). Then place both hands down together by bending at the waist while kicking the other leg up into a handstand position (R). As the trail leg catches up to the lead leg (legs together), the arms elevate the body with a strong push off the floor (R). The hips are extended through the rotation phase as the feet snap down to the floor with the back arched [demonstrate] (R). Think *hurdle, kick, snap, arch, land.* As an assist, the front handspring can be done off a stacked mat to allow for more rotation time to bring the feet down for a better landing (E). [As in the preceding skills, spotting in the early stages gives students feelings of success. Spotting is the same as in the front walkover.]

- *Back handspring* (E): Begin the back handspring from a semisquat position (R). Lean back as though sitting in a chair (knees over feet) (R). As soon as you feel a loss of balance, thrust the arms up and back while the legs push off the floor (R). The head also moves back as you begin to look for the floor (R). At this point the back is arched and the arms reach for the floor, thumbs in (R). Place the hands on the mat, shoulder-width apart, as the legs snap down (R). As the legs snap, the arms also extend and thrust up off the floor (R). The final position is an erect stand with arms stretched out [demonstrate] (R). Think *sit, throw, reach, snap, land.* [Spotting is the same as in a back walkover and is recommended in the beginning stages. As students get more skill they can approach the mat, do a round-off, and finish with a back handspring in a line.]

Spotting or assisting is critical for these advanced moves. As a teacher, you can't spot for every child every time. Children can be taught to help each other. Parent aides and high school students can help as well.

"OK, I want everyone to come back together again. We'll work on a final sequence for this learning experience (A). Each of you is to select one of the skills we learned and put it into a short sequence. Your rotation skill may come at the beginning or end of your sequence. I want you to include a beginning and an ending balance and use good transitions throughout the sequence. For example, balance in a headstand, forward roll, return to feet, steps, hurdle, front handspring, and balance. Or balance in a back bend with hands on the floor and feet on a bench, back walkover away from the bench, and finish in a balance. [Demonstrate.] Work for quality in your sequence. Although this is an individual sequence, work with a partner. Take turns and spot for each other. When you're ready, we'll have half the class present their sequences to the other half, and vice versa. Work hard! [Signal go. Allow practice. Signal stop.] Showtime! [After performances] Thanks. You're really putting together some challenging work."

Ideas for Assessment

- Use a checklist to determine who has the readiness skills to perform the more difficult skills beyond the first three stations—arm strength, back flexibility, ability to perform a cartwheel with good form, and so forth.

- Quality of body mechanics is important in all advanced skill work. Look for powerful hurdle actions and arm-thrusting actions. Good body lines are essential. Legs must be stretched and the back arched. Legs must be snapped to the floor. Check for form and timing on each skill.

How Can I Change This?

- Not all children can work at the same level. Be willing to modify activities to allow for varying ability levels. Some students could be rolling over a rolled mat. Others could be doing a round-off over a bench. Be sensitive to everyone's abilities.

- Add a piece of equipment to the sequence. For example, a front walkover on the floor can be an approach to a bench, box, horse, or beam. Mount the equipment, balance, travel (jump, hop), perform a cartwheel or round-off as a dismount, and finish in a balance.

Ideas for Teaching Fitness

- Performing any of the skills in this learning experience requires the development of strength in the arms and shoulder girdle. Students can do push-ups, stand on their hands, or perform other exercises in which they take the body weight on their arms and hands in an upright or inverted position.

- Performing any of the skills in this learning experience requires the development of back flexibility. Students can practice pushing up into a back bend and holding the position for increasingly longer periods. They can do back bends entirely on the floor or with the hands or feet elevated on a piece of equipment such as a folded mat or bench.

Ideas for Integrated Curriculum

- These are difficult gymnastics skills. Students have to learn to make responsible decisions about whether they are ready to attempt a given skill. This is not a time to goof off or be a daredevil. Talk to students about responsibility, trust, risk, and cooperation. Teach them how to spot for and help each other. When they are ready, teach them how to risk learning a new skill by knowing they have worked up to it.

- Point out that these rotation skills serve as the basis for tumbling, cheerleading, diving, and advanced gymnastics work. As students perform these skills, they need to learn to use their eyes to focus on a point of reference on a wall to know where their body is located in space.

- Have the students watch the performances of advanced or Olympic gymnasts, analyze their floor exercise and apparatus routines, and write down the rotation skills they see. To check if the students understand what they need to strive for in learning to perform the skills themselves, ask them to write out or explain elements of form they see the advanced gymnasts use.

- Have the students write out their routines using a code, specific words, or simple drawings to describe each of the skills in their sequences.

- Students can write about their feelings when they take weight on their hands and perform more advanced gymnastics skills using principles of rotation.

ADDITIONAL IDEAS FOR LEARNING EXPERIENCES

ROCKING AND ROLLING

Hard as a Rock

- Hug your knees and tuck your chin, keeping your body in a tight, round shape. Rock back, then up to a sitting position again. Do the rock twice more.
- Sit and put your thumbs under your ears. Make the palms of your hands face the ceiling. Point your fingers backward. This time you will have to hold your body in that round shape by contracting your abdominal muscles. Now, rock back and forward three times. Rock far enough back so that your hands are touching flat or almost flat on the mat by your head. Each time your hands touch the floor, push hard on them to rock back to a sitting position. On the third rock, rock forward to stand up without pushing on the floor with your hands. To accomplish this, tuck your heels close under your seat, keep your head forward with your chin to our chest, push your arms forward as strongly as possible to reach out in front of you, and push up hard with your legs.
- From a log (arms by your side) or pencil position (arms stretched above your head), rock first in one direction and then in the other. Start from lying on your belly as well as your back. Keep your body stiff and tight. Rock with your arms stretched over your head (pencil). Rock with your arms held tight at your sides (log). Keep muscles tight and concentrate on rocking the whole body as a unit.
- Curl up very small in a ball like an egg. Rock in one direction and then the other.
- Start in a balance of your choice. Then choose a rocking action that is logical or provides a smooth transition, and perform the rocking action three times. Finish in a new balance.
- Sit next to a partner and try to match any of the previous rocking motions.

We're on a Roll

- Curl up very small and close to the floor. Roll along the floor curled up like an egg.
- Using a pencil roll or log roll, travel down the end of the mat and return. Use tight muscles as if your legs are glued together. Try to roll as straight as possible. Pretend the mat is a road and you have to stay between the lines (sides of the mat) without rolling into the ditch (off the mat).
- Run in and out of mats. When you come to a free mat, curl up and roll on it. Try sideways, forward, and backward directions in your rolls. Get up and continue on. Be careful of others.
- Bounce with two feet together (jump) between mats. When you get to a mat, curl up and roll across the mat in backward, forward, or sideways directions. Get up and continue on.
- Run, jump, land. Then sink down and roll away sideways. Use a log or pencil roll or an egg roll. Repeat to the other side.

- Face the mat. Put your hands and feet on the mat with your feet together. Move your feet slowly nearer and nearer to your hands. Put your chin on your chest and overbalance forward to roll over. Remember to curl up as soon as you lose your balance. Round your back and keep your head off the floor. If you are successful at that, can you stand up without pushing from your hands?

- Stand with your back to the mat. Sink down, do a backward shoulder roll or backward roll, and recover to your feet.

- Rock backward and forward several times with your hands up beside your head in the correct place—thumbs in, palms facing the ceiling. When you feel you are almost rocking over backward, swing back hard and push on your hands to roll over backward onto your feet. Remember to push up hard with your hands and arms to provide clearance for your head as it comes through. The head should not take any weight.

- Roll in a forward direction in slow motion. When I hit the drum, roll in fast motion. When I hit the drum again, change to slow motion. Choose another roll and change the speed on my drum beat.

- Choose a favorite way to roll and roll all the way down the length of the mat without stopping. Combine two rolls by using one roll to go one direction down the mat and another to return to the starting position.

- Travel in and out of the equipment provided (boxes and benches) on your feet. When you come to a free piece of equipment, use a roll of your choice to move toward it. Climb on. Then perform a balance on the equipment.

- Travel in and out of the equipment on different body parts. When you come to a clear piece, roll toward it, climb on, and balance. Then jump off and roll away again.

- Travel in and out of the equipment any way you choose. When you come to a clear piece, roll toward it, climb on, and balance. Then leave the equipment in a roll by taking weight on your hands first—weight on hands, tuck chin to chest, slowly lower into the roll. As you overbalance, curl up tight and keep your head off the floor.

- Travel in a bouncing way between pieces of equipment. Then jump up onto the equipment and balance. Lower yourself down and use the equipment in a sliding way. Slide down off the equipment and roll away.

- Travel in and out of the equipment in different ways. When you come to a clear piece, mount it and perform a balance. Then jump down with a quarter or half turn to land on the floor. Sink down and roll away.

TURNING AND SPINNING

Dizzy Izzy

- Stand on one foot and spin around on the ball of that foot. Throw your arms and look in the direction of the spin. Spin with your arms outstretched, showing good extension. Spin with your arms tucked in. Start with the arms close and then extend them as you spin. Under which conditions do you spin faster? Slower? Why?

- Find other body parts on which you can spin. Try your knees, belly, seat, two feet, and so forth. Let the children try different ideas.

A Long Axis

- Working in pairs, shake hands and lean away to spin around each other. Stop, release hands, and run in and out of everyone in class. Each time a command is given, find a new partner, shake hands, and take a short spin around before moving on.

- Imagine a line—the vertical axis—is running straight through your body from your head to your toes. Can you find several ways of turning your body around that line while remaining in one spot? While moving? Which body parts can initiate the movements? Give the children time to experiment with and demonstrate different ideas. Can any other body parts take your weight as you turn or spin around the long axis of your body?

- Run and jump high in the air to turn around as far as possible before landing. Turn clockwise. Turn counterclockwise. Remember to land safely on your feet. What happens when you change the shape of your body while in the air? What are the best ways of entering into the jumps?

- Start by lying in a long, flat position on the floor. Find ways of turning around your long axis in that position.

- Create a short sequence of movements, turning around your long axis while your body is stretched or curled. Use various body parts to produce the rotation.

- Use a piece of equipment such as a box or bench. Travel to the piece of equipment using steplike actions of the feet. When you arrive at the equipment, use a jumping action to travel over it while turning around your long axis. Always land safely on your feet. Next, mount the equipment with a turning action. Dismount the equipment with a turning movement. Finally, create a sequence. Turn around your long axis as you mount the apparatus. Balance on the equipment. Then turn again as you dismount. Link the movements together smoothly.

Head Over Heels

- Imagine that a line runs through your body from one hip to the other. This is called your side or horizontal axis. Find different ways of turning your body around that line. Try various rocking and rolling actions. See if you can turn around this side axis in a forward or backward direction from a balance on your shoulders, then from a kneeling position, then from a sitting position.

- Use a piece of equipment such as a balance beam or horizontal bar. Can you find anywhere on the apparatus where you can spin around your long axis or turn around your side axis? Can you dismount the equipment while turning around your side axis? Teach those who are skilled enough to perform hip circles around the bar. For a forward hip circle, cast away. Come back to the bar and lean forward with a straight body. Lead with the chin, with chest out. Keep the bar close to your hips and return to the starting front support position. Or start in a front support position and initiate a front hip circle; finish it in a hanging position under the bar. For a backward hip circle, cast away, then come back to the bar swinging the legs forward while leaning back. Keep the bar close to your hips and return to your starting front support position.

- Join two movements together—one turning around your long axis and one turning around your side axis. Add balance positions to start and finish your sequence. Look for continuity of movement.

Wheeling and Dealing

- Imagine you have a line from the front of your belly to your backbone (spine). That is called your transverse axis. In what ways can you turn your body around that line? Crouch close to the floor on your feet. Roll sideways across your shoulders and back to your starting crouch position. Try rolling both to the left and to the right. Sit on the floor with your legs in a straddle position. Roll sideways across your shoulders and back to your straddle position. Can you do that several times in a row, making a half turn each time? Can you perform it in both directions—to the left and to the right?

- From a crouched position on the floor, place your hands to one side and take your body weight onto them while lifting your seat high. Do this to the left and to the right. Add a small piece of equipment such as a jump rope, a wand raised 6 inches (15 cm) off the floor, or a hula hoop and perform the same action over or into and out of the equipment. Perform the same activity while going along a bench from end to end.

- Try cartwheels to the left and to the right. Make them simple if necessary, taking weight on the hands in a wheeling motion and allowing the legs to be in a bent or pike position. Encourage those who are capable to wheel the legs over the top in a vertical alignment. Try cartwheels on a line on the floor. Try cartwheels on a raised surface such as a bench that is 10 to 12 inches (25-30 cm) wide (for safety, provide raised or folded mats on each side of the bench to reduce the impact of any possible falls). Start a cartwheel on the bench and land on the floor. Perform a cartwheel over the bench from one side to the other.

- Travel on the floor and equipment while performing turning and spinning movements where possible. Make up and perform a sequence that shows a turning action through each of the three axes.

CHAPTER 8

Designing Gymnastics Sequences

As noted in chapter 3, children typically learn gymnastics in stages (Nilges 1997, 1999). In stage I, children learn basic individual skills. These skills cross all three skill themes of traveling, statics, and rotation and are evidenced in such skills as a hop, cartwheel, front support, tip-up, headstand, forward roll, and backward shoulder roll. These individual skills serve as a basis for skill combinations in stage II and beginning sequence work in stage III. In the younger grades, children should learn simple sequences consisting of three or fewer options. Older children can become involved in more advanced levels of skill development at stage I and place their skills into increasingly complicated sequence work at stage IV. Older children are better able to choose and use additional skills and process variables, developing rather sophisticated work. The options should be broad enough so that all students can develop a sequence regardless of their skill level.

As in dance, sequences are process oriented; they have a beginning, a middle, and an end. They are movement sentences. In beginning and ending positions, gymnasts often stand in erect balances that signal control and draw attention. These positions say, "Watch me," or "I am finished now." Rather than standing in an alert (erect) position, beginning and ending shapes also can easily draw on other body shapes as a means of starting and finishing a sequence. In the middle of a sequence or routine, children are given options involving skills from the main themes of traveling, balance, and rotation and from the process variables (BSER). For example, children are told that the sequence must consist of a travel on the feet, a roll, and a symmetrical balance; two rolls using two different body shapes; or three balances at three different levels.

Designing sequences is a good way for children to consolidate work, reviewing previous movements and adding one new element. All sequence work should focus on good linking actions and transitions from one skill to another. Start sequence work by allowing the children time to explore the possibilities after you state the task. Children need to discover what works at their level and what doesn't. From among the many options, the work should next be narrowed to choices the children like or can perform best. At this point, have the children repeat the sequences several times so that they can memorize the sequence, finally performing it without errors.

Sequences help children integrate skills from each of the three main themes and should be used on an informal, developmental basis in every lesson. Occasionally, such as at the end of a work unit, sequences may be used for more formal assessments. Chapter 4 discusses the topic of assessment in greater depth.

WHAT MAKES A GOOD GYMNASTICS SEQUENCE

Just as in the area of games, children learn basic skills first. When learning to play baseball, a player has to learn to bat, field, and throw. In tennis, a player has to learn to serve and hit forehand and backhand strokes. Learning basic skills, however, doesn't hold their attention for long. They want to play a game. The same thing holds true in gymnastics. Children soon want to combine skills and put them into a sequence or routine. Therein lies the fun.

So, what factors or concepts do you as a teacher need to focus on to help children understand what it takes to build a good sequence? The following ideas should serve as a basis for developing sequence work with children.

Fall Within the Guidelines of Sequence Requirements

All sequences should have specified requirements. Beginning sequences may have only two or three requirements. As children develop as gymnasts, sequences may become as complex as the children can handle. Sequences should focus on an intended unit of work or a final way for children to demonstrate what they have learned. For example, if the unit of work has been on linking balance positions with rolling actions, that is what you should see. If a child uses traveling actions such as a hop or jump, those actions should be refocused according to the nature or intent of the task. If the unit of work involves a child using a piece of equipment such as a box or bench to approach, mount, balance on, and dismount, that is what you should see. If a child's work is beside the piece of equipment or entirely on the piece of equipment without a mount or dismount, those actions too should be refocused according to the nature or intent of the task.

You can remind the children about the requirements of the sequence or you can provide them with written checklists of what should be in the sequence.

Formal Way to Begin and End

As stated previously, sequences must have a good beginning and ending position or shape. While this may be an erect (alert) standing position, it may also be a balance pose. The intent is to say, "I am ready to start," or "I am finished."

The beginning or ending may be a traveling action, static pose, or rotation. For example, children might use a run to initiate a vault. They can use any number of balance poses to signal the start or end of a sequence. Likewise, they can use a rotary action such as a sit-spin or roll could to start or end a sequence. Whatever choices the children make, the movements must be done with control, intent, and precision.

If a skill involves a partner or a piece of equipment, the beginning or ending may be a mount or dismount. For example, one partner may go from an erect standing position into a leaning handstand supported by the assisting partner. Or, a child may cartwheel or jump with a quarter, half, or full rotation while dismounting off a bench. In either case, the beginning or ending should be controlled and practiced to perfection.

No matter what, the beginning or ending should not contain any extraneous movement. No wobbling, extra steps, staring off into space, fixing hair, adjusting clothing, or wandering off. The beginning and ending should be focused and done with intent.

Still Poses Held Long Enough to Show Control

No one would ever expect a gymnast to hold a position for a long time. Many held poses require a tremendous amount of strength. For example, standing on one leg in what is commonly called a stork stand is a balance with a small base of support. Similarly, a tip-up, headstand, and handstand are difficult to hold for a long time. Many balances on equipment or even partner balances are also difficult to hold for any duration. However, that is not the point of gymnastics. The point is for gymnasts to show that they have mastered the skills and have control. Then, they need to move on in their sequence.

In general, holding a pose for three to five seconds is enough to show control. So a gymnast should move smoothly into the chosen balance pose, hold it for a short time, and then move smoothly out of the balance into the next move.

What is not desired is a child attempting a balance and doing it poorly by wobbling all over the place or taking extra steps. Often this leads to stumbling or falling over, thus creating an unsafe situation. When this happens, encourage a child to leave that move out of the sequence at this time and substitute it with another balance that she has mastered. Also encourage the child to continue working on the more difficult skill and provide her with help and spotting. Then, at a later time when she has mastered the difficult skill, she can include that skill in a future sequence.

Smooth Transitions

In developing sequence work, the big question is how to get from here to there in the smoothest, most logical way without any unnecessary movement. The answer often depends on the starting position. If the first position is a tall, upright position, the next move might involve sinking the body by bending at the knees and hips and smoothly going into a forward, backward, or sideways rocking or rolling action to lead into the next balance. It could involve dropping forward into a front support or using a steplike wheeling action to end up on a knee and foot. If a child starts in a balance on the floor on one of a number of bases of support, the most logical transition move may be a rocking, rolling, or sliding action into the next position. Here are the big questions to ask: "Where am I now?" "Where do I want to go?" "How can I smoothly and logically get there?"

In working with a piece of equipment or with a partner, the questions are the same, but the solutions are more challenging. A child must consider the direction of approach to the equipment, the distance away from the equipment, how one partner can assist or stabilize and support the other, how one partner can assume or release the partial or complete weight of the other partner, and how to synchronize movement with a partner. Think smooth, logical, no extra or unnecessary steps or movement.

Challenging Work at an Individual Level of Expertise

Unlike sequence or routine work in Olympic gymnastics where everyone is held to the same standard of performance, sequence work in educational gymnastics should encourage children to develop their individual, unique work based on their level of ability. As long as students meet the requirements of a stated routine (verbal or written), they can get a high score and feel a sense of accomplishment.

Let's face it: In any given class of children, there may be some who are at a low level of skill and strength, some at a middle level, and perhaps a few who have the potential to be high-level performers. The trick is to challenge students in the development of their sequences to work at their level. If you see some students putting together a sequence that is above their ability level, work with them and offer suggestions for alternative moves. For example, a shoulder roll could be used in place of a forward or backward roll. Or, a balance on two hands and one foot with the free leg extended could be substituted for an inverted three-point balance. In other instances you may see students at medium or higher levels of ability who are not challenging themselves. You know the level of work that they are capable of. Don't let them be lazy. Challenge them accordingly to work at their level of ability. They will take great pride and have a sense of accomplishment when they achieve an appropriate goal.

Novelty and Contrast

When given a sequence to develop and perform, encourage children to think for themselves. Encourage them to try novel ideas. They can try to balance in a new way, move into or out of a balance in a new way, approach a piece of equipment from a different direction, or perform a partner balance that is unique. While what they are doing may not be truly new or novel, it is new to them. Thus they feel a sense of ownership and pride in their accomplishments.

In educational gymnastics it is acceptable for each child to come up with his or her unique way to solve a problem. Encourage children to try several ways to complete their gymnastics sequences. Try one way. Try another. Which way works best? Which feels best? Encourage them to challenge themselves and not look around to see what a friend or an adjacent gymnast is doing.

Depending on the nature of the sequence, contrast is also an important concept to focus on. Most often, sequence work will involve comparing a minimum of two options: body shapes, bases of support, levels, directions, symmetry and asymmetry, dimensions, time, relationship to a partner or piece of equipment. Whatever the nature of the sequence, make sure that the children show contrast in their work. For example, a child could create an upright balance, then an inverted balance. In a different sequence, a child could move out of one balance quickly, then out of the next balance slowly.

For both the performer and the observer, moving in novel ways makes the experience interesting. Likewise, including contrast in a sequence makes the experience more fun to perform and to watch.

Complete Body Awareness

Regardless of whether a child is performing an individual skill or a complete gymnastics sequence, the child must have complete body awareness at all times. From head to toe, the child must be in complete control. Anything less than that may look sloppy, which can also compromise safety. For example, what is the head doing? Is the child tucking the chin to initiate a roll? Did he turn the head to begin a spinning action? Where are the eyes focused—forward, to the side, behind? It makes a difference when holding a balance or performing a rotation action. With respect to the torso, is the child concentrating on the best straight, curved, or bent body shape possible? What are the arms and legs doing? Are they straight with extensions out through the fingers and toes? Are they bent at specific angles or curved with an intended purpose?

When working with a piece of equipment or a partner, it is even more important to have complete body awareness at all times. Children must make conscious decisions of where they place their body weight partially or completely on the equipment or partner. In general, weight should be supported from positions of strength. For example, placing shoulders over arms with elbows locked, knees over feet or hips over feet while on equipment and placing weight on a partner over the knees or shoulders rather than in the middle of the back or front are good principles to follow. The point is that children must be conscious of making decisions that will affect the quality of their performance and make them safe at all times.

SAMPLE GYMNASTICS SEQUENCES

What follows are some sample gymnastics sequences. The sequences provided are divided into four categories:

1. Individual sequences on a mat

2. Partner sequences on a mat

3. Individual sequences with a piece of equipment on a mat

4. Partner sequences with a piece of equipment on a mat

Because individual sequences on a mat may be the most widely practiced, six sequences are provided. Three sequences are provided for each of the other categories.

We are not suggesting that these examples are the best or only gymnastics sequences possible. On the contrary, as is the purpose of this whole book, they are a starting point. They give you and the children involved a place to begin generating ideas for further development.

Individual Sequences on a Mat

Sequence 1
Individual Sequence–Floor Work

1. Link shapes ABC, DEF, GHI (rows).
2. Link shapes ADG, BEH, CFI (columns).
3. Link shapes AEI, CEG (diagonals).
4. Link shapes ABCFI, ADGHI (any five shapes).

- Hold each shape for 3 seconds.
- Make transitions from one shape to another as smoothly as possible.
- Make each shape with quality—precise, bend or stretch, and so on.

Figure 8.1 Individual sequence on a mat.

Reach–Rock–Return

Try each of the following sequences. From the beginning shape rock into the rounded shape and then return to the beginning shape.

1. Sequence A
2. Sequence B
3. Sequence C

- Remember to fully extend and reach for 3 seconds when performing the beginning and ending shapes.
- Make body parts curved for a smooth rocking action.

Figure 8.2 Reach–rock–return.

Try each of the following sequences.
1. Sequence A—Balance–pencil roll–balance
2. Sequence B—Balance–egg roll–balance

Sequence
Balance–Roll–Balance

- Remember to perform quality balances (center of gravity over base of support, good lines, and tight muscles).
- Hold each balance for 3 seconds.
- Use good techniques when rolling and perform smooth transitions between balances and rolls.

Figure 8.3 Balance–roll–balance.

Create a Sequence 1: Balance–Pencil Roll–Balance

Select a beginning balance from A, B, or C. Use a pencil roll for transitioning into an ending balance selected from D, E, or F. Now repeat the above selecting a different beginning and ending balance.

- Remember to perform quality balances (center of gravity over base of support, good lines, and tight muscles).
- Hold each balance for 3 seconds.
- Use good technique when rolling and perform smooth transitions between balance and rolls.

Figure 8.4 Pencil roll sequence.

Create a Sequence 2: Balance–Forward Shoulder Roll–Balance

Select a beginning balance from A, B, or C. Use a forward shoulder roll for transitioning into an ending balance selected from D, E, or F. Now repeat the above selecting a different beginning and ending balance.

- Remember to perform quality balances (center of gravity over base of support, good lines, and tight muscles).
- Hold each balance for 3 seconds.
- Use good technique when rolling and perform smooth transitions between balance and rolls.

Figure 8.5 Balance–forward shoulder roll sequence.

Create a Sequence 3: Balance–Backward Shoulder Roll–Balance

Select a beginning balance from A, B, or C. Use a backward shoulder roll for transitioning into an ending balance selected from D, E, or F. Now repeat the above selecting a different beginning and ending balance.

- Remember to perform quality balances (center of gravity over base of support, good lines, and tight muscles).
- Hold each balance for 3 seconds.
- Use good technique when rolling and perform smooth transitions between balance and rolls.

Figure 8.6 Balance–backward shoulder roll sequence.

Partner Sequences on a Mat

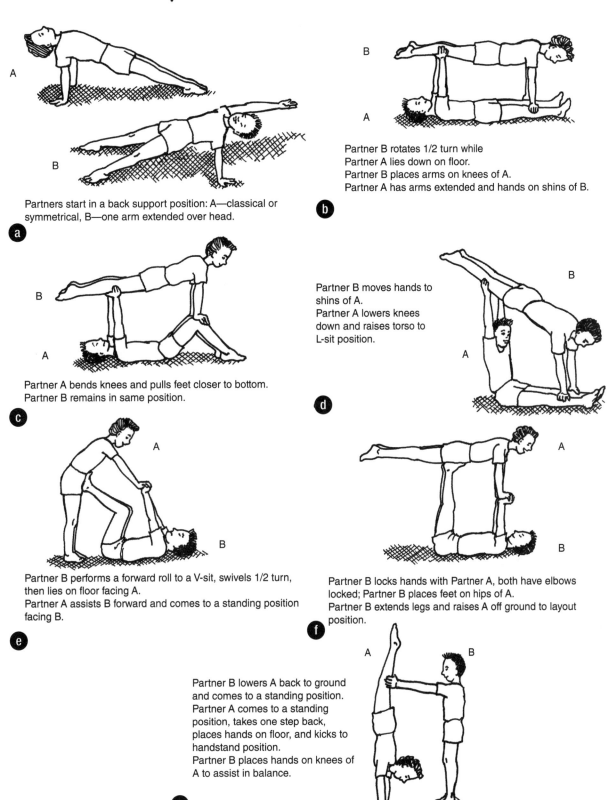

Partners start in a back support position: A—classical or symmetrical, B—one arm extended over head.

a

Partner B rotates 1/2 turn while Partner A lies down on floor. Partner B places arms on knees of A. Partner A has arms extended and hands on shins of B.

b

Partner A bends knees and pulls feet closer to bottom. Partner B remains in same position.

c

Partner B moves hands to shins of A. Partner A lowers knees down and raises torso to L-sit position.

d

Partner B performs a forward roll to a V-sit, swivels 1/2 turn, then lies on floor facing A.
Partner A assists B forward and comes to a standing position facing B.

e

Partner B locks hands with Partner A, both have elbows locked; Partner B places feet on hips of A.
Partner B extends legs and raises A off ground to layout position.

f

Partner B lowers A back to ground and comes to a standing position.
Partner A comes to a standing position, takes one step back, places hands on floor, and kicks to handstand position.
Partner B places hands on knees of A to assist in balance.

g

Figure 8.7 Partner sequence without equipment: taking partial and complete weight with individual balances.

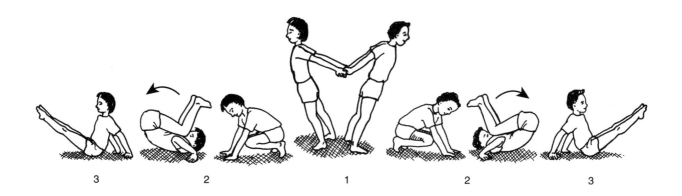

3   2   1   2   3

Partner Sequence
Counterbalance/Countertension–Roll–Balance

Try the following sequence:
1. Beginning: Counterbalance
2. Middle: Forward roll away from partner (parting)
3. Ending: Individual balance
4. Practice the sequence until you and your partner are synchronized throughout and end simultaneously.

For a quality sequence remember to
- communicate and cooperate (synchronize your movements),
- lean away from your partner for counterbalance, and
- use smooth transitions into and out of your balances and rolls.

Figure 8.8 Partner sequence with counterbalance.

Creating Partner Sequences
Parting and Meeting Using Counterbalance/Countertension

Create a partner sequence: Parting
  1. Select a counterbalance or countertension from A–F below; roll away from your partner (parting); and, end in an individual balance.
  2. Practice the sequence until you and your partner are synchronized throughout and end simultaneously.
Create another partner sequence: Parting and Meeting
  1. Select a different counterbalance or countertension: roll away from partner (parting); perform an individual balance; reverse roll to return to partner (meeting); and, end with the same counterbalance.
  2. Practice the sequence until you and your partner are synchronized throughout and end simultaneously.

For a quality sequence remember to
  • communicate and cooperate (select balances you can both perform and synchronize your movements),
  • lean away from your partner for counterbalance or press toward your partner for countertension, and
  • use smooth transitions into and out of your balances and rolls.

Figure 8.9 Creating partner sequences.

Individual Sequences With a Piece of Equipment on a Mat

a Begin in symmetrical star standing shape: legs straddled, arms Y position; left or right side to the middle of the bench.

b Cartwheel to left or right to arrive at bench; standing two feet together. Drop down to a knee and foot—torso erect—one arm up, inside arm extended out sideways.

c Bend forward—inside shoulder on bench. Outside arm hand on the floor—push up into a shoulder or handstand with torso inverted. Tall erect, legs together, toes pointed.

d Forward roll onto the bench and into a V-sit—legs straddled wide apart. Sit-spin push from left, right, left spin 1/2, 1, 1-1/2 times around.

e Come out of sit-spin into a shoulder stand—one leg straight up, toes pointed, other leg knee bent with foot against calf of opposite leg. Rock down out of shoulder stand, 1/4 turn to get body with shoulders parallel with bench.

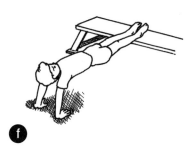

f Reach for floor with arms and go into a back support position with legs on the bench—body extended.

g Go into a front support position—one leg raised other in contact with the bench. Rotate to right or left 1/2 turn.

h Slide legs off bench and smoothly go into a forward roll. End in a V-sit on the floor legs together—extended straight, toes pointed—arms resting back on floor.

Figure 8.10 Individual sequence with equipment: three types of rotation with poses.

Gymnastics Routine

Perform the following gymnastics routine using an apparatus (bench, box, beam, or folded mat).

Next, create your own routine. Your routine should include the following:

1. Starting balance
2. Form of travel to the piece of apparatus (locomotor skill or a rotation movement such as a roll or cartwheel)
3. A mount onto the apparatus (such as a jump or a leap)
4. Performance on the apparatus must include at least one mode of travel, one balance different from the starting balance, and one rotational movement such as a spin or a jump turn
5. A dismount with either a shape in flight (wide, narrow, curled or twisted) or a change of direction (jump turn)
6. An ending balance different from the other two balances

For a quality routine remember to include:

- A variety of movement qualities by making changes in the base of support, level, direction, shape, and/or speed within the routine.
- At least one inverted balance.
- Quality balances (center of gravity over base of support, good lines, and tight muscles).
- Good technique on all movements.
- Smooth transitions between movements.

Figure 8.11 Individual gymnastics routine using a bench.

Individual Gymnastics Routine on Equipment 1

Perform the following gymnastics routine using a box or folded mat:

1. V-sit
2. Skip to box
3. Jump onto box (mount)
4. Scale balance on box
5. Jump off of box (dismount)
6. Knee scale

Next, create your own routine. Include the following:

1. Starting balance
2. Travel to box
3. Mount
4. Balance on box
5. Dismount
6. Ending balance

For a quality routine remember to
- include quality balances (center of gravity over base of support, good lines, and tight muscles, and hold for 3 seconds),
- use good technique on all movements, and
- use smooth transitions between movements.

Figure 8.12   Individual gymnastics sequence on equipment.

Partner Sequences With a Piece of Equipment on a Mat

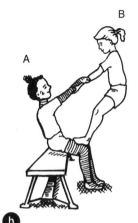

(a) Partners begin on the floor away from each other and the bench. Partner A is in an L-sit position with back toward the bench, shoulders parallel to the bench. Partner B is standing in an X position away from the bench, shoulders parallel to the bench.

(b) Partner A performs a backward roll or shoulder roll to arrive at the bench and comes to a seated position on the bench. Partner B performs a cartwheel to arrive in a standing position in front of Partner A. Partner B then joins hands with Partner A and also places one foot at a time on Partner A's lower thighs. Partner A pulls Partner B up while Partner B leans back a little. Because Partner B is leaning back, Partner A's seat comes off the bench.

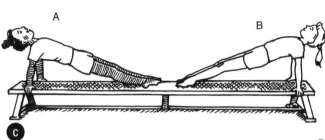

(c) Partner B steps or jumps off of Partner A's legs and lands on two feet facing the bench. Partner A sits back on the bench and swivels 1/4 turn to allow the feet to move toward the middle of the bench while the hands are placed near the end of the bench. Partner A pushes up into a back support position. At the same time the swiveling action is taking place with Partner A, Partner B jumps 1/4 turn with two feet onto the bench with her feet near Partner A's and then lowers self to a mirroring back support position.

(d) Partner B comes out of the back support position and performs a V-sit with a 1/2 turn into a lying position on the bench. Partner A comes out of the back support position by straddling her legs, tucking her legs, rocking forward, placing her hands on the bench, and coming to a squat position and then standing position facing Partner B. Partner A then jumps or spins 1/2 turn and begins a back bend with arms extended over her head. Partner B raises her legs, places feet on the lower back or seat of Partner A, and at the same time reaches and joins hands with Partner A while pulling them up into a full extended support position.

(e) Partner B lowers Partner A back to the bench in a standing position. Partner A makes a 1/4 turn and jumps down to the floor, squats and does a forward roll and ends in a knee and foot support with inside arm extended up and outside arm extended out. Partner B comes to a sitting position, does a 1/4 swivel to face the same direction as Partner A, goes into a forward roll, and ends on a knee and foot with inside arm extended up and outside arm extended out. Inside hands are touching at the apex.

Figure 8.13 Partner routine with equipment.

| 5 | 4 | 3 | 2 | 1 | 2 | 3 | 4 | 5 |

Partner Routine
Counterbalance/Countertension Routine Using Equipment (bench or beam)

Try the following sequence:
1. Start on the bench performing the partner countertension/counterbalance.
2. Travel away from your partner using a crossover step.
3. Turn, facing the end of the bench.
4. Jump/half-turn (180˚), land in a balanced pose facing partner.
5. Practice the routine until you and your partner are synchronized throughout and end simultaneously.
6. You may choose to change roles and repeat the sequence.

Next, with a partner, create a routine using equipment. Include the following:
1. Starting countertension/counterbalance
2. Travel away from partner
3. Dismount (rotations, shape in flight, and so on)
4. Ending pose or balance

For a quality routine remember to
• communicate and cooperate (select balances you can both perform and synchronize your movements),
• lean away from your partner for counterbalance or press toward your partner for countertension,
• bend knees on landings to absorb force, and
• use good technique on all movements.

Figure 8.14 Partner balance routine with countertension and equipment.

Partner Routine Using Equipment (folded mat and two wedge mats)

Try the following sequence:
1. Beginning: Perform a partner balance with partner A in supporting role (left) and partner B in balance (right).
2. Middle: A parting roll with Partner B performing a forward roll down the wedge and Partner A performing a backward roll down the other wedge.
3. End: Land in standing pose.
4. Practice the routine until you and your partner are synchronized throughout and end simultaneously.
5. You may choose to change roles and repeat the sequence.

Next, with a partner, create a routine using equipment. Include the following:
1. Starting partner balance (A, B, C, or D)
2. A parting roll
3. Ending pose or balance

For a quality routine remember to
• communicate and cooperate (select balances you can both perform and synchronize your movements),
• lean away from your partner for counterbalance or press toward your partner for countertension,
• bend knees on landings to absorb force, and
• use good technique on all movements.

Figure 8.15 Partner routine using equipment.

APPENDIX

Forms and Handouts

As a teacher, you may find this series of forms helpful for promoting and developing your gymnastics program. It begins with a gymnastics report card, which you might send home with a child's academic report card. When you are completing the report card, a simple asterisk (*) can denote the skills a child has learned during the grading unit. In addition, you can use an M, P, or B to denote level of mastery of a skill or concept (see key at bottom of report card). Space at the bottom of the card allows you to write short comments about routines, sequence work, and cognitive and affective assessment.

Next is a series of task cards that serve as examples for you to use with individual or station work in a gymnastics setting. A series of balance puzzles, a gymnastics notation system, and a learning center sheet contain additional ideas for promoting individual and station work in gymnastics.

A sample award certificate for children's work in gymnastics, an individual sequence, and a partner sequence are items that encourage the development of high-quality routines. Teachers, parents, older students, or peers can learn to use the subjective rating scale provided, in much the same manner as regular gymnastics is judged. As long as they challenge themselves within their own levels of ability, less-skilled students can achieve high scores just as the high-skilled students can; all students receive recognition for effort. Finally, as states move toward high-stakes assessment in physical education, two sample rubrics are included to represent what might be assessed for gymnastics students in grades K to 2 and grades 3 to 5.

Gymnastics Report Card

Name _____ School _____

Teacher _____ Grade _____

Unit Work or Skills Mastered

Traveling			
Steplike (using feet)	**Steplike (using hands, feet, and knees)**	**Weight transfer**	**Flight**
____ Walking	____ Crawling	____ Rocking, rolling	____ Takeoff
____ Running	____ Bear walk	____ Twisting, turning	____ Suspension
____ Hopping	____ Crab walk	____ Sliding	____ Landing
____ Jumping	____ Bunny hop	____ Tumbling	____ Minitramp work
____ Skipping	____ Mule kick		____ Vaulting
____ Galloping	____ Coffee grinder		
____ Sliding	____ Walkover (front, back)		
____ Other locomotion	____ Wheeling		
	____ Springing		

Statics		
Characteristics of balance	**Principles of balance**	**Types of balance**
____ Moments of stillness	____ Base of support	____ Upright, inverted
____ Tightness of body	____ Center of gravity	____ Symmetrical, asymmetrical
____ Controlled	____ Balance, counterbalance	____ Hangs
	____ Linking actions	____ Supports
	____ Movement into and out of balance	____ Relationship to equipment
		____ Individual, partner

Rotation		
Principles of rotation	**Movement around three axes**	**Rotation of the body**
____ Radius of rotation	____ Vertical	____ In space
____ Eye focus	____ Horizontal	____ Around equipment
	____ Transverse	

Level of Mastery

M denotes that your child has mastered this skill or concept.

P denotes that your child is practicing or working toward mastering this skill or concept.

B denotes that your child is currently below developmental level in regard to this skill or concept.

Routine and sequence work: components of sequence _____

_____

_____

Knowledge assessment: _____

_____

_____

Attitude and values assessment: _____

_____

_____

Note: An asterisk (*) indicates work during this grading period and level of mastery.

From P.H. Werner, L.H. Williams, and T.J. Hall, 2012, *Teaching Children Gymnastics,* 3rd edition (Champaign, IL: Human Kinetics).

Examples of Station Task Cards
That Link Themes in Educational Gymnastics

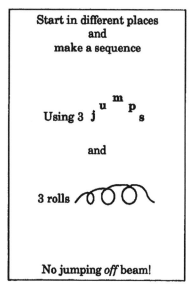

Start in different places
and
make a sequence

Using 3 j u m p s

and

3 rolls

No jumping *off* beam!

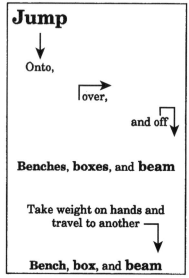

Jump

↓

Onto,

over,

and off

Benches, boxes, and **beam**

Take weight on hands and
travel to another

Bench, box, and **beam**

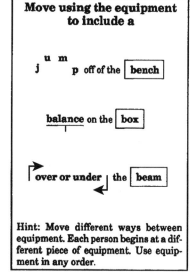

**Move using the equipment
to include a**

j u m p off of the | bench |

balance on the | box |

over or under the | beam |

Hint: Move different ways between
equipment. Each person begins at a different piece of equipment. Use equipment in any order.

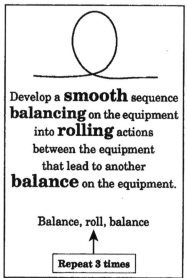

Develop a **smooth** sequence
balancing on the equipment
into **rolling** actions
between the equipment
that lead to another
balance on the equipment.

Balance, roll, balance

| Repeat 3 times |

From P.H. Werner, L.H. Williams, and T.J. Hall, 2012, *Teaching Children Gymnastics,* 3rd edition (Champaign, IL: Human Kinetics).

Balance Puzzles

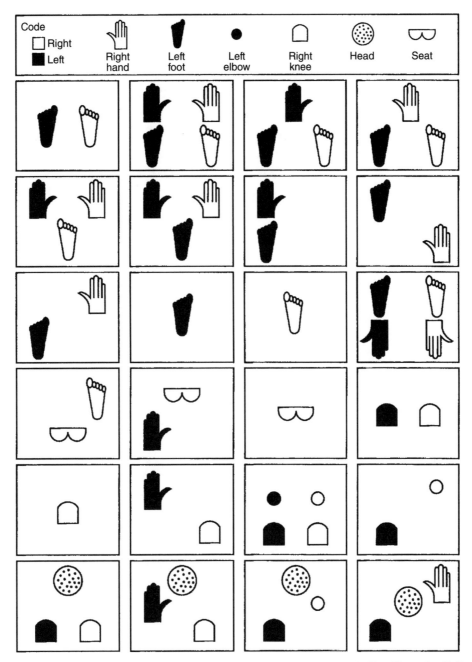

From P.H. Werner, L.H. Williams, and T.J. Hall, 2012, *Teaching Children Gymnastics*, 3rd edition (Champaign, IL: Human Kinetics). From P. Werner, and L. Rini, 1976, *Perceptual motor development,* vol. 1. (New York: Wiley), 13-14. Copyright © 1976 by Wiley. Reprinted by permission of John Wiley & Sons, Inc.

Write Your Sequence Using Gymnastics Notation

Gymnastics Symbols for Movements and Concepts

Traveling actions
Feet: Walking   – – –
     Running ᴡᴡᴧ
     Leaping ⌒
     Jumping ∧
     Hopping ꟾꟾꟾ
     Skipping ⊥
     Sliding ▷

Weight transfer and rotation
     Cartwheel x
     Round-off x̲
     Bunny hop ʌ
     Walkover ⫽
     Roll ⲟⲟⲟ

Balance
Hanging ⋎
Swinging ⊥
Support T
Back bend ⌒
Headstand ⊥⊥
Handstand ᴛᴛ

Concepts

Direction
Up ↑
Down ↓
Forward →
Backward ←
Sideways ↔

Pathway
Straight —
Curved ∿
Zigzag ⵗ

Relationship
Over ⌒
Under ⌣
Around 𝒪

Level
Low ⊓
Medium ⊟
High ⊔

Speed
Fast ⫽
Slow •••

Symmetry
Symmetrical Δ
Asymmetrical ⋈

Invent your own symbols: _____ **3•** = 3 times _____

_____ **I** = inverted _____

_____

_____

_____

_____

_____

_____

_____

Sample sequence: _____ ꟾꟾꟾ→3• _____ Hop forward 3 times

_____ ⲟⲟⲟ _____ Roll backward

_____ ⋈I _____ Asymmetrical balance, inverted

Your sequence:

1. _____

2. _____

3. _____

4. _____

5. _____

From P.H. Werner, L.H. Williams, and T.J. Hall, 2012, *Teaching Children Gymnastics,* 3rd edition (Champaign, IL: Human Kinetics). Original ideas presented by Stephen W. Sanders, J.T. Walker School, Marietta, Georgia, at the Southern District AAHPERD Conference, Nashville, Tennessee, February 1980. Printed by permission.

Learning Center: Designing a Sequence

Objective

When you have completed these activities, you will be able to perform a gymnastics sequence on the equipment provided.

Equipment

This learning center can be performed on any of the pieces of equipment in the gym, such as a box, bench, beam, bar, or table.

What to Do

1. After you choose a piece of equipment, try several ways of getting on, or *mounting,* safely. Try various ways of jumping or hopping, using hands and feet, or even a rolling or wheeling action. Use a forward, backward, or sideways direction.
2. Choose the mount you like best, then *balance* in a symmetrical body shape on two, three, or four body parts. Count to three while you hold your balance.
3. *Change* your balance to an asymmetrical balance using various body parts.
4. Find a way to get off, or *dismount,* your equipment safely.
5. Practice the whole sequence: mount, balance, change, dismount. Do it several times until it is easy. Then go to number 6.

Check for Quality

6. Is your sequence smooth with good linking actions? Are there extra steps, pauses, or hesitations?
7. Check your balance shapes for stillness and control.
8. Are you challenging yourself? If part of your sequence is too easy, change that part to make it more difficult.

How Can I Change My Sequence?

9. Change the balance shapes—stretch, curl, twist.
10. Change the level of the balances.
11. Change the place you get on and off the equipment (end, side).
12. Vary the speed during the sequence—start slowly and end quickly or start quickly and end slowly.
13. As you dismount the equipment, finish the sequence by adding a roll and a new balance on the floor.

From P.H. Werner, L.H. Williams, and T.J. Hall, 2012, *Teaching Children Gymnastics,* 3rd edition (Champaign, IL: Human Kinetics).

This certificate for

Excellence in Gymnastics

is awarded to

_____

Child's name

for

_____

Name of routine

School _____ Grade _____

Teacher _____

From P.H. Werner, L.H. Williams, and T.J. Hall, 2012, *Teaching Children Gymnastics,* 3rd edition (Champaign, IL: Human Kinetics).

Gymnastics Routine

Individual Sequence Using Bench or Box and Mats

Develop a floor exercise sequence on the bench and mats that includes the following components:

- A minimum of five balances will be included in the routine.
- The sequence is to begin and end in a gymnastics posture position.
- Balances should show changes of shape, symmetry and asymmetry, and changes of bases and the number of bases of support.
- One balance must be inverted.
- One balance must include taking weight completely or partially on the bench or box.
- One traveling action must be steplike.
- One traveling action must involve taking weight on the hands.
- Other traveling actions may include rocking, rolling, and sliding.

Other considerations in the routine should include

- changes in the use of air and floor pathways,
- changes in speed (time),
- changes in level, and
- the use of relationships (from one body part to another; to the equipment as you approach or move away from it; or to the bench as you move on, over, or off it).

Be aware of linking actions from one balance to another. What works smoothly to take you from one position to another? Be aware of line and technique in your work. Are your stretched shapes extended? Are your curved shapes rounded and smooth? Have you eliminated any unnecessary actions?

You will be graded on these factors:

Balancing actions: 2 points

Traveling actions: 2 points

Use of the bench or box: 2 points

Linking actions, transitions: 2 points

Variety in use of BSER process characteristics and aesthetic appeal: 2 points

From P.H. Werner, L.H. Williams, and T.J. Hall, 2012, *Teaching Children Gymnastics,* 3rd edition (Champaign, IL: Human Kinetics).

Gymnastics Routine

Partner Balances With Mat

With your partner, develop a sequence on the mat that includes the following components:

- The sequence must include a clear beginning position and ending position that show you are ready to begin the sequence and that you have ended your work.
- Your sequence must include three partner balances.
- At least one of the three partner balances will include one person taking the complete weight of the second person.
- The remaining two balances may include partially taking your partner's weight through balance and counterbalance.
- The routine must include a minimum of two individual balances.
- You must show the use of process characteristics in your sequence. This includes body and spatial awareness, effort, and relationships. Some examples include changes in base of support, method of traveling, or a body shape; changes in level, direction, extension, or pathway; changes in time or use of force; and changes in relationships with a focus on mirroring, matching, or contrasting work.
- Give consideration to logical movement that provides for smooth transitions (linking actions) among traveling, balances, and rotation work. Pay particular attention to how you use your weight-transfer actions to arrive at and move away from your partner and how you can move smoothly into and out of the individual and partner balances.

Be aware of linking actions from one balance to another. What works smoothly to take you from one position to another? Be aware of line and technique in your work. Are your stretched shapes extended? Are your curved shapes rounded and smooth? Have you eliminated any unnecessary actions?

You will be graded on these factors:

Clear beginning and ending and smooth transitions: 2 points

Partner balances: 2 points

Individual balances: 2 points

Traveling, weight-transfer actions: 2 points

Variety in BSER process characteristics: 2 points

From P.H. Werner, L.H. Williams, and T.J. Hall, 2012, *Teaching Children Gymnastics,* 3rd edition (Champaign, IL: Human Kinetics).

Gymnastics Rubric

Grades K to 2

Assessment Task

Demonstrate a gymnastics sequence that includes a minimum of three action verbs and three BSER movement concepts.

Choices of action verbs	Choices of movement concepts
Steplike traveling action	Body awareness: body shape
Step, jump, hop, skip, slide, gallop	Spatial awareness: change level, direction, pathway, extension
Transfer weight from feet to hands to feet	Effort: time, force, space
Bunny hop, cartwheel	Relationship: body parts to equipment
Balance	

Examples

Action verb	Movement concept
Jump	Forward to and into a hoop
Balance	Low level, symmetrical in hoop
Roll	Change direction or speed away from hoop
Action verb	**Movement concept**
Cartwheel	Time: fast, slow
Roll	Direction: forward, backward, sideways
Balance	Shape, level
Action verb	**Movement concept**
Balance	Shape, level, base of support
Roll	Time, direction
Balance	Change shape, level, base of support

Write in or draw your sequence:

Action verb	Movement concept

(continued)

Criteria for Assessment

- Balances must show good, clear shapes and straight, angular, and curved lines, and they must be held for three seconds.
- Traveling actions must show good form and technique.
- Rotation actions must show good form and technique.
- Sequence must show use of three different movement concepts.
- Transitions must be smooth and logical.
- The beginning and end of sequence positions must be clear.

Level 3

Proficiently performs action verbs with form and technique; consistently shows a clear beginning and ending; shows variety and contrast in movement concepts; consistently shows smooth, logical transitions; consistently repeats same sequence.

Level 2

Performs action verbs with good form and technique; usually shows a clear beginning and ending; shows some variety and contrast in movement concepts; usually shows smooth, logical transitions; usually repeats same sequence.

Level 1

Performs action verbs with some technique and control; sometimes shows a clear beginning and ending; shows little variety or contrast in movement concepts; rarely shows smooth, logical transitions; rarely repeats same sequence.

Level 0

Performs action verbs with poor technique; rarely shows a clear beginning and ending; shows no variety or contrast in movement concepts; rarely shows smooth, logical transitions; never repeats the same sequence.

From P.H. Werner, L.H. Williams, and T.J. Hall, 2012, *Teaching Children Gymnastics,* 3rd edition (Champaign, IL: Human Kinetics).

Gymnastics Rubric

Grades 3 to 5

Assessment Task

Create, write, and perform a six-part gymnastics sequence using a piece of equipment (e.g., box, bench, beam, horse, bars).

The sequence must include three of the following four elements:

- Traveling actions used to mount, travel along, and dismount the apparatus
- Upright and inverted balance positions
- Aerial movement, including a vaulting action and shape in flight
- A skill requiring some transfer of weight to hands and back to feet

You must choose and perform all sequence work while giving thought to showing a variety of action verbs and a variety of choices among the BSER movement concepts.

Examples

1. Beginning position: standing upright away from bench with side of body to the end of the bench, alert, ready to begin—body in star position, cartwheel sideways quickly to arrive at the bench.	2. Swivel a quarter turn to face bench. Use a slow forward roll to mount the bench.
3. End the roll in a V-sit with seat and two hands supporting body weight on bench with legs in a straddle position; hold the position for 3 seconds.	4. Swivel a half turn, lie down on the bench, and move into an inverted shoulder stand with one leg stretched and the other bent, with the foot next to the knee of the straight leg.
5. Rock out of the shoulder stand with the body in a curled-up position; when feet make contact with the bench, rise to a standing position.	6. Ending position: jump powerfully off the bench; while in the air perform a tuck shape; land softly on the ground with side facing the bench. Stand in a controlled, alert position to show you are finished.

Write in or draw your sequence:

1. Starting position	2.
3.	4.
5.	6. Ending position

(continued)

Criteria for Assessment

- Three of the four parts must be included in the sequence—traveling, upright and inverted balances, aerial movement, and weight transfer to hands and back to feet.
- Action verbs must show consideration for using a variety of movement concepts.
- Transitions must be smooth and logical.
- The sequence must have clear beginning and ending positions.

Level 3

Proficiently performs a minimum of three of four action verbs with form and technique; consistently shows a clear beginning and ending; shows variety and contrast in movement concepts; consistently shows smooth, logical transitions; consistently repeats same sequence; written narrative description consistently matches performance.

Level 2

Performs a minimum of three of four action verbs with form and technique; usually shows a clear beginning and ending; shows some variety and contrast in movement concepts; usually shows smooth, logical transitions; consistently repeats same sequence; written narrative description consistently matches performance.

Level 1

Performs a minimum of two of four action verbs with some technique and control; sometimes shows a clear beginning and ending; shows little variety or contrast in movement concepts; rarely shows smooth, logical transitions; rarely repeats same sequence; written narrative description usually matches performance.

Level 0

Performs fewer than two action verbs with poor technique; rarely shows a clear beginning and ending; shows no variety or contrast in movement concepts; rarely shows smooth, logical transitions; never repeats the same sequence; written narrative description rarely matches the performance.

From P.H. Werner, L.H. Williams, and T.J. Hall, 2012, *Teaching Children Gymnastics,* 3rd edition (Champaign, IL: Human Kinetics).

REFERENCES

Belka, D. 1993. Educational gymnastics: Recommendations for elementary physical education. *Teaching Elementary Physical Education* 4 (2): 1-6.

Brown, M. 1987. *D.W. flips.* Boston: Little, Brown.

Buschner, C. 1994. *Teaching children movement concepts and skills: Becoming a master teacher.* Champaign, IL: Human Kinetics.

Coelho, J. 2010. Gymnastics and movement instruction: Fighting the decline in motor fitness. *Journal of Physical Education, Recreation and Dance* 81 (1).

Cooper, P.S., and M. Trnka. 1989. *Teaching basic gymnastics: A coeducational approach.* 2nd ed. New York: MacMillan.

Graham, G. 2008. *Teaching children physical education: Becoming a master teacher.* 3rd ed. Champaign, IL: Human Kinetics.

Graham, G., S. Holt/Hale, and M. Parker. 2010. *Children moving: A reflective approach to teaching physical education.* 8th ed. Mountain View, CA: Mayfield.

Hacker, P., E. Malmberg, J. Nance, A. Tilove, and S. True. 1993. *Sequential gymnastics for grades 3-6.* 3rd ed. Indianapolis: U.S. Gymnastics Federation.

Hopple, C. 2005. *Elementary physical education teaching and assessment: A practical guide.* 2nd ed. Champaign, IL: Human Kinetics.

Kelly, L.E. 1989. Instructional time: The overlooked factor in PE curriculum development. *Journal of Physical Education, Recreation and Dance* 60 (6): 29-32.

Mitchell, D., B. Davis, and R. Lopez. 2002. *Teaching fundamental gymnastics skills.* Champaign, IL: Human Kinetics.

National Association for Sport and Physical Education (NASPE). 1995. *Moving into the future: National standards for physical education.* Reston, VA: Author.

National Association for Sport and Physical Education (NASPE). 2004. *Moving into the future: National standards for physical education.* 2nd ed. Reston, VA: Author.

National Association for Sport and Physical Education (NASPE). 2010. *Appropriate instructional practice guidelines for elementary school physical education.* Reston, VA: Author.

Nilges, L. 1997. Educational gymnastics: Stages of content development. *Journal of Physical Education, Recreation and Dance* 68 (3): 50-55.

Nilges, L. 1999. Refining skill in educational gymnastics: Seeing quality through variety. *Journal of Physical Education, Recreation and Dance* 70 (3): 43-48.

Nilges, L. 2000. Teaching educational gymnastics. *Teaching Elementary Physical Education* 11 (4): 6-35.

Nilges-Charles, L.M. 2008. Assessing skill in educational gymnastics. *Journal of Physical Education, Recreation and Dance* 79 (3): 41-51.

Physical Education Association of Great Britain and Northern Ireland. 1991. Gymnastics—ideals for the 1990's? *British Journal of Physical Education* 22 (3): 8-35.

Ravegno, I. 1988. The art of gymnastics: Creating sequences. *Journal of Physical Education, Recreation and Dance* 59 (3): 66-69.

Rikard, G.L. 1992. Developmentally appropriate gymnastics for children. *Journal of Physical Education, Recreation and Dance* 63 (6): 44-46.

Rink, J. 2010. *Teaching physical education for learning.* 6th ed. Boston: McGraw-Hill.

Shulman, L.S. 1987. Knowledge and teaching: Foundations of the new reform. *Harvard Educational Review* 57 (1): 1-22.

Siedentop, D. 1991. *Developing teaching skills in physical education.* 3rd ed. Palo Alto, CA: Mayfield.

U.S. Department of Health and Human Services, Centers for Disease Control and Prevention. 2008. *2008 Physical activity guidelines for Americans.* www.health.gov/paguidelines.

SUGGESTED READINGS

Baumgarten, S., and K. Pagnano-Richardson. 2010. Educational gymnastics: Enhancing children's physical literacy. *Journal of Physical Education, Recreation and Dance* 81 (4): 18-25.

This article defines educational gymnastics, stresses the role of educational gymnastics in a physical education program, and emphasizes a movement framework that contributes to a child's physical literacy. Concepts of body, space, effort, and relationships are discussed from a gymnastics perspective.

Belka, D. 1993. Educational gymnastics: Recommendations for elementary physical education. *Teaching Elementary Physical Education* 4 (2): 1-6.

This article compares educational gymnastics with Olympic gymnastics, pointing out how educational gymnastics is more appropriate in elementary school settings. It describes eight movement themes: weight bearing and weight transfer, dynamic and static balance, steplike movements, rocking and rolling, sliding, flight and landings, hanging and swinging, and climbing.

Brown, M. 1987. *D.W. flips.* Boston: Little, Brown.

This is a beginning book for children's reading. It features D.W. who loves to do flips and all sorts of gymnastics activities.

Carroll, M.E., and D.R. Garner. 1988. *Gymnastics 7-11: A lesson-by-lesson approach.* New York: Falmer Press.

This popular title views gymnastics from the perspective of education or body management, providing primary teachers with practical assistance in structuring meaningful lessons for young children. The lesson-by-lesson approach covers the four-year period from 7 to 11 years. Specific skills are taught for regular use throughout the program.

Franck, M., G. Graham, H. Lawson, T. Loughrey, R. Ritson, M. Sanborn, and V. Seefeldt. 1991. *Physical education outcomes: A project of the National Association for Sport and Physical Education.* Reston, VA: Author.

This project attempts to define the physically educated person, K to 12, in terms of the psychomotor, cognitive, and affective domains. Benchmarks for each grade level are described in such terms as *has learned specific skills, is physically fit, does participate regularly, knows cognitive information*, and *values physical activity*.

Graham, G. 2008. *Teaching children physical education: Becoming a master teacher.* 3rd ed. Champaign, IL: Human Kinetics.

This text for the pedagogy course of the American Master Teacher Program for Children's Physical Education integrates research-based information with firsthand teaching experience. The book is an excellent resource of practical skills and techniques to help teachers motivate children to practice, build positive feelings, minimize off-task behavior and discipline problems, and create an atmosphere conducive to learning. It also aids in developing lesson content and problem solving, observation and analysis, feedback, and assessments.

Graham, G., S. Holt/Hale, and M. Parker. 2010. *Children moving.* Mountain View, CA: Mayfield.

This book develops skill themes that children can use as they move through levels of proficiency. The chapters on traveling, jumping and landing, rolling, balancing, and weight transfer are particularly appropriate for educational gymnastics.

Hacker, P., E. Malmberg, J. Nance, A. Tilove, and S. True. 1993. *Sequential gymnastics for grades 3-6.* 3rd ed. Indianapolis: U.S. Gymnastics Federation.

This book presents a guideline to establishing a safe, noncompetitive environment in schools. Skill sequences require little or no spotting and are taught in progressive order, one skill building on another. Activities use mats, low balance beams, vault boards, and horizontal bars.

Hopple, C. 2005. *Elementary physical education teaching and assessment: A practical guide.* 2nd ed. Champaign, IL: Human Kinetics.

This unique resource is divided into two parts. Part I introduces the concept of purposeful planning (creating curriculum goals or outcomes that are realistic and achievable for your particular situation) and then shows how to assess those goals using portfolio and performance task assessments. Teachers will find the many hints helpful, especially concerning the use and scoring of these assessments. Part II is organized according to the concepts (including fitness concepts) and skills taught in physical education. It also contains sample performance and portfolio tasks. Teachers can use many of these in directly assessing NASPE benchmarks, which are referenced when applicable. The learnable pieces are detailed for each skill and concept, along with activity ideas and hints for teaching them at the varying grade levels. Part III centers on actual assessment tasks and curriculum ideas for the classroom. Each chapter reflects additions and revisions to the first edition as a result of how much more is known about assessment.

Kirchner, G., J. Cunningham, and E. Warrell. 1978. *Introduction to movement education.* 2nd ed. Dubuque, IA: Brown.

A fundamentally sound text, this book does not have separate chapters on games, dance, or gymnastics. Rather, it presents illustrated chapters on Laban themes of movement qualities (shape, direction, effort, and range) and the use of small and large apparatus.

Kruger, H., and J. Kruger. 1977. *Movement education in physical education.* Dubuque, IA: Brown.

Taking a new look at physical education, this book gives attention to using 16 Laban themes. These fundamental themes serve as the basis for work in games, dance, and gymnastics.

Learmouth, J., and K. Whitaker. 1977. *Movement in practice.* Boston: Plays.

The authors present 14 educational gymnastics lessons. Each lesson includes a theme or combination of themes, an introductory exploratory phase, development of the theme through extensions and refinements, and the linking of the theme with apparatus work.

Mauldon, E., and J. Layson. 1979. *Teaching gymnastics.* 2nd ed. London: MacDonald and Evans.

The authors examine the relevance of gymnastics in a historical context and in the context of the school curriculum. Based on educational gymnastics themes, the book serves physical education specialists as well as classroom teachers.

Morrison, R. 1974. *A movement approach to educational gymnastics.* Boston: Plays.

The material in this book covers the full range of educational gymnastics for primary and secondary students. The actions emphasize locomotion and balance. Subthemes for locomotion include transfer of weight, traveling, and flight. Subthemes for balance include weight bearing, balancing skills, actions of arriving, and on- and off-balance actions. Partner and group work appear in a separate section.

Nilges, L. 1997. Educational gymnastics: Stages of content development. *Journal of Physical Education, Recreation and Dance* 68 (3): 50-55.

Rink's four stages of game playing are interpreted into content development in gymnastics. The first stage is the exploration and variation of individual skills. The second stage is the combination of individual skills. Gradually children combine individual skills into beginning sequences in stage 3. During stage 4 advanced sequences are developed.

Nilges, L. 1999. Refining skill in educational gymnastics: Seeing quality through variety. *Journal of Physical Education, Recreation and Dance* 70 (3): 43-48.

This article focuses on how teachers create refining and extending tasks for students in an attempt to improve on the efficiency and variety of responses shown in students' work. In the refining process, teachers focus on the correctness and mechanics of performance and the use of smooth transitions between movements. During the extension process, teachers focus on the variety of student choices in the performance of a given problem-solving task to indicate an understanding of the number of responses available in an open movement task.

Nilges, L. 2000. Teaching educational gymnastics. *Teaching Elementary Physical Education* 11 (4): 6-35.

This journal edition is a special feature on educational gymnastics. It is written and edited by Nilges. Coauthors are Belka, Hardin, Lathrop, Murray, and Ratliffe. Topics in the feature include safety tips; teaching rolling, steplike, flight, and balance actions; assessment; and facilitating inclusion.

O'Quinn, G. 1978. *Developmental gymnastics.* Austin, TX: O'Quinn.

This is a sequential model for Olympic gymnastics stunts, tumbling, and beginning apparatus work. Skills are presented in a developmental progression and illustrated well. Descriptions of the proper mechanics for each skill include performance cues for execution. The book is oriented to beginners (ages 5 and 6) through children in the elementary years.

Physical Education Association of Great Britain and Northern Ireland. 1991. Gymnastics—ideals for the 1990's? *British Journal of Physical Education* 22 (3): 8-35.

This special issue presents the best of theory and issues concerning educational gymnastics. It is a series of articles written by England's leading authorities on educational gymnastics.

Ravegno, I. 1988. The art of gymnastics: Creating sequences. *Journal of Physical Education, Recreation and Dance* 59 (3): 66-69.

This article presents a clear outline of how to help children build sequences in gymnastics and includes several examples.

Rikard, G.L. 1992. Developmentally appropriate gymnastics for children. *Journal of Physical Education, Recreation and Dance* 63 (6): 44-46.

Included in a special issue on developmentally appropriate physical education practices for children, this article gives many suggestions for teaching gymnastics. Rikard identifies inappropriate practices and suggests corrections.

Ryser, O., and J. Brown. 1990. *A manual for tumbling and apparatus stunts.* 8th ed. Dubuque, IA: Brown.

This guide is an excellent resource for physical education teachers on class organization and skill techniques in Olympic gymnastics. It also serves coaches of competitive gymnastics teams by providing competitive rules, background information, and skill progressions on the various competitive events.

Stanley, S. 1977. *Physical education: A movement orientation.* 2nd ed. Toronto: McGraw-Hill.

Following the Laban movement framework, this book emphasizes the use of body awareness, spatial awareness, effort, and relationships in the teaching of games, dance, and gymnastics. The chapters on gymnastics offer selected lessons for children in the primary through the intermediate years.

Wemer, P., and T. Sweeting. 1991. Gymnastics in schools. *The Physical Educator* 48 (2): 86-92.

This article is based on the theoretical approach to modern educational gymnastics, which uses the themes of traveling, rotation, and static work as the foundation for gymnastics content. These themes are supported by the Laban process variables of body awareness, spatial awareness, effort actions, and relationships.

Williams, J. 1987. *Themes for educational gymnastics*. 3rd ed. London: Black.

This established book is a very practical reference. Teachers can use its material as detailed lesson plans or as starting points.

ABOUT THE AUTHORS

Peter H. Werner, PED, is a retired distinguished professor emeritus from the department of physical education at the University of South Carolina. His area of expertise is physical education for children, including gymnastics, dance, and interdisciplinary learning. Dr. Werner has presented at numerous national conferences for the American Alliance for Health, Physical Education, Recreation and Dance and for the National Association for Sport and Physical Education. He has presented a session on educational gymnastics at an international conference as well.

Dr. Werner served as senior editor for *Teaching Elementary Physical Education* and has served in editorial roles for many other physical education publications. He has been recognized numerous times for his contributions to physical education, including receiving the Ada B. Thomas Outstanding Faculty Advisor Award in 2001 from the University of South Carolina, the Margie Hanson Service Award in 2002 from the Council on Physical Education for Children, and the Hall of Fame Joy of Effort Award from the National Association for Sport and Physical Education in 2008. He is a coauthor of *Interdisciplinary Teaching Through Physical Education* (2009), *Seminar in Physical Education* (2008), and *Geocaching for Schools and Communities* (2010), all with Human Kinetics. He has also written hundreds of articles.

Dr. Werner and his wife make their home in Black Mountain, North Carolina, where he enjoys whitewater canoeing, running, biking, and hand-crafting brooms.

Lori H. Williams, PhD, is an assistant professor at the Citadel in Charleston, South Carolina. She has taught physical education at the elementary, middle school, and college levels. Her 25 years of teaching experience include 14 years in public schools. Gymnastics has always been part of her curriculum. She coauthored *Schoolwide Physical Activity* (2010) and several articles for refereed publications. Williams has presented at numerous state, regional, and national conferences, many of which included a focus on gymnastics. She has been an active participant in collecting and analyzing assessment data at the state level with the South Carolina Physical Education Assessment Program, and she has been a member of the NASPE Assessment Task Force.

Tina J. Hall, PhD, is an associate professor in the department of health and human performance at Middle Tennessee State University. She has taught since 1985, spending 18 of those years at the elementary and middle school levels. Her experience in gymnastics includes teaching gymnastics as an integral part of her elementary and middle school physical education curriculum, conducting an afterschool gymnastics club, and teaching educational gymnastics to future physical educators at the college level. Hall has conducted numerous workshops and in-services focusing on gymnastics. She is a coauthor of *Schoolwide Physical Activity* (2010) and several articles for refereed publications.